The School of Niklaus Wirth

László Böszörményi • Jürg Gutknecht • Gustav Pomberger (Eds.)

The School of Niklaus Wirth

The Art of Simplicity

dpunkt.verlag

MK

László Böszörményi
laszlo@itec.uni-klu.ac.at

Jürg Gutknecht
gutknecht@inf.ethz.ch

Gustav Pomberger
pomberger@swe.uni-linz.ac.at

Editor: Gerhard Rossbach
Copy Editing: Naomi Wilson
Cover Design: Helmut Kraus, Düsseldorf
Production: Josef Hegele, Dossenheim
Printing: Koninklijke Wöhrmann B.V., Zutphen, The Netherlands

Die Deutsche Bibliothek – CIP-Einheitsaufnahme:

The school of Niklaus Wirth : the art of simplicity / László Böszörményi ... – Heidelberg : dpunkt-Verl. 2000
ISBN 3-932588-85-1

Ringstrasse 19
69115 Heidelberg
Germany

Outside Germany, Switzerland and Austria this book is available through
Morgan Kaufmann Publishers
340 Pine Street, Sixth Floor, San Francisco, CA 94104-3205, USA
http://mkp.com

ISBN 3-932588-85-1 (dpunkt.verlag)
ISBN 1-55860-723-4 (Morgan Kaufmann Publishers)

Preface

In the age-old art of painting, we identify certain extraordinary masters of the art, whose contributions form a turning point in history, and whose name separates all that came before from all that comes after. Their pervasive influence is due in large part to the further contributions and wider teaching of a small band of their immediate followers, who enjoyed the privilege of apprenticeship in the same studio or school, and acquired their learning and skills directly from the words and from the example of the master.

In the short history of computing, there has been time enough to recognise the pioneering achievements of Niklaus Wirth in the complex field of computer system design. His expertise covers the whole range of the subject, from electronic hardware and processor architecture, through kernels and operating systems to utilities and selected applications. But his genius is most clearly and most widely recognised in the design and implementation of programming languages. Their unmatched quality is supported by the excellence of the implementing architecture, and they inspire the highest quality in the body of software designed with their aid. Motivated throughout by a deep repugnance for all forms of complexity, and empowered by a deep analysis of all its causes, he repeatedly wins through to a framework of underlying principles and structures of remarkable simplicity and elegance.

The determined pursuit of simplicity requires the repeated courage to throw away all achievements of the past, and start again from a newer and simpler foundation. So at a time when few experts have produced even a single practicable programming language, Niklaus has made a progression from Euler through PL360, ALGOL W, and PASCAL, to Modula (two versions) and Oberon. These form a scale of quality against which one can chart the progress of commercial languages such as C, C++, Visual Basic and Java. The later members of the commercial series are beginning to approach the quality of the earlier languages designed by Niklaus.

Systems designed in Zurich have always been of the highest quality, recognised by those most qualified to assess it, and adopted for daily use by those who have full freedom to choose. To implement his systems, he has enlisted the long-term aid of many students, colleagues and followers. This book has been written by them to convey to a wider community of engineers and scientists a feeling for the excitement and novelty of those pioneering exploits, and for the continuing relevance of what was achieved then to the problems of the present day.

The book is dedicated in respect and affection to Niklaus Wirth, master of the far from simple art of simplicity, by those who have studied in his school, among whom I am proud to number myself as one of the earliest.

Tony Hoare

Contents

Introduction

This book presents Niklaus Wirth as a teacher.

Wirth has often been praised for his excellent work as a designer of programming languages, of compilers, of operating systems and even of hardware – in short, as an *engineer.* I suspect that his own self-image is primarily that of an engineer. As a child he admired trains and airplanes. And now, in the status of a professor emeritus, he still has this capability of *admiration* for the technically new and exciting, which is probably one of his secrets that will keep himself and his inspiration young.

It is less widely known, however that Niklaus Wirth is an outstanding teacher. He is a member of a teacher dynasty with long traditions, but one who has never felt a specific vocation to be a teacher. Nevertheless, as a university professor he has assisted many young people to understand technology, and more importantly, to discover their own individual style and relationship to this technology.

With the exception of some of his closer colleagues – Prof. Dijkstra, Prof. Hoare and Prof. Rechenberg – the contributors of this book are disciples of Wirth. Some of them have become university professors following the example of Wirth himself; some have become scientists in industrial laboratories; while others have moved to the most diverse corners of the world in pursuit of commercial careers in various fields. This book gives a kaleidoscopic mélange of views into programming language theory, compiler construction, software engineering, operating system design and hardware construction – just to mention the main areas. These are all fields where Wirth set basic initiatives and his pupils have expanded on these with own ideas and applications. We hope that the reader of this book acquires some insight into the recent past and near future of some core technologies of computer science, and into the personality of the man who has so influenced these technologies.

Many of the papers touch on one persistent and pervasive quality of all his works: his unequivocal demand for *simple* solutions. Wirth's predilection for simplicity can be attributed, in my opinion, to a natural *honesty*: he does not talk about topics he does not really understand; and he readily admits to not understanding something. This rare characteristic has allowed him to preserve his ability to see and learn and invent; it has been his greatest asset in leading others to discover the obvious and to discard the complicated.

The authors and the editors of this book hope to pass on this love for honesty and enthusiasm for simple engineering solutions to the reader and their feeling for a man to whom we are all so indebted.

László Böszörményi

Part I

Niklaus Wirth – a Pioneer of Computer Science

Niklaus Wirth – a Pioneer of Computer Science

Gustav Pomberger, Hanspeter Mössenböck, Peter Rechenberg
Johannes Kepler University of Linz

Abstract

Niklaus Wirth is one of the most influential scientists of the early computer age. His ideas and especially his programming languages have shaped generations of programmers worldwide. This paper tries to acknowledge the scientific achievements of Niklaus Wirth and to honor him as a person. A small part of the paper is also devoted to Wirth's influence on computer science at the Johannes Kepler University of Linz.

1 Introduction

Ask computer specialists anywhere – be it in Europe or America, in Asia or Australia – who the most important computer scientists in the world are, and you can bet that the name Niklaus Wirth will be on every list. Ask programming language experts about the person with the greatest influence on the development of programming languages, and they would agree on Niklaus Wirth. Ask students, teachers and computer hobbyists about the most important programming languages, and you can be sure that even today Pascal will be on every list. Finally, examine the literature of computer science in the elite circle of books with the greatest number of copies printed, the widest distribution, and the most translations, and you will find books by Niklaus Wirth, especially the prominent book on Pascal.

These few examples show that Professor Niklaus Wirth is one of the world's leading computer scientists. It is our honor and pleasure to acknowledge his achievements as a scientist, educator and person as well as his influence on research and teaching all over the world.

We begin by reviewing Wirth's scientific career and by recognizing his most important work as well as the honors that the computer world has bestowed upon him. Wirth's work had significant impact on the development of computer science and the work of other researchers worldwide. Needless to say, he has also influenced research and teaching at the Johannes Kepler University of Linz, and part of this paper sketches this influence. Finally, we take particular pleasure in acknowledging Niklaus Wirth as a person and a contemporary.

2 Wirth's Scientific Career

Niklaus Wirth was born in 1934 in Winterthur, Switzerland. After graduating from ETH Zurich in electrical engineering in 1959 he completed his master's degree at Laval University in Quebec, Canada, in 1960 and went on to complete his Ph.D. in programming languages in 1963 under professor H. D. Huskey at the University of California at Berkeley. Wirth served as an assistant professor at the newly founded computer science department at Stanford University from 1963 to 1967. During this time he became intensely involved with questions regarding programming-language development.

In 1967 Wirth returned as a professor to Zurich, first to the university, then in 1968 to ETH, where he co-founded the Department of Computer Science. The development of computer science as an academic major and as a research field at ETH was and is decidedly influenced by Wirth. In March 1999 Wirth retired as professor at ETH with a much-acclaimed parting lecture [47].

The guiding aspiration of Wirth's work has been to exploit to the limits of technical feasibility the possibilities offered by the computer for solving problems, all the while striving for simplicity and comprehensibility. This attitude arises from his insight into interrelations, and presents a sharp contrast to today's prevailing tendency to make programs, systems and organizations increasingly huge and complex, and thus opaque and dangerous [42].

Wirth does not belong to the ever growing number of scientists who publish simple (sometimes trivial) phenomena in an inflated, scientifically padded representation without offering much innovation. Quite the contrary, his work contributed to simplifying the understanding of complex interrelations and to providing clean solutions to existing problems.

The following subsections describe five periods in Wirth's scientific work, each lasting for about a decade and each crowned with major contributions to the development of computer science.

The Early Years

Shortly before 1960, the first Fortran compiler was completed, Algol was defined and some years later implemented. But – strangely enough – this pioneering work was hardly reflected in the open literature. Till the end of the decade only one coherent book about compiler construction appeared [2]. It was understandable that IBM was not interested in the publication of the techniques applied in Fortran compilers, but why did so little appear about the implementation of Algol? Only fragments such as the translation of arithmetic expressions and parsing methods were published. The reason for this reservation was perhaps that the implementers felt their work yet to be immature and poorly suited for publication. General principles and methods were scarcely recognized; and if they were, how could they be described? Assembler code was unreadable, Algol was known only to a small minority, and Fortran was taboo in the Communications of the ACM.

This was the situation when Wirth's and Weber's paper "Euler: A Generalization of Algol and its Formal Definition" appeared in 1966 [3]. Contrary to all the patchy work before, it contained the syntactic and semantic description of a complete language with a size similar to Algol. Moreover, the description of syntax and semantics were not intermingled as usual at this time but clearly separated, and the semantic description was quite formal. This was new! The paper also contained a lot of other interesting things: An outline and a judgement of contemporary suggestions of semantic descriptions, a definition of precedence grammars (which were invented by Floyd shortly before [1]), and, last but not least, the formal description of an interpreter that served as back end in the Euler compiler.

This description method was so sound that Wirth from thereon always put his faith in it. His technique to separate syntax and semantics may have been a model for Knuth's attributed grammars. It was also new to build the syntax of a programming language in accordance with a particular parsing method, and, of course, to combine the definition and an implementation of the language. This combination also characterizes Wirth's later work: not only to define a language but to implement it as well and to experiment with it before publication. Here we encounter the old and humble craftsmanship which today's computer scientists would need so much.

Two years later Wirth developed PL360 [5], an algorithmic language for the IBM 360 machines. This work showed how steadily he went his own way, building innovations on top of experienced grounds. We believe that PL360 must have been a revelation for the assembler programmers of the IBM 360. It is remarkable that Wirth developed the PL360 compiler as a cross compiler, since no 360 machine was available to him at this time. He wrote:

> At the time when the project to develop a compiler for PL360 was started, no 360 computer was available to the author, nor did the facilities promised with the forthcoming machine look too enticing to use. It was therefore decided to use the available Burroughs B5500 computer for the design and testing of the compiler, which was completed by the author within two months of part time work. It accepted a preliminary version of PL360 which contained the basic features of the presently described language.
>
> The compiler was then reprogrammed in its own language. Through a loader and supervisor program (written in assembly code), the program, recompiled on the B5500, became immediately available on the 360 computer.

> The experiment of describing the compiling algorithm in PL360 itself proved to be the most effective test on the usefulness and appropriateness of the language and it influenced the subsequent development of the language considerably. During this process, several features which seemed desirable were added to the language, and many were dropped again after having proved to be either dubious in value, inconsistent with the design criteria, or too involved and leading to misconceptions. The leading principle and guideline was to produce a conceptionally simple language and to keep the number of features and facilities minimal.

Don't these sentences embody the program of Wirth's further scientific life? Didn't he apply the same methods in the development of Pascal, Modula and Oberon?

When we read the PL360 paper anew we were astonished by how carefully he motivated his design decisions. Read for instance the section "Addressing and Segmentation" which discusses base register addressing, a property of the 360 that led to many difficulties and programming errors.

From Euler to Pascal

Wirth's work on Euler attracted the interest of an IFIP working group whose goal was to propagate and further develop Algol60. In 1965 three recommendations for a successor were submitted. During the deciding meeting in the fall of 1966 in Warsaw, the proposal of van Wijngaarden was favored over Wirth's recommendation and was developed further to receive IFIP ratification in 1970 as Algol68. While Algol68 was a completely new language, Wirth's recommendation had strived to improve Algol60. Together with Hoare, Wirth refined his proposal into a language called Algol-W [4] and implemented it at Stanford on an IBM/360 using his systems programming language PL360. Algol-W was widely distributed among universities and contributed to spreading the spirit of Algol.

In 1968 Wirth began with the development of Pascal [7, 8, 10, 11, 14]. This happened to be the beginning of a whole series of great contributions to the development of computer science and laid the foundation of Wirth's reputation as a computer pioneer. He writes of his work on Pascal:

> Freed of the constricting influence of a workgroup consensus, the language Pascal was conceived in Zurich. The foundation was provided by Algol-W and the desire to develop a language that can be implemented efficiently and that meets the requirements for building system programs (compilers, operating systems). Furthermore, we gave top priority to a base of clear, mathematically and machine-independently defined concepts so that the language could be employed to the advantage of instruction in computer science.

These goals were more than achieved. Pascal was first used for teaching at ETH in 1972 and grew to be one of the most popular teaching languages in the world. Not only teachers but also practitioners learned to appreciate Pascal's concepts. Hardly any other programming language has been the subject of so much literature.

In the development of Pascal, a major aim was to show that structured languages need not take a back seat to older languages such as Fortran with respect to the efficiency of the generated code as long as proper attention was paid to the implementation of the compiler. Unfortunately the computer industry and industrial users, who should have had a particular interest in this kind of engineering, took many years to recognize the value of this work, and some never did.

A new Pascal compiler project at ETH served as a proving ground for the technique of stepwise refinement in program development, which was also postulated by Wirth [6]. This provided the welcome opportunity for other universities to assist in porting the Pascal compiler to other computers. The machine-independent parts of the new compiler generated code for a virtual machine, which could then be implemented rather easily as an interpreter on other machines. This virtual machine was called Pascal-P (for portable) [24] and became the basis of the many Pascal implementations that first became available for mainframes (IBM, DEC, UniVac, Siemens). The breakthrough for Pascal, however, came with the rise of the microcomputer and the realization that Pascal-P could be implemented there as well.

Even then Wirth did not confine himself to just the design and implementation of programming languages. In 1970 ETH acquired a mainframe, a CDC 6000. The priority for selecting the machine was to meet the demands of scientific computing (number crunching). While time sharing systems were spreading worldwide, the software of this computer was not well-suited to this approach. Under the direction of Wirth and in cooperation with the ETH computing center, the new time sharing system Venus was developed and successfully met the demands of multiple terminal access without a noticeable reduction in computing performance.

From Pascal to Modula-2 and Lilith

In 1973 Wirth committed himself to the development of concepts and tools for the design of modular multiprogramming systems. The rules postulated here forced the formulation of language elements to express the creation and synchronization of such processes. Embedding these rules into a minimal environment led to the language Modula [17, 18, 19], which was implemented on a PDP-11. The first application was the Hexapus system, which permitted the direct connection of small computers to the computing center.

In a sabbatical year spent at the Xerox Palo Alto Research Center in 1976, Wirth encountered a fundamentally new kind of computer, the personal workstation. It was programmed in a language called Mesa [16], which was based on the concepts of modules and separate compilation. Back at ETH Wirth launched a research project with the goal of developing such a computer together with an appropriate programming language and system software. The result was the workstation Lilith [23, 27], the programming language Modula-2 [25], the operating system Medos [26] and a couple of other tools. Despite the apparently enormous scope of the project, the determined work of up to seven team members achieved the goal in only three years. This is a result that is hard to beat.

In addition to an operating system and a compiler, a program development system requires an interactive editor. All these tools had to be developed from scratch for the Lilith in order to be able to exploit the high-resolution monitor and the mouse. Wirth himself programmed the prototypical text editor Dina as well as the graphics editor Sil for producing figures and schematic diagrams for documenting the Lilith hardware. Dina proved to be the model for the later editors Andra and Lara [28], which allowed the simultaneous creation of multiple documents with various fonts and were inspired by Xerox' Bravo editor [22]. Although tools of this kind are standard for every computer today, at that time they were revolutionary.

The most significant contribution of the Lilith project was to enable solutions that were unthinkable with commercially available products of the time. The first ten Liliths were put into operation in 1980, years before similar systems became commercially available. Lilith computers were subsequently employed not just at the ETH Zurich, but throughout the world (one of the first Liliths outside of ETH was shipped to the University of Linz). Seldom have the results of a university research project been translated so directly into practical use.

The development of a complete system like Lilith in such a short time was made possible in part by the deliberate availability of only one programming language. The choice was a modified Pascal called Modula-2, a language inspired by Mesa that consciously sacrificed backward compatibility. The new concepts included the module as the programming unit for separate compilation, the coroutine as the basic component of parallel processes, and an encapsulated set of types and procedures to enable access to machine-dependent properties.

The first Modula-2 compiler was completed in 1979 on the PDP-11; it was then ported to the Lilith. Interest in Modula-2 grew quickly because it had obvious advantages over Pascal, especially for the design of complex systems in teams. Furthermore, Modula-2 was simpler and more elegant than Ada, a language developed at the same time with nearly the same goals. Not only was the PDP-11 compiler distributed to hundreds of universities and companies, compiler companies also began to develop and sell their own compilers. The advantages of Modula-2 already became evident in the development of the Lilith software. The compiler, the operating system, the editors, and all other tools were programmed exclusively in Modula-2. This showed that the restriction to a single language was not only possible, but even brought significant advantages.

A personal workstation gains value when it is connected to other computers via a network, especially with servers and shared resources such as printers and file servers. Under the direction of Wirth, a network interface was designed on the basis of Ethernet. This was the first fast local area network in Switzerland and was well ahead of its time.

Although Wirth had already experienced the multifaceted use of laser printers in 1976 at Xerox PARC, these printers only became affordable in 1982, and even then they lacked the interface to computers that could make use of their advantages. That same year Wirth acquired the first two laser printers in Europe. He designed the hardware and software interfaces himself as well as the formatting program Skylla/Zeus, with which he produced his book *Programming in Modula-2* on the Lilith to camera-ready copy. Again Wirth was a harbinger.

Another important contribution in the seventies was Wirth's proposal for a new syntax notation [21], to become known as EBNF. With Algol, PL/I and other languages a bunch of different notations had been developed, all variations of the Backus-Naur form (BNF), some of them enriched by new metasymbols, some even written in two dimensions (PL/I). Wirth proposed a new notation that at one blow made all the others look baroque and inappropriate. It allowed expressing recursion by repetition, the removal of empty alternatives, and it was easily parsable by a machine. Wirth used this notation for the description of his own languages. We wonder why it did not become a world wide standard. Unfortunately, Ada, Java and other new languages use different syntax notations again.

From Modula-2 and Lilith to Oberon and Ceres

With Modula-2 and Lilith, Wirth set a milestone in computer science. But he would not have been Wirth if he had been satisfied with that and rested on his laurels. Guided by his knowledge and experience from the Modula-2 project, and with the support of his colleague Jürg Gutknecht and a small project team, he developed the programming language and operating system Oberon [34, 35, 36, 39, 40] and the Ceres workstation (Model 1 1984-86, Model 2 1988, and Model 3 1990 [32, 37]). These developments, like their precursors, stood out by advancement and simplification of the status quo without uneasy compromises. Oberon enhanced Modula-2 by the concept of type extension [33], and thus by object-oriented concepts; at the same time it is a leaner Modula-2 trimmed down to what is most important. The language Oberon is seductive in its simplicity and minimality, as is the operating system.

Likewise, the Ceres workstation is exemplary of consistent development in terms of overview and understanding. In his challenging requirements definition Wirth demanded, among other things, energy-saving and quiet operation. He achieved this with such an extremely low energy consumption level that a noisy ventilation fan became superfluous. The Ceres-3 consumes only 15 watts in continuous operation without a monitor.

In order to make Oberon available on all modern computers of that time, a new project [43] was launched in 1989 in which the Oberon compiler was split into a machine-independent front end and a machine-specific back end. The back end was implemented for the IBM PC, for the Macintosh as well as for workstations from Sun, DEC, IBM and HP. This established full source code compatibility of Oberon programs across a multitude of platforms. In the course of this project, the Oberon language was slightly extended to Oberon-2 [38], which supports type-bound procedures. The Oberon-2 compilers were distributed via the newly popular Internet and were picked up by many universities and companies all over the world.

Wirth's recent work

In recent years Wirth has been involved in developing programming languages and tools for Field Programmable Gate Arrays (FPGAs) [45, 46]. These are components that afford an array of processors of a single type. Each processor handles one or more very simple logical operations and is connected with its neighbors. By programming the array, any hardware circuit can be implemented in software. The circuit proves somewhat slower than a real hardware circuit, but has the advantage that it can be reprogrammed at run time. Wirth's assistants employed this technique to build a simple workstation in which individual hardware components assume different functions. Wirth successfully used FPGAs in his lectures on Digital Circuit Design [41], which allowed students to design and test circuits in software. This proved to be an inexpensive alternative to hardware laboratories and shows how Wirth applies his endeavor for efficiency, simplicity and elegance to all conceivable fields.

Before receiving his emeritus status, Wirth once again let his engineering talent flare up. He conceived and implemented hardware and software for the control of model helicopters – of course in Oberon. This project proved that there is no reason for not applying modern high-level languages to even such specialized fields as low-level real-time systems.

Publications and academic honors

Wirth's outstanding character is also reflected in his publications, which, like his other work, are distinguished by clarity and concentration on what is relevant. Wirth has authored numerous publications, among them more than 10 books that have been translated into many languages and have become classics in computer literature.

After this necessarily incomplete list of Wirth's achievements, it should be no surprise that any selection of the top ten computer scientists in the world almost certainly includes his name. The international computer science community has bestowed special recognition on Wirth and honored him with numerous awards, prizes and honorary doctorates. Eight honorary Ph.D.s from seven nations have been conferred upon him, and with at least ten high awards, Wirth is certainly one of the most decorated computer scientists in the world. We mention only the following distinctions as representative of Wirth's many honors:

- The ACM's A.M. Turing Award is the highest distinction that a computer scientist can achieve. Wirth received this award in 1984.
- The IEEE Emanuel R. Piore Award for achievement in the field of Information Processing contributing to the advancement of science and the betterment of society went to Wirth in 1983.
- In 1987 Wirth was decorated with the IEEE Computer Pioneer Award.
- The Prix Max Petitpierre, an award presented to a person whose political, diplomatic or economic activities, or scientific or artistic works, have made a contribution to improving the relationship of Switzerland with the rest of the world, was extended to Wirth in 1990.
- The Marcel Benoit Prize was imparted to Wirth in 1991 in recognition of the computer languages introduced by him that realized new concepts of structured programming and had a lasting influence on the multifaceted use of computers worldwide and in all fields of knowledge.
- In 1994 Wirth was inducted into the U.S. National Academy of Engineering.
- In 1999 Wirth was awarded the Outstanding Research Award in Software Engineering by ACM SIGSOFT and the Leonardo da Vinci Medal from the Societe Europeenne pour la Formation des Ingenieurs (SEFI).

3 The Person Niklaus Wirth

One of the sources of Wirth's many successes, indeed perhaps the primary source, has been a rare combination of personal characteristics. On the one hand, he is by nature an inventor with a tremendous feeling for what will be of importance in the future. On the other hand, he has the ability to combine theory and practice in a most advantageous way. He not only defined his programming languages and tools on paper, but also built compilers and implemented tools so that they could be used by the rest of us. He even designed and built his own computer systems that were tailored to his programming languages, thus merging hardware and software to an inseparable unit. There are few computer scientists who feel at home in both hardware and software engineering to the same extent, and we know of no other person who can combine the construction of software and hardware in such an advanced way.

Another characteristic of Wirth is the inevitability of his continuing development work. We are tempted to say that he is obsessed with striving for simplicity, efficiency and elegance. For example, after it became clear in 1982–83 that existing

Modula-2 compilers, including those at ETH, failed to fully exploit the advantages of the language, Wirth decided to design a new compiler, which he implemented himself. The new compiler was based on the one-pass principle, made possible by the larger memory capacity of modern computers, and drastically reduced the frequency of slow access to secondary storage. The new compiler proved attractive in its clear and simple design and its efficiency. It encompassed 5000 lines of code, compared to 10,000 for its predecessor and more than 100,000 for other comparable languages. It compiled itself in less than 2 minutes, compared to 30 minutes for its predecessor and hours for other compilers of comparable languages. These advantages not only become obvious in daily use, they also refute the frequent claim that modern languages need gigantic, complex compilers.

Considering all that Wirth has achieved as an individual researcher and in cooperation with team members whom he often sparked to special achievements, it is easy to be astonished at his great success, and some might feel some degree of envy. Then some tend to look for negative characteristics that are so often associated with such outstanding talent. Could he be reclusive or conceited, or one-sided in his computer orientation, or a lunatic, or unapproachably arrogant? Quite the contrary, we can assure that none of this applies.

To give a very personal picture of Niklaus Wirth, one of the authors of this paper (Gustav Pomberger) remembers how he first met Wirth and how he became a disciple and a friend of him:

> As I arrived at his institute in 1982 for a research position, my reverence for him made me afraid to knock at his door. But when I first met this great scientist with quickened pulse, the friendly, pleasant-natured and modest man stretched out his hand to me and dissipated my nervousness. He did not speak down to others, as many much less creative persons in such positions often do. Wirth turned out to be not just a brilliant scientist but also a very special person in many fields. Let me share some episodes to show what I mean.
>
> The occasion was the awards presentation of the Austrian Computer Society. I was quite surprised as Wirth recognized after only a few notes that the orchestra was opening the ceremonies with Mozart's Linz Symphony, certainly not one of the composer's more important works. Wirth then began his talk on processor architecture with some comments on the Linz Symphony that showed that he was a profound music lover.
>
> Although Wirth claims not to be into sport and likes to smoke his pipe regularly, he has always been in excellent physical shape. He astounded me on our tour through South America in 1987 as he challenged me to a race at an elevation of 4800 meters in the Peruvian highlands. Although I had done a lot of running not long before, my astonishment grew as my 15 years' senior friend outclassed me without effort. His toleration of the elevation and his condition were sensational.

Wirth is also a language talent – and this is not limited to programming languages. He speaks several languages and amazed me on our South America trip when we arrived in Lima as he began to employ excellent Spanish to converse with a lovely Peruvian lady.

Wirth's interests also extend to politics and literature – not just computer literature, of which I suspect that he reads very little. Over the years he has called my attention to many highly interesting books. I was always amazed how much time he had for things other than computer science, although his scientific productivity is well above average. In many discussions that I recall, Wirth impressed us not only with his astuteness and analytical talent, but ever again with his broad education and his wit and sense of humor.

Often intellectuals prove to be quite clumsy when it comes to any manual work, but not Niklaus Wirth. He shows splendid craftsmanship. His home is filled with not just tools for software and hardware, but also with classical tools for precision engineering and other crafts. For example, he enjoys building model airplanes, but he also demonstrated flight talent on real planes. I recall sharing a glider flight with him. After only a little instruction, he could handle the glider almost perfectly, and some time later he took flight training in the U.S.

4 Wirth's Influence on Teaching and Research in Linz

Wirth's work influenced computer scientists at many universities all over the world. As an example we show how Wirth's research shaped our own work at the University of Linz.

The eldest of the three authors (Rechenberg) grew up with Fortran and PL/I and had used mainly IBM machines when he came to Linz in 1975 to take a chair for software development. He knew Wirth from his publications and highly valued his work but he did not become a particular friend of Pascal because the Pascal of that time – like Algol – did not allow separate compilation of procedures. This seemed to be a severe disadvantage for practical use because it prevented the modularization of large programs.

This situation changed all of a sudden with the advent of Modula-2 and personal computers. In Modula-2 we found everything we needed for research and teaching in compiler construction and software engineering: A new small language with all the modern constructs of Pascal, and, in addition, a wonderful module concept with encapsulation, import and export.

In the early eighties – at the beginning of the microcomputer age – our group in Linz decided to write a Modula-2 compiler for such a small machine. A "modern" computer was acquired (an Intel 8085 with 128 Kbytes of memory and still without a hard disk) at a price for which you could get 20 high-end PCs today. Since half of the memory was already taken by the operating system it was clear that our compiler would not fit into memory as a whole. We had to divide it into 7 passes. Although the compiler became too clumsy and slow to be used in practice, the project was a great experience and a kind of apprenticeship for us. For the first time we had the opportunity to study Wirth's way of writing compilers in detail. We were lucky to obtain the sources of the ETH 4 pass Modula-2 compiler that had just been developed for the Lilith. We learned about Wirth's way of parsing, error handling, type checking, attribute management and code generation. What we learned was immediately integrated into our lectures, so that our students in Linz obtained first hand knowledge about modern compiler technology.

As the computers became bigger and cheaper, it was feasible to think about one-pass compilers. In 1984 Wirth developed a single-pass Modula-2 compiler for the Lilith, which was an incentive for us to start a follow-up project, in which we ported this compiler to our mainframe, an IBM/370, which we still used for teaching at that time. Again we were stunned by the simplicity and elegance of Wirth's code. Since there was no Modula-2 compiler on the IBM/370 so far, we had to cross-develop our compiler on a Macintosh and transfer the generated code over a 300 baud modem line to the mainframe. Although every bug fix caused a recompilation on the Macintosh and a multi-hour transfer of the new object code to the mainframe, we got a first version of the compiler running within just a few weeks – a fact which can partly be put down to the clear structure of Wirth's compiler.

Our compiler projects in the eighties also led to personal contacts between Zurich and Linz. Visits of Rechenberg were followed by a longer stay of Pomberger in Wirth's group in 1982. From 1984 to 1987 Pomberger served as a professor at the University of Zurich, which allowed an even closer contact between Wirth and him. Finally, Mössenböck joined Wirth's group as an assistant professor from 1988 to 1994.

Since 1994, Oberon became the major work horse for many of our research projects in Linz. We ported the Oberon system to the Power Macintosh and to Linux, we used it in Ph.D. projects on object-oriented databases, static program analysis and distributed object systems, and extended it by a number of mechanisms such as metaprogramming, exception handling, and concurrency.

Wirth had also a substantial influence on teaching in Linz. Generations of students were educated with his programming languages. In 1982, Pascal became the primary teaching language, which was followed by Modula-2 in 1986, and finally by Oberon-2 in 1994. The simplicity and clearness of these languages make them ideal for beginners, but Modula-2 and Oberon-2 also have all the features that are necessary to teach advanced software engineering concepts.

More than anybody else from outside, Wirth has shaped teaching and research in Linz. Not only many of the professors and researchers but also the students can be called his disciples. For this reason, Wirth received a honorary doctorate from the Johannes Kepler University of Linz in 1993.

5 Conclusion

Niklaus Wirth is certainly one of the most remarkable characters in computer science. During his 40 years of professional life he has contributed some of the most influential programming languages, but also compilers, system software, computer systems and a number of pioneering software engineering practices [9, 12, 15, 20]. An uncontested pioneer in computer science and a multifaceted individual in every way, Wirth influenced many of us and still continues to enrich the world around him.

References

1. Floyd R.W.: Syntactic Analysis and Operator Precedence. Journal of the ACM, 10(3):316-333, 1963
2. Randell B., Russell L.J.: Algol 60 Implementation: The Translation and Use of Algol 60 on a Computer, Academic Press, 1964
3. Wirth N., Weber H.: Euler: A Generalization of Algol and Its Formal Definition. Comm. ACM 9(1): 11-23, and 9(2): 89-99, 1966
4. Wirth N., Hoare C.A.R.: A Contribution to the Development of Algol. Comm. ACM 9(6): 413-432, 1966
5. Wirth N.: PL360, A Programming Language for the 360 Computers, Journal ACM 15(1): 37-74, 1968
6. Wirth N.: Program Development by Stepwise Refinement. Comm. ACM 14(4): 221-227, 1971
7. Wirth N.: The Programming Language Pascal. Acta Informatica 1(6): 35-63, 1971
8. Wirth N.: The Design of a Pascal Compiler. Software – Practice & Experience 1(4): 309-333, 1971
9. Wirth N.: Systematic Programming. Prentice Hall, 1973
10. Hoare C.A.R., Wirth N.: An Axiomatic Definition of the Programming Language Pascal. Acta Informatica 2: 335-355, 1973
11. Jensen K., Wirth N.: Pascal – User Manual and Report. Springer-Verlag, 1974
12. Wirth N.: On the Composition of Well-Structured Programs. ACM Computing Surveys 6(4): 247-259, 1974
13. Wirth N.: On the Design of Programming Languages. IFIP Congress 1974, 386-393
14. Wirth N.: An Assessment of the Programming Language Pascal. Trans. Software Engineering 1(2): 192-198, 1975
15. Wirth N.: Algorithms + Data Structures = Programs. Prentice Hall, 1975
16. Mesa Language Manual. Xerox PARC, Oct. 1976.
17. Wirth N.: Modula: A Language for Modular Multiprogramming. Software – Practice & Experience 7(1): 3-35, 1977
18. Wirth N.: The Use of Modula. Software – Practice and Experience 7(1): 37-65, 1977
19. Wirth N.: Design and Implementation of Modula. Software – Practice and Experience 7(1): 67-84, 1977
20. Wirth N.: Towards a Discipline of Real-Time Programming. Comm. ACM 20(8): 577-583, 1977

21. Wirth N.: What Can We Do about the Unnecessary Diversity of Notations for Syntactic Definitions? Comm. ACM 20(11): 822-823, 1977
22. Lampson B.W.: Bravo Manual. Alto User's Handbook. Xerox PARC, 1978
23. Wirth N.: The Personal Computer Lilith. Proc. 5th Intl. Conf. on Software Engineering 1981, 2-16
24. Nori K.V., Amman U., Jensen K., Nägeli H.H., Jacobi Ch.: Pascal-P Implementation Notes. In: Pascal -The Language and its Implementation, Ed. D. W. Barron, John Wiley & Sons, 1981
25. Wirth N.: Programming in Modula-2. Springer-Verlag, 1982
26. Knudsen S.E.: Medos-2: A Modula-2-Oriented Operating System for the Personal Computer Lilith. Diss ETH 7346, ETH Zürich, 1983
27. Wirth N.: From Programming Language Design to Computer Construction (Turing Award Lecture). Comm. ACM 28(2): 159-164, 1985
28. Gutknecht J.: Concepts of the Text Editor Lara. Comm. ACM 28(9): 942-960, 1985
29. Wirth N.: Algorithms and Data Structures. Prentice Hall, 1986
30. Wirth N.: Microprocessor Architectures: A Comparison Based on Code Generation by Compiler. Comm. ACM 29(10): 978-990, 1986
31. Wirth N.: Hardware Architectures for Programming Languages and Programming Languages for Hardware Architectures. Proc. ASPLOS '87, 2-8
32. Eberle H.: Development and Analysis of a Workstation Computer. Dissertation, ETH Zurich, 1987.
33. Wirth N.: Type Extensions. ACM TOPLAS 10(2): 204-214, 1988
34. Wirth N.: The Programming Language Oberon. Software – Practice and Experience 18(7): 671-690, 1988
35. Wirth N., Gutknecht J.: The Oberon System. Software – Practice and Experience19(9): 857-893, 1989
36. Wirth N.: Designing a System from Scratch. Structured Programming 10(1): 10-18, 1989
37. Wirth N.: Ceres-Net: A Low-Cost Computer Network. Software – Practice & Experience 20(1): 13-24, 1990
38. Mössenböck H., Wirth N.: The Programming Language Oberon-2. Structured Programming 12(4): 179-195, 1991
39. Reiser M., Wirth N.: Programming in Oberon: Steps Beyond Pascal and Modula. Addison-Wesley, 1992
40. Wirth N., Gutknecht J.: Project Oberon – The Design of an Operating System and Compiler. Addison-Wesley, 1992
41. Wirth N.: Digital Circuit Design. Springer-Verlag, 1995
42. Wirth N.: A Plea for Lean Software. IEEE Computer 28(2): 64-68, 1995
43. Brandis M., Crelier R., Franz M., Templ J.: The Oberon System Family. Software – Practice and Experience 25(12): 1331-1366, 1995
44. Wirth N.: Theory and Techniques of Compiler Construction. Addison-Wesley, 1996
45. Wirth N.: The Language Lola, FPGAs and PLDs in Teaching Digital Circuit Design. Proc. Ershov Memorial Conference 1996, 2-20
46. Wirth N.: Hardware Compilation: Translating Programs into Circuits. IEEE Computer 31(6): 25-31, 1998
47. Erfindungen der Informatik: Ein Plädoyer für Zuverlässigkeit anstelle von Innovationitis. Abschiedsvorlesung von Niklaus Wirth. Neue Zürcher Zeitung, 29.1.1999

Part II
Niklaus Wirth and Edsger W. Dijkstra

From Programming Language Design to Computer Construction[1]

Niklaus Wirth

From NELIAC (via ALGOL 60) to Euler and ALGOL W, to Pascal and Modula-2, and ultimately Lilith, Wirth's search for an appropriate formalism for systems programming yields intriguing insights and surprising results.

It is a great pleasure to receive the Turing Award, and both gratifying and encouraging to receive appreciation for work done over so many years. I wish to thank ACM for bestowing upon me this prestigious award. It is particularly fitting that I receive it in San Francisco, where my professional career began.

Soon after I received notice of the award, my feeling of joy was tempered somewhat by the awareness of having to deliver the Turing lecture. For someone who is an engineer rather than an orator or preacher, this obligation causes some noticeable anxiety. Foremost among the questions it poses is the following: What do people expect from such a lecture? Some will wish to gain technical insight about one's work, or expect an assessment of its relevance or impact. Others will wish to hear how the ideas behind it emerged. Still others expect a statement from the expert about future trends, events, and products. And some hope for a frank assessment of the present engulfing us, either glorifying the monumental advance of our technology or lamenting its cancerous side effects and exaggerations.

In a period of indecision, I consulted some previous Turing lectures and saw that a condensed report about the history of one's work would be quite acceptable. In order to be not just entertaining, I shall try to summarize what I believe I have learned from the past. This choice, frankly, suits me quite well, because neither do I pretend to know more about the future than most others, nor do I like to be proven wrong afterwards. Also, the art of preaching about current achievements and misdeeds is not my primary strength. This does not imply that I observe the present computing scene without concern, particularly its tumultuous hassle with commercialism.

1. This Turing Award Lecture of Niklaus Wirth was published in February of 1985 in Volume 28, Number 2 of the *Communications of the ACM* and is reprinted with the permission of the ACM.

Certainly, when I entered the computing field in 1960, it was neither so much in the commercial limelight nor in academic curricula. During my studies at the Swiss Federal Institute of Technology (ETH), the only mention I heard of computers was in an elective course given by Ambros P. Speiser, who later became the president of IFIP. The computer ERMETH developed by him was hardly accessible to ordinary students, and so my initiation to the computing field was delayed until I took a course in numerical analysis at Laval University in Canada. But alas, the Alvac III E machinery was out of order most of the time, and exercises in programming remained on paper in the form of untested sequences of hexadecimal codes. My next attempt was somewhat more successful: At Berkeley, I was confronted with Harry Huskey's pet machine, the Bendix G-15 computer. Although the Bendix G-15 provided some feeling of success by producing results, the gist of the programming art appeared to be the clever allocation of instructions on the drum. If you ignored the art, your programs could well run slower by a factor of one hundred. But the educational benefit was clear: You could not afford to ignore the least little detail. There was no way to cover up deficiencies in your design by simply buying more memory. In retrospect, the most attractive feature was that every detail of the machine was visible and could be understood. Nothing was hidden in complex circuitry, silicon, or a magic operating system.

On the other hand, it was obvious that computers of the future had to be more effectively programmable. I therefore gave up the idea of studying how to design hardware in favor of studying how to use it more elegantly. It was my luck to join a research group that was engaged in the development – or perhaps rather improvement – of a compiler and its use on an IBM 704. The language was called *NELIAC*, a dialect of ALGOL 58. The benefits of such a "language" were quickly obvious, and the task of automatically translating programs into machine code posed challenging problems. This is precisely what one is looking for when engaged in the pursuit of a Doctorate. The compiler, itself written in NELIAC, was a most intricate mess. The subjec seemed to consist of 1 percent science and 99 percent sorcery, and this tilt had to be changed. Evidently, programs should be designed according to the same principles as electronic circuits, that is, clearly subdivided into parts with only a few wires going across the boundaries. Only by understanding one part at a time would there be hope of finally understanding the whole.

This attempt received a vigorous starting impulse from the appearance of the report on *ALGOL 60*. ALGOL 60 was the first language defined with clarity; its syntax was even specified in a rigorous formalism. The lesson was that a clear specification is a necessary but not sufficient condition for a reliable and effective implementation. Contact with Aadrian van Wijngaarden, one of ALGOL's codesigners, brought out the central theme more distinctly: Could ALGOL's principles be condensed and crystallized even further?

Thus began my adventures in programming languages. The first experiment led to a dissertation and the language Euler – a trip with the bush knife through the jungle of language features and facilities. The result was academic elegance, but not much of practical utility – almost an antithesis of the later data-typed and structured programming languages. But it did create a basis for the systematic design of compilers that, so was the hope, could be extended without loss of clarity to accommodate further facilities.

Euler caught the attention of the IFIP Working Group that was engaged in planning the future of ALGOL. The language ALGOL 60, designed by and for numerical mathematicians, had a systematic structure and a concise definition that were appreciated by mathematically trained people but lacked compilers and support by industry. To gain acceptance, its range of application had to be widened. The Working Group assumed the task of proposing a successor and soon split into two camps. On one side were the ambitious who wanted to erect another milestone in language design, and, on the other, those who felt that time was pressing and that an adequately extended ALGOL 60 would be a productive endeavor. I belonged to this second party and submitted a proposal that lost the election. Thereafter, the proposal was improved with contributions from Tony Hoare (a member of the same group) and implemented on Stanford University's first IBM 360. The language later became known as ALGOL W and was used in several universities for teaching purposes.

A small interlude in this sizable implementation effort is worth mentioning. The new IBM 360 offered only assembler code and, of course, FORTRAN. Neither particularly were loved, either by me or my graduate students, as a tool for designing a compiler. Hence, I mustered the courage to define yet another language in which the ALGOL compiler would be described: A compromise between ALGOL and the facilities offered by the assembler, it would be a machine language with ALGOL-like statement structures and declarations. Notably, the language was defined in a couple of weeks; I wrote the cross compiler on the Burroughs B-5900 computer within four months, and a diligent student transported it to the IBM 360 within an equal period of time. This preparative interlude helped speed up the ALGOL effort considerably. Although envisaged as serving our own immediate needs and to be discarded thereafter, it quickly acquired its own momentum. PL360 became an effective tool in many places and inspired similar developments for other machines.

Ironically, the success of PL360 was also an indication of ALGOL W's failure. ALGOL's range of application had been widened, but as a tool for systems programming, it still had evident deficiencies. The difficulty of resolving many demands with a single language had emerged, and the goal itself became questionable. PL/l, released around this time, provided further evidence to support this contention. The Swiss army knife idea has its merits, but if driven to excess, the knife becomes a millstone. Also, the size of the ALGOL-W compiler grew beyond the limits within which one could rest comfortably with the feeling of having a grasp, a mental understanding, of the whole program. The desire for a more concise yet more appropriate formalism for systems programming had not been fulfilled. Systems programming requires an efficient compiler generating efficient code that operates without a fixed, hidden, and large so-called run-time package. This goal had been missed by both ALGOL-W and PL/I, both because the languages were complex and the target computers inadequate.

In the fall of 1967, I returned to Switzerland. A year later, I was able to establish a team with three assistants to implement the language that later became known as Pascal. Freed from the constraints of obtaining a committee consensus, I was able to concentrate on including the features I myself deemed essential and excluding those whose implementation effort I judged to be incommensurate with the ultimate benefit. The constraint of severely limited manpower is sometimes an advantage.

Occasionally, it has been claimed that Pascal was designed as a language for teaching. Although this is correct, its use in teaching was not the only goal. In fact, I do not believe in using tools and formalisms in teaching that are inadequate for any practical task. By today's standards, Pascal has obvious deficiencies for programming large systems, but 15 years ago it represented a sensible compromise between what was desirable and what was effective. At ETH, we introduced Pascal in programming classes in 1972, in fact against considerable opposition. It turned out to be a success because it allowed the teacher to concentrate more heavily on structures and concepts than features and peculiarities, that is, on principles rather than techniques.

Our first Pascal compiler was implemented for the CDC 6000 computer family. It was written in Pascal itself. No PL6000 was necessary, and I considered this a substantial step forward. Nonetheless, the code generated was definitely inferior to that generated by FORTRAN compilers for corresponding programs. Speed is an essential and easily measurable criterion, and we believed the validity of the high-level language concept would be accepted in industry only if the performance penalty were to vanish or at least diminish. With this in mind, a second effort-essentially a one-man effort was launched to produce a high-quality compiler. The goal was achieved in 1974 by Urs Ammann, and the compiler was thereafter widely distributed and is being used today in many universities and industries. Yet the price was high; the effort to generate good (i.e., not even optimal) code is proportional to the mismatch between language and machine, and the CDC 6000 had certainly not been designed with high-level languages in mind.

Ironically again, the principal benefit turned up where we had least expected it. After the existence of Pascal became known, several people asked us for assistance in implementing Pascal on various other machines, emphasizing that they intended to use it for teaching and that speed was not of overwhelming importance. Thereupon, we decided to provide a compiler version that would generate code for a machine of our own design. This code later became known as P-code. The P-code version was easy to construct because the new compiler was developed as a substantial exercise in structured programming by stepwise refinement and therefore the first few refinement steps could be adopted unchanged. Pascal-P proved enormously successful in spreading the language among many users. Had we possessed the wisdom to foresee the dimensions of this movement, we would have put more effort and care into designing and documenting P-code. As it was, it remained a side effort to honor the requests in one concentrated stride. This shows that even with the best intentions one may choose one's goals wrongly.

But Pascal gained truly widespread recognition only after Ken Bowles in San Diego recognized that the P-system could well be implemented on the novel microcomputers. His efforts to develop a suitable environment with integrated compiler, filer, editor, and debugger caused a breakthrough: Pascal became available to thousands of new computer users who were not burdened with acquired habits or stifled by the urge to stay compatible with software of the past.

In the meantime, I terminated work on Pascal and decided to investigate the enticing new subject of multiprogramming, where Hoare had laid respectable foundations and Brinch Hansen had led the way with his Concurrent Pascal. The attempt to distill concrete rules for a multiprogramming discipline quickly led me to formulate them in terms of a small set of programming facilities. In order to put the rules to a genuine test, I embedded them in a fragmentary language, whose name was coined after my principal aim: modularity in program systems. The module later turned out to be the principal asset of this language; it gave the abstract concept of information hiding a concrete form and incorporated a method as significant in uniprogramming as in multiprogramming. Also, Modula contained facilities to express concurrent processes and their synchronization.

By 1976, I had become somewhat weary of programming languages and the frustrating task of constructing good compilers for existing computers that were designed for old-fashioned "by-hand" coding. Fortunately, I was given the opportunity to spend a sabbatical year at the research laboratory of Xerox Corporation in Palo Alto, where the concept of the powerful personal workstation had not only originated but was also put into practice. Instead of sharing a large, monolithic computer with many others and fighting for a share via a wire with a 3KHz bandwidth, I now used my own computer placed under my desk over a 15MHz channel. The influence of a 3000-fold increase in anything is not foreseeable; it is overwhelming. The most elating sensation was that after 16 years of working for computers, the computer now seemed to work for me. For the first time, I did my daily correspondence and report writing with the aid of a computer, instead of planning new languages, compilers, and programs for others to use. The other revelation was that a compiler for the language Mesa, whose complexity was far beyond that of Pascal, could be implemented on such a workstation. These new working conditions were so many orders of magnitude above what I had experienced at home that I decided to try to establish such an environment there as well.

I finally decided to dig into hardware design. This decision was reinforced by my old disgust with existing computer architectures that made life miserable for a compiler designer with a bent toward systematic simplicity. The idea of designing and building an entire computer system consisting of hardware, microcode, compiler, operating system, and program utilities quickly took shape in my imagination – a design that would be free from any constraint to be compatible with a PDP-11 or an IBM 360, or FORTRAN, Pascal, UNIX, or whatever other current fad or committee standard there might be.

But a sensation of liberation is not enough to succeed in a technical project. Hard work, determination, a sensitive feeling of what is essential and what ephemeral, and a portion of luck are indispensable. The first lucky accident was a telephone call from a hardware designer enquiring about the possibility of coming to our university to learn about software techniques and acquire a Ph.D. Why not teach him about software and let him teach us about hardware? It didn't take long before the two of us became a functioning team, and Richard Ohran soon became so excited about the new design that he almost totally forgot both software and Ph.D. That didn't disturb me too much, for I was amply occupied with the design of hardware parts; with specifying the micro- and macrocodes, and by programming the latter's interpreter; with planning the overall software system; and in particular with programming a text editor and a diagram editor, both making use of the new high-resolution bit-mapped display and the small miracle called Mouse as a pointing device. This exercise in programming highly interactive utility programs require the study and application of techniques quite foreign to conventional compiler and operating system design.

The total project was so diversified and complex that it seemed irresponsible to start it, particularly in view of the small number of part-time assistants available to us, who averaged around seven. The major threat was that it would take too long to keep the enthusiastic two of us persisting and to let the others, who had not yet experienced the power of the workstation idea, become equally enthusiastic. To keep the project within reasonable dimensions, I stuck to three dogmas: Aim for a single-processor computer to be operated by a single user and programmed in a single language. Notably, these cornerstones were diametrically opposed to the trends of the time, which favored research in multiprocessor configurations, time-sharing multiuser operating systems, and as many languages as you could muster.

Under the constraints of a single language, I faced a difficult choice whose effects would be wide ranging, namely, that of selecting a language. Of existing languages, none seemed attractive. Neither could they satisfy all the requirements, nor were they particularly appealing to the compiler designer who knows the task has to be accomplished in a reasonable time span. In particular, the language had to accommodate all our wishes with regard to structuring facilities, based on 10 years' experience with Pascal, and it had to cater to problems so far only handled by coding with an assembler. To cut a long story short, the choice was to design an offspring of both proven Pascal and experimental Modula, that is, Modula-2. The module is the key to bringing under one hat the contradictory requirements of high-level abstraction for security through redundancy checking and low-level facilities that allow access to individual features of a particular computer. It lets the programmer encapsulate the use of low-level facilities in a few small parts of the system, thus protecting him from falling into their traps in unexpected places.

The *Lilith* project proved that it is not only possible but advantageous to design a single-language system. Everything from device drivers to text and graphics editors is written in the same language. There is no distinction between modules belonging to the operating system and those belonging to the user's program. In fact, that distinction almost vanishes and with it the burden of a monolithic, bulky resident block of code, which no one wants but everyone has to accept. Moreover, the Lilith project proved the benefits of a wellmatched hardware/software design. These benefits can be measured in terms of speed: Comparisons of execution times of Modula programs revealed that Lilith is often superior to a VAX 750 whose complexity and cost are a multiple of those of Lilith. They can also be measured in terms of space: The code of Modula programs for Lilith is shorter than the code for PDP-11, VAX, or 68000 by factors of 2 to 3, and shorter than that of the NS 32000 by a factor of 1.5 to 2. In addition, the code generating parts of compilers for these microprocessors are considerably more intricate than they are in Lilith due to their ill-matched instruction sets. This length factor has to be multiplied by the inferior density factor, which casts a dark shadow over the much advertised high-level language suitability of modern microprocessors and reveals these claims to be exaggerated. The prospect that these designs will be reproduced millions of times is rather depressing, for by their mere number they become our standard building blocks. Unfortunately, advances in semiconductor technology have been so rapid that architectural advances are overshadowed and have become seemingly less relevant. Competition forces manufacturers to freeze new designs into silicon long before they have proved their effectiveness. And whereas bulky software can at least be modified and at best be replaced, nowadays complexity has descended into the very chips. And there is little hope that we have a better mastery of complexity when we apply it to hardware rather than software.

On both sides of this fence, complexity has and will maintain a strong fascination for many people. It is true that we live in a complex world and strive to solve inherently complex problems, which often do require complex mechanisms. However, this should not diminish our desire for elegant solutions, which convince by their clarity and effectiveness. Simple, elegant solutions are more effective, but they are harder to find than complex ones, and they require more time, which we too often believe to be unaffordable.

Before closing, let me try to distill some of the common characteristics of the projects that were mentioned. A very important technique that is seldom used as effectively as in computing is the bootstrap. We used it in virtually every project. When developing a tool, be it a programming language, a compiler, or a computer, I designed it in such a way that it was beneficial in the very next step: PL360 was developed to implement ALGOL W; Pascal to implement Pascal; Modula-2 to implement the whole workstation software; and Lilith to provide a suitable environment for all our future work, ranging from programming to circuit documentation and development, from report preparation to font design. Bootstrapping is the most effective way of profiting from one's own efforts as well as suffering from one's mistakes.

This makes it mandatory to *distinguish early between what is essential and what ephemeral.* I have always tried to identify and focus in on what is essential and yields unquestionable benefits. For example, the inclusion of a coherent and consistent scheme of data type declarations in a programming language I consider essential, whereas the details of varieties of for-statements, or whether the compiler distinguishes between upper- and lowercase letters, are ephemeral questions. In computer design, I consider the choice of addressing modes and the provision of complete and consistent sets of (signed and unsigned) arithmetic instructions including proper traps on overflow to be crucial; in contrast, the details of a multichannel prioritized interrupt mechanism are rather peripheral. Even more important is ensuring that the ephemeral never impinge on the systematic, structured design of the central facilities. Rather, the ephemeral must be added fittingly to the existing, well-structured framework.

Rejecting pressures to include all kinds of facilities that "might also be nice to have" is sometimes hard. The danger that one's desire to please will interfere with the goal of consistent design is very real. I have always tried to weigh the gains against the cost. For example, when considering the inclusion of either a language feature or the compiler's special treatment of a reasonably frequent construct, one must weigh the benefits against the added cost of its implementation and its mere presence, which results in a larger system. Language designers often fail in this respect. I gladly admit that certain features of *Ada* that have no counterparts in Modula-2 may be nice to have occasionally, but at the same time, I question whether they are worth the price. The price is considerable: First, although the design of both languages started in 1977, Ada compilers have only now begun to emerge, whereas we have been using Modula since 1979. Second, Ada compilers are rumored to be gigantic programs consisting of several hundred thousand lines of code, whereas our newest Modula compiler measures some five thousand lines only. I confess secretly that this Modula compiler is already at the limits of comprehensible complexity, and I would feel utterly incapable of constructing a good compiler for Ada. But even if the effort of building unnecessarily large systems and the cost of memory to contain their code could be ignored, the real cost is hidden in the unseen efforts of the innumerable programmers trying desperately to understand them and use them effectively.

Another common characteristic of the projects sketched was the *choice of tools*. It is my belief that a tool should be commensurate with the product; it must be as simple as possible, but no simpler. A tool is in fact counterproductive when a large part of the entire project is taken up by mastering the tool. Within the Euler, ALGOL W, and PL360 projects, much consideration was given to the development of table-driven, bottom-up syntax analysis techniques. Later, I switched back to the simple recursive-descent, top-down method, which is easily comprehensible and unquestionably sufficiently powerful, if the syntax of the language is wisely chosen. In the development of the Lilith hardware, we restricted ourselves to a good oscilloscope; only rarely was a logic state analyzer needed. This was possible due to a relatively systematic, trick-free concept for the processor.

Every single project was primarily *a learning experiment*. One learns best when inventing. Only by actually doing a development project can I gain enough familiarity with the intrinsic difficulties and enough confidence that the inherent details can be mastered. I never could separate the design of a language from its implementation, for a rigid definition without the feedback from the construction of its compiler would seem to me presumptuous and unprofessional. Thus, I participated in the construction of compilers, circuity, and text and graphics editors, and this entailed microprogramming, much high-level programming, circuit design, board layout, and even wire wrapping. This may seem odd, but I simply like hands-on experience much better than team management. I have also learned that researchers accept leadership from a factual, in-touch team member much more readily than from an organization expert, be he a manager in industry or a university professor. I try to keep in mind that teaching by setting a good example is often the most effective method and sometimes the only one available.

Lastly, each of these projects was carried through by the enthusiasm and the desire to succeed in the knowledge that the endeavor was worthwhile. This is perhaps the most essential but also the most elusive and subtle prerequisite. I was lucky to have team members who let themselves be infected with enthusiasm, and here is my chance to thank all of them for their valuable contributions. My sincere thanks go to all who participated, be it in the direct form of working in a team, or in the indirect forms of testing our results and providing feedback, of contributing ideas through criticism or encouragement, or of forming user societies. Without them, neither ALOGL W, nor Pascal, nor Modula-2, nor Lilith would have become what they are. This Turing Award also honors their contributions.

On the transitive closure of a wellfounded relation

by
Edsger W. Dijkstra

Dedicated to
Niklaus Wirth

0 Notation, terminology, and imported mathematics

We use the term "predicates" for the elements of a boolean algebra, their standard model being boolean functions defined on some space. Besides the usual boolean operators $(\neg, \wedge, \vee, \Rightarrow, \Leftarrow, \equiv)$, we use for predicates the "everywhere operator" $[\ldots]$ of type predicates $\rightarrow \{$<u>true</u>$,$ <u>false</u>$\}$: $[p]$ is only <u>true</u> if p is, for all other p, $[p] \equiv$ <u>false</u>. In the standard model, $[\ldots]$ corresponds to universal quantification over the underlying space.

In what follows, f is a so-called "predicate transformer", i.e. a function f: predicates $\rightarrow$ predicates. When we then wish to consider the boolean expression $[f.x]$ as an equation to be solved for the unknown x, we denote that equation by $x\colon [f.x]$. If

$$x\colon ([f.x] \wedge \langle \forall y\colon [f.y]\colon [x \Rightarrow y]\rangle)$$

has a solution, it is unique and is called "the strongest solution of $x: [f.x]$"; similarly, if

$$x: ([f.x] \wedge \langle \forall y: [f.y]: [x \Leftarrow y] \rangle)$$

has a solution, it is unique and is called "the weakest solution of $x: [f.x]$".

A predicate transformer f being "monotonic" means that for all predicates x, y

$$[x \Rightarrow y] \Rightarrow [f.x \Rightarrow f.y] \quad .$$

The famous Theorem of Knaster-Tarski tells us that for monotonic f, the equations $x: [f.x \Rightarrow x]$ and $x: [f.x \equiv x]$ have the same strongest solution

$$\langle \forall y: [f.y \Rightarrow y]: y \rangle \quad ,$$

while the equations $x: [x \Rightarrow f.x]$ and $x: [x \equiv f.x]$ have the same weakest solution

$$\langle \exists y: [y \Rightarrow f.y]: y \rangle \quad .$$

The "relation calculus" is obtained from the predicate calculus by adding to it two operators ("composition" and "converse") and one constant (the identity element of composition). In this note we only need the composition, which will be denoted by an infix ";" with a syntactic binding power between $\neg$ and the logical infix operators. We shall use that composition is associative and that in either argument it distributes over $\vee$; the latter property implies that composition is monotonic in either argument. In the standard model of the relation calculus, the predicates are boolean functions of two variables of the same type —the underlying space has the structure of a "Cartesian square"— and the composition of the relations p and q is modelled by

$$\alpha(p;q)\beta \equiv \langle \exists \gamma :: \alpha p \gamma \wedge \gamma q \beta \rangle \quad .$$

(As is usually done, we have treated the relations as infix symbols.)

Relation $\sqsupset$ being (left-)wellfounded means no more and no less than that for any P

$$\langle \forall \alpha :: \langle \forall \gamma : \alpha \sqsupset \gamma : P.\gamma \rangle \Rightarrow P.\alpha \rangle \Rightarrow \langle \forall \alpha :: P.\alpha \rangle \; ,$$

i.e. that proof by mathematical induction is valid: instead of showing $P.\alpha$ for arbitrary α , it suffices to show that it follows from the assumption that P holds for all "smaller" values γ . Taking a contrapositive, denoting $\neg P$ by x (a relation that need not depend on its second argument), and $\sqsupset$ by r , we can express the (left-)wellfoundedness of r by the fact that for all x

(0) $[x \Rightarrow r;x] \Rightarrow [\neg x]$.

In other words, (left-)wellfoundedness of r means that <u>false</u> is the only, and hence the weakest solution of $x: [x \Rightarrow r;x]$. But then, thanks to Knaster-Tarski, <u>false</u> is also the weakest, and hence the only, solution of $x: [x \equiv r;x]$, so that we can also characterize the (left-)wellfoundedness of r by the fact that for all x

(1) $[x \equiv r;x] \Rightarrow [\neg x]$.

The two alternative formulations for r being (left-)wellfounded explain our interest in the boolean expressions $[x \Rightarrow r;x]$ and $[x \equiv r;x]$.

<u>Remark</u> Other characterizations of wellfoundedness are in terms of minimal elements of subsets or lengths of decreasing chains. In view of their explicit reference to the elements of the domain, the existence of the point-free characterizations (0) and (1) comes as a surprising simplification. (End of Remark.)

1 The nonreflexive transitive closure

The nonreflexive transitive closure s of

a relation r can be defined as the strongest s satisfying

(2) $[r \vee r;s \equiv s]$.

(Because of Knaster-Tarski, there are alternative definitions, but we chose (2) because, all by itself, it has interesting consequences.)

<u>Lemma 0</u> For any pair r, s of relations satisfying (2) we have

$$\langle \forall x :: [x \Rightarrow r;x] \Rightarrow [x \Rightarrow s;x] \rangle \quad .$$

<u>Proof</u> We observe for any r, s satisfying (2) and any x

$[x \Rightarrow s;x]$

$\equiv$ {(2)}

$[x \Rightarrow (r \vee r;s);x]$

$\Leftarrow$ {pred. calc. and monotonicity of ;}

$[x \Rightarrow r;x]$

(End of Proof)

Combining Lemma 0 with the characterization (0) of left-wellfoundedness, we conclude

<u>Corollary 0</u> If the nonreflexive transitive closure of a relation is left-wellfounded,

so is the relation itself.

<u>Lemma 1</u> For any pair r,s of relations satisfying (2) we have

$$\langle \forall x :: [x \equiv s;x] \Rightarrow [x \equiv r;x] \rangle$$

<u>Proof</u> We observe for any r,s satisfying (2) and any x satisfying

(3) $[x \equiv s;x]$

x
$\equiv$ {(3)}
$s;x$
$\equiv$ {(2)}
$(r \vee r;s);x$
$\equiv$ {; distributes over $\vee$ and is associative}
$r;x \vee r;s;x$
$\equiv$ {(3)}
$r;x \vee r;x$
$\equiv$ {pred. calc.}
$r;x$

(End of Proof)

Combining Lemma 1 with the characterization (1) of left-wellfoundedness, we conclude

<u>Corollary</u> 1 If a relation is left-wellfounded,

so is its nonreflexive transitive closure.

Remark It is worth noting that neither of our Lemmata requires r to be wellfounded or s to be the strongest s satisfying (2). (End of Remark.)

2 Uniqueness

Finally, we show that for left-wellfounded r, (2) determines s uniquely, i.e. given

(4) $[r \vee r;s \equiv s]$

(5) $[r \vee r;t \equiv t]$

(6) $\langle \forall x :: [x \Rightarrow r;x] \Rightarrow [\neg x] \rangle$,

then $[s \equiv t]$ holds.

Proof For reasons of symmetry, it suffices to show $[t \Rightarrow s]$. We observe

$[t \Rightarrow s]$

$\equiv$ {pred. calc.}

$[\neg(t \wedge \neg s)]$

$\Leftarrow$ {(6) with $x := t \wedge \neg s$}

$[t \wedge \neg s \Rightarrow r;(t \wedge \neg s)]$

$\equiv$ {shunting}

$[t \Rightarrow s \vee r;(t \wedge \neg s)]$

$\equiv$ {(4)}

$[t \Rightarrow r \vee r;s \vee r;(t \wedge \neg s)]$

$\equiv$ { ; distributes over $\vee$ and pred. calc }
$[t \Rightarrow r \vee r;(t \vee s)$
$\Leftarrow$ { monotonicity of ; }
$[t \Rightarrow r \vee r;t]$
$\equiv$ { (5) }
true

(End of Proof.)

I gratefully acknowledge the contribution of Rutger M. Dijkstra (viz. the isolation of Lemma 1) and that of Wim Feijen and Netty van Gasteren (viz. the final proof of unicity).

Austin, 10 January 2000

Part III

The Teachings of a Scholar as Told by his Pupils – Common Work in Retrospect

Oberon – The Overlooked Jewel

Michael Franz
University of California, Irvine

Abstract

Niklaus Wirth has received much deserved fame for the creation of Pascal, but in many ways, he subsequently became a victim of Pascal's success. In an age of rising specialization, in which most researchers are trying to define themselves as experts in increasingly narrow domains, Wirth stands out as a rare generalist, almost an "Universalgenie" of our discipline. Sadly, the larger computer science community has been unable or unwilling to recognize Wirth's broader horizon as a builder of systems, and throughout his career has pigeonholed him as a "language and compiler guy".

But ever since Pascal, the language aspect has been almost secondary to Wirth's work. Modula(-2) and Oberon both came out of larger system-level design projects that simultaneously also developed workstation computers, modular operating systems, and suites of innovative application programs. Unfortunately, these other important contributions were overshadowed by the programming languages they were associated with, and hence never received the recognition they deserved.

This article presents selected facets of Project Oberon, the latter of Wirth's two large system-level design efforts. The leitmotiv of this project was a quote from Einstein, "make it as simple as possible, but not simpler". And if any further evidence was still needed, Oberon provided the conclusive proof for Wirth's mastery of The Art of Simplicity.

1 Introduction

The world at large will remember Niklaus Wirth primarily as "that language guy", and associate his name with *Pascal*, the programming language he created in the late 1960s. But the fame that the widespread success of Pascal brought to Wirth was at best a mixed blessing, as it overshadowed all of his subsequent accomplishments, some of them even greater than Pascal itself.

This was, of course, partially a problem of Wirth's own making. In his modest Swiss Engineer's manner, and quite untypical for a celebrated academic, Wirth consistently avoided exploiting the initially high-speeding Pascal bandwagon for the purpose of "marketing" his subsequent ideas. Indeed, he even refrained from giving his later programming-language creations names such as "Pascal-2", "Pascal Plus", or "Pascal-2000" but instead opted first for "Modula", and then "Oberon". Both of these languages would probably have been considerably more successful if the connection to the Pascal legacy had been made in their name[1] but this would have run counter to Wirth's view that a marketer he is not.

Unfortunately, in an academic culture of increasingly flatulent self-promotion, such modesty eventually almost inevitably leads to a certain degree of self-imposed obscurity. In Wirth's case, the world continued to clamor for "more Pascal" for quite a while, but Wirth had long moved on to new horizons and more or less ignored these requests. Eventually, the world lost interest, and it, too, moved on to new horizons, which unfortunately were not always compatible with Pascal and its successor languages.

The principal reason why Wirth did not immediately respond to clamors for "more Pascal" was of course simply that he did *not* view himself primarily as a "language guy". Indeed, Wirth's publication record quite conclusively demonstrates that his talent has always been much broader and focused chiefly at the *system* level. Twice in his career, Wirth was instrumental in building a complete computer system "from scratch", each consisting of a hardware platform, a modular operating system and related systems-level software such as compilers and assemblers, and also a limited amount of highly innovative application software.

Both of these systems, **Lilith**/Medos/Modula[2] in 1981, and Ceres/**Oberon** in 1988 were years ahead of their time and could at the point of their inception be rivalled by only a small number of far more complex research systems being developed at places such as Xerox' Palo Alto Research Laboratory[3]. For example, the Oberon System of almost ten years ago anticipated such innovations as a hypertext-based user interface, living "applets" embedded within documents, target-machine independent mobile code, and document-centric computing. And Oberon

1. Wirth himself makes this observation in [Wir93].
2. The Lilith/Medos/Modula-2 system is usually summarily referred to as the "Lilith system" while the "Ceres/Oberon" system is commonly known as "The Oberon System". This probably reflects the greater relative importance of the hardware aspects at the time of Lilith, as well as the fact that Oberon soon emancipated itself of the Ceres hardware platform by being ported to several alternative architectures as well.
3. The Lilith and Oberon projects were in fact both inspired by systems that Wirth had encountered at Xerox PARC, namely the Mesa and Cedar systems. Wirth succeeded in replicating many of the key characteristics of these advanced systems with considerably less effort, achieving this remarkable reduction in complexity to some extent by leaving out some inherently complex features, such as preemptive multitasking. As a consequence, comparisons with the much larger research systems existing at the time aren't entirely fair.

provided not just the vision, but also executed that vision in a robust implementation that could actually be and consequently *was* used on a day-to-day basis – quite unlike some of today's "research" systems.

In retrospect, both the Lilith and Oberon systems were probably *too far* ahead of their time, which is why they did not receive the enthusiastic responses they should have deserved. In both cases, the situation was exacerbated by the fact that the research community was expecting a *language* from Wirth, while he delivered a *system*. As a consequence, the predictable result in both instances was that the world at large focused only on the language component of Wirth's offering, and more or less ignored the remainder that was at least as important.

The story of Lilith is for someone else to tell. This article presents my hindsight view of The Oberon System, from the highly subjective perspective of having been one of the early members of Wirth's Oberon group (since early 1989)[4]. I will try to illuminate certain aspects of Oberon that were relevant then and still are relevant today, concentrating on the lesser-known facets rather than the previously published ones. The most important influence throughout was of course Wirth's insistence on simplicity of design, which finally seems to be finding a resonance in the world of computing. I believe that Wirth's ultimate impact will be felt even stronger ten years from now than it is today, and that the legacy of his accomplished career devoted to The Art of Simplicity will be enduring.

2 The Oberon Compiler

Niklaus Wirth is widely known as the creator of several programming languages. What is less well known is that he also personally wrote several compilers, including the first single-pass compiler for Modula-2 that later evolved into the initial compiler for Oberon[5]. These compilers distinguished themselves by their particularly simple design – they didn't aspire to tickle the last possible bit of achievable performance out of a piece of code, but aimed to provide adequate code quality at a price-point of reasonable compilation speed and compiler size. At the time, this was in stark contrast to almost all other research in compilers, which generally had been characterized by an enormous and ever-increasing complexity of optimizations to the detriment of compilation speed and overall compiler size.

In order to find the optimal cost/benefit ratio, Wirth used a highly intuitive metric, the origin of which is unknown to me but that may very well be Wirth's

4. To the best of my knowledge, when I started my Diploma Thesis in the Fall of 1988, I actually became only the third day-to-day user of Oberon (after J. Gutknecht and N. Wirth himself). At that time, all other members of the Institute for Computer Systems were still using Modula-2, and the Oberon System and language themselves were still undergoing minor revisions.
5. The initial compilers for Pascal were written by E. Marmier, U. Ammann, and R. Schild [Wir93], and the initial Modula-2 compiler by L. Geissmann.

own invention. He used the compiler's *self-compilation speed* as a measure of the compiler's quality. Considering that Wirth's compilers were written in the languages they compiled, and that compilers are substantial and non-trivial pieces of software in their own right, this introduced a highly practical benchmark that directly contested a compiler's complexity against its performance. Under the self-compilation speed benchmark, only those optimizations were allowed to be incorporated into a compiler that accelerated it by so much that the intrinsic cost of the new code addition was fully compensated[6].

And true to his quest for simplicity, Wirth continuously kept improving his compilers according to this metric, even if this meant throwing away a perfectly workable, albeit more complex solution. I still vividly remember the day that Wirth decided to replace the elegant data structure used in the compiler's symbol table handler by a mundane linear list. In the original compiler, the objects in the symbol table had been sorted in a tree data structure (in identifier lexical order) for fast access, with a separate linear list representing their declaration order. One day Wirth decided that there really weren't enough objects in a typical scope to make the sorted tree cost-effective. All of us Ph.D. students were horrified: it had taken *time* to implement the sorted tree, the solution was *elegant*, and it worked *well* – so why would one want to throw it away and replace it by something *simpler*, and even worse, something as prosaic as a linear list? But of course, Wirth was right, and the simplified compiler was both smaller and faster than its predecessor.

And fast these compilers were – not just Wirth's original compiler, but also the Oberon compilers that were subsequently developed by his students for a variety of target architectures [BCF95]. Every single one of these compilers outperformed the respective manufacturer's recommended compiler for the particular architecture by several orders of magnitude in compilation speed, and on several of the platforms, also in code quality. Only on the newer RISC platforms could the Wirth-style compilers not quite compete, mainly because they used a linear-scan register allocation mechanism rather than the more advanced graph-coloring variants employed by their competitors [Cha82]. It is quite ironic that in the current trend towards "just-in-time" compilation for Java, in which compilation speed is more important than the last bit of execution speed, Wirth-style compilation is making a grandiose comeback – unfortunately sometimes without proper attribution[7].

6. A more detailed discussion of this and related metrics, and an example application of the metric, can be found in [Fra94b].
7. For example, Adl-Tabatabai et al. [ACL98] describe a compilation strategy for Java that they might just as well have copied from one of Wirth's books [WG92, Wir96], but they present it as a new invention and give it the new name "lazy code selection". Wirth has been teaching the identical method at least since the mid-1980's, calling it "delayed code emission".

3 The Oberon Libraries and Application Program Interface

The fact that they had no prior experience in operating system design turned out to be a blessing when Niklaus Wirth and Jürg Gutknecht were designing the interfaces of the core modules of the Oberon system. Unconstrained by any preconceived notions of how "things should work", they designed a thoroughly novel system architecture that exhibits quite a few little strokes of genius throughout.

For example, anyone who has ever had the opportunity to use Oberon's file system is likely to find most other file system interfaces lacking. Unlike conventional file systems, Oberon's differentiates between the abstractions of a *data file* and an access mechanism to it. The latter is called a "Rider" and maintains the current position[8]. An arbitrary number of these Riders may operate concurrently on the same file, sharing just one set of buffers with full synchronization. In other file systems, these two abstractions are intertwined, making the "current position" a property of the file itself. Worse still, these other file systems often permit the creation of several unsynchronized access paths to the same file by allowing "multiple opening of the same file" – this may of course lead to corruption of the associated data file if the ranges of several concurrent access paths inadvertently overlap.

Oberon also separates the directory operations from the file operations. When a new file is created in Oberon, no entry is made into the directory, making the file anonymous. A name can be entered into the directory at any time, which makes the file permanent on the disk and possibly shadows an existing file with the same name. At any given moment, a directory lookup will simply return the instance of the file that was last registered. In my experience, this separation of directory and file operations makes programming much more intuitive and simple.

As a third example from among the many contributions that simplify the task of programming, the Oberon System allows an arbitrary number of files to be open simultaneously, and they neither need to be explicitly closed, nor deleted. Instead, file closing (with concomitant buffer flush to disk) is delegated to the garbage collector: files whose descriptors become unreachable from the executing code are automatically closed, and if such a file is also no longer accessible via the directory (either because it has never been registered or because another file with the same name was subsequently registered) it is automatically deleted and its storage space reclaimed.

The file system is only one example of how Oberon solved some age-old problems in a novel and practical manner. Future system designers would do well to study Oberon's application program interfaces more closely.

---

8. C. Szyperski [Szy92b, Szy98] later generalized this separation of concerns into the "Carrier/Rider" design pattern and applied it successfully to domains other than the file system.

4 Oberon's Hypertext-Based User Interface

At the time of its creation, Oberon's user interface was highly unusual and outright intimidating to newcomers. In the initial absence of introductory tutorials for beginning users, it also had a very steep learning curve – in short, this was a system for "power users" (and yet was used very successfully for many years by ETH's undergraduate population).

However, revisiting the Oberon user interface ten years later, one finds that it no longer seems so intimidating. Oberon-style interaction has become ubiquitous, since today every web browser and even Microsoft's Windows desktop has many similarities with the Oberon system of yore. Furthermore, people have become much more accustomed to initiating complex commands by mouse actions.

But even today, Oberon's design is unrivalled in its simplicity and complete avoidance of modal dialogs. For example, a file being displayed in a Viewer (window) could be saved under a different name in the original Oberon system simply by editing the name displayed in the Viewer's title bar and then clicking the save command in the menu. To this date, I find this more intuitive than any "save as" command offered in any modern system that then will pop up a modal dialog box to enter a new name.

Oberon's steep learning curve was due to the fact that it used a three-button mouse, in which almost all combinations of simultaneous mouse-clicks (and "interclicks") had separate meanings. Oberon also differentiated between a current focus (a user-set coordinate on a screen, most often used to mark a whole window for a subsequent command), a text entry position, and multiple text selections. In almost all other systems, these points of attention are combined, but separating them is what makes powerful commands (such as "replace all occurrences of the second most recent text selection in the document currently marked by the focus by the text selected most recently") possible.

But the real power behind Oberon's original user interface[9] came from the pervasive use of *text as a unifying abstraction*. All text in Oberon behaved the same, whether it was a file name displayed in a Viewer's title bar, a command in a menu bar, the output of a "list directory" command, or the contents of an editor window. And almost all operations offered by the system operated on such abstract texts rather than on "passive" character arrays or data files. For example, if one had wanted to, one could have run the Oberon compiler directly on the text representing a Viewer's title bar, or one could have compiled the associated menu bar

9. J. Gutknecht and H. Marais subsequently developed an enhanced graphical user interface for Oberon System 3 [Gut94] that makes the end users' experience far more pleasant. Not surprisingly, however, this increased end-user convenience comes at the price of a somewhat higher complexity on the programmers' side. It also brings with it a certain loss of the rigid regularity of the original text-based system, because the user interface now contains a multitude of data types other than text.

(although neither of this would have made much sense). Oberon's approach of incorporating text as a fundamental abstraction was a major improvement over the traditional "pipe" solution as found in Unix-like systems, simultaneously more powerful and intuitively simpler.

5 Extensibility and Document-Centric Approach

The Oberon System was designed with *extensibility* in mind – the ability to augment the system's functionality, possibly even at run-time, without having to modify or recompile any of the existing parts [PS94]. This naturally leads to an operational model founded on the principle of *dynamic loading* of code modules. Oberon refines this model considerably by allowing multiple entry points (so-called "commands") into each dynamically loaded module that can be activated by the end-user individually, and by preserving a module's global state across multiple invocations of such individual commands.

Remarkably, Oberon's architecture from the very beginning offered a still greater degree of extensibility, beyond the mere provision of additional commands in supplementary modules. By adopting a document-centric approach based on a generalization of the classic Model-View-Controller (MVC) design pattern [KP89], Wirth and Gutknecht arrived at a highly flexible and elegant system structure, permitting end-users to create wholly separate Model-View-Controller triplets that could nevertheless share the display space and other system resources with the built-in MVC-triplet supporting the text abstraction.

The key to this flexibility was a departure from the traditional object-oriented model of class-based dynamic dispatch with implementation inheritance[10]. Oberon replaced this model with an architecture in which the messages themselves were represented by objects[11]. This had two important consequences: First, the message hierarchy used in the system became independent of the object hierarchy and could be evolved independently of it. This in turn made a *generic broadcast mechanism* possible by which messages could be routed through the inner layers of the system even though they originated and were ultimately processed in an outer layer[12].

---

10. H. Mössenböck, J. Templ, and R. Griesemer later incorporated the class construct of traditional object-oriented programming languages (along with implementation inheritance) into a variant strain of Oberon [MJG89, MW92].
11. In the classification by Gamma et al. [GHJ95], this is the *Command (233)* design pattern.
12. In a traditional object-oriented design, the generic recipient of a message is modelled using an abstract class. This limits the range of messages that can be sent – although the concrete recipient in an extension of the original system may "understand" additional messages, these cannot be routed through the core system that predates the extension. For a more detailed discussion of this issue, see [Fra98].

It is precisely this architecture that makes Oberon so powerful at such comparably small size and complexity. Interestingly enough, the structure of the Oberon System cannot be replicated using class-based dynamic dispatch all by itself. Unfortunately, critics of the Oberon language who deplored its lack of automated type-based dispatch and method inheritance apparently never realized that these features would not have been of any use in supporting the architecture of the Oberon System[13].

Szyperski later demonstrated that Oberon's particular message dispatch mechanism was a sufficiently powerful foundation to support true "compound documents" [Szy92a], in which different and mutually unaware software components are jointly responsible for the display of a document containing a multitude of complex data items. Apparently, the Oberon system has always had all the mechanisms in place to be called a software component framework [Szy98], although Wirth and Gutknecht, in their dislike of marketing, neglected to advertise this fact properly.

6 Cross-Platform Computing

Niklaus Wirth and Jürg Gutknecht initially conceived the Oberon System as a didactic tool that could actually be understood in its entirety by a single person. As a consequence, although Oberon was written specifically as the native operating system for the Ceres workstation, its simplicity of design and orthogonality of concepts made it surprisingly simple to port onto other computer platforms.

Ironically, Gutknecht, and to some extent also Wirth had some serious reservations about this in the beginning, as they feared that due to the necessity of having to build on top of existing operating system software, the performance on other platforms would be so bad as to give Oberon a bad name. But since the group of graduate students around them was so enthusiastic about the prospect of bringing Oberon "to the rest of the world" (Ceres machines existed only at ETH in Zurich), they soon gave the go-ahead for alternative implementations of Oberon.

So some of us graduate students started porting Oberon to other platforms, first writing a compiler for the target architecture, and then re-building the Oberon system on top of the native operating system. And surprisingly, Oberon turned out to be not only highly portable, but (after some fine-tuning of the connections to the respective native operating systems[14]) also quite efficient on other platforms. By

13. On the contrary, Oberon's *architecture* is sufficiently interesting to perhaps warrant more specific language support of *its* particular mechanisms. The ongoing design of the experimental programming language Lagoona [Fra97] is an attempt to lift some of these mechanisms to the source-language level.

14. A representative selection of the engineering challenges (and their solutions) encountered when porting the Oberon System to run "on top of" another operating system is presented in [Fra93].

late 1990, several versions of Oberon were available, for Apple Macintosh computers based on MC68000 series microprocessors, for Sun Microsystems workstations using the SPARC architecture, and for MIPS-based workstations from Digital Equipment Corporation. Eventually, there were also implementations for Intel i86-based personal computers, for IBM's RISC System/6000, and for Hewlett-Packard's HP-RISC architecture[15].

Unfortunately, the cross-platform aspect of the Oberon project has never been fully appreciated by the wider research community. This is unfortunate because Oberon offered a level of cross-platform portability that was unprecedented and with the possible exception of Java has never been achieved again. Excluding a handful of low-level modules, every Oberon source program could be compiled and executed on any of the platforms, and produce exactly the same results. Wirth and Gutknecht realized the importance of portability early on, and after the first Oberon ports were finished and the implementors came back to report incompatibilities and inconsistencies, they went back to refine the Oberon system interface to remove these obstacles to true portability. Quite remarkably, for example, about half of the machines that Oberon ran on used little-endian byte-ordering, while the other half used big-endian addressing, yet this was abstracted away completely at Oberon's application program interface.

Oberon's extraordinary cross-platform capabilities extended not only to the source code, but also to the data formats used within the system. For example, complex documents could be shared freely among platforms, preserving not only all of the formatting across all target platforms, but even supporting the same editor extensions (today we would call them "applets") on every platform. In contrast, there are still commercial software packages today that use different file formats for each of the platforms on which they are available.

7 Machine-Independent Mobile Code

Another domain in which Oberon provided pioneering work was in the area of machine-independent mobile code along with just-in-time code generation. As early as 1991, I had published a paper [FL91] at the annual Modula-2 conference (with Stefan Ludwig, who was doing his Diploma Thesis under my supervision at the time), advocating *dynamic compilation at load-time* from a target-architecture independent, compiler-oriented intermediate representation.

This work eventually led to my dissertation [Fra94a], the central thesis of which was that one could obtain *machine independence effectively for free* if only one could manage to find a sufficiently dense intermediate representation so that the additional computational effort required for just-in-time code generation could be compensated entirely by reduced I/O overhead due to much smaller "object

15. For a more detailed history and implementation background, see Brandis et al. [BCF95].

files". My dissertation proposed such a representation, subsequently christened "Slim Binaries" [FK97].

True to Wirth's spirit of creating *usable* research, this work in the ensuing period matured beyond being simply a research prototype, as would perhaps have been its fate almost everywhere else but ETH. With the help of Thomas Kistler, who later became my own student at UC Irvine, the Slim Binary format was turned into the *main* software distribution format for the two different processor architectures that Apple's Macintosh operating system ran on. This meant that almost all of the Oberon system was dynamically compiled at load-time on these platforms, with the only major exception of the dynamic compiler itself, and the Oberon storage allocator and garbage collector.

As a result, by the end of 1994, the users of MacOberon were routinely employing dynamic just-in-time compilation at load time from a machine-independent representation, although most of them probably simply didn't notice (nor should they have noticed!). At the time, dynamic compilation was largely considered a "cute curiosity" without many practical consequences. Until, of course, in 1995, Java "happened", which had not only the effect of making just-in-time compilation a "hot topic", but whose publicity assault also more or less completely drowned all prior or simultaneous research of a similar nature.

8 Daily Life With Oberon

Oberon never became a household name, but even among those who did learn of Oberon, only a select few realized that it was not just simply a research prototype, but actually the one and only system that almost all members of the Institute for Computer Systems (including the secretary!) used on a daily basis for all their computing tasks. And as a result of the daily use by its designers, Oberon became extraordinarily reliable[16].

I believe that at the time, the members of the Institute for Computer Systems never fully appreciated the reliability of the Oberon System, because they had nothing else to compare it with. But those of us who have since been forced to work with commercial software will look back to our Oberon years as a golden era

16. True to Wirth's maxim that software designers should be forced to use the products of their labor themselves, each of the Ph.D. students who had ported Oberon onto a new platform subsequently used Oberon on that particular platform as his main (and often sole) work environment. Only recently is this sentiment making a comeback in the software developer community, under the somewhat flippant moniker of "eating one's own dog-food". Hence, after having created the code-generating loader for my machine-independent code-transportation format, I actually wrote my doctoral dissertation using a version of Oberon's document processing software that was generated afresh on-the-fly by dynamic compilation each time that I started it.

without the frequent glitches, unexpected crashes, and data losses that users of other systems are accustomed to.

And the phrase that Oberon was used "for all computing tasks" should be taken literally. For example, almost every scientific article that came out of the Institute for Computer Systems in the 1990's was written using one of Oberon's several document-processing systems. Almost incredibly, even the *fonts* used to type-set these articles on the Oberon-driven laser printer were designed in-house by the resident typographer, H. E. Meier[17]. Similarly, the Institute ran its own network protocols, file servers, print servers, and mail servers, all of which (along with the respective client software) had been developed entirely in-house, and to the greatest extent by N. Wirth himself. I estimate that the Institute spent less than one thousand dollars on commercial software during the whole decade.

Moreover, few people know that Ceres and Oberon not only provided the backbone of all *research* at the Institute for Computer Systems, but also for most of the *education*. ETH was probably the only university in the Western world that in the 1990's conducted the majority of its undergraduate education in Computer Science using workstation computers (of the Ceres family) built in-house, running an operating system (Oberon) developed in-house, and teaching a programming language (Oberon) created by one of the resident professors. And the resulting education was arguably better than anywhere else, because instead of merely explaining to students *how to use* the available educational computer systems, at ETH the educational system's architects were at hand to explain *the motivation* behind individual design decisions.

On the research side, having a system developed in-house meant independence. Rather than calling a telephone hot-line when a problem occurred, one could simply walk over to the author of the code that caused the problem. And in the resulting dialogue, the problem would usually be identified and corrected on the spot. Alternatively, since the complete source code of the Oberon System was readily available to everyone within the Institute (which is currently a highly fashionable idea), one would correct the error oneself and then inform the original author of the correction so that the master copy of the code was updated. Either way, the code base soon achieved its legendary robustness.

9 Conclusion

The Oberon System was well ahead of its time, anticipating many developments in software that most of the rest of the world is beginning to address only now. It is to be hoped that future researchers study Oberon closely, because in many instances,

17. The fonts and font design system go back to the earlier Lilith project, but H. E. Meier continued working at the Institute for Computer Systems throughout most of the Oberon project.

they will find inspirations that will prevent them from having to re-invent a wheel here or there. And just like a wheel is superior to more complex alternatives, Oberon's design contains many simple and elegant solutions that are unlikely to ever be surpassed, at any level of complexity.

Dedication

This article is dedicated to N. Wirth, whose radiant example has shaped my professional thinking profoundly. It was his books that I read during high-school that prompted me to choose ETH to study for my undergraduate degree. It was Wirth's classes there that encouraged me to continue onwards for a Ph.D. And finally, it was his example as a Ph.D. advisor and professor that persuaded me to pursue an academic career of my own. Thank you, Niklaus, for leading the way.

References

[ACL98] A.-R. Adl-Tabatabai, M. Cierniak, G.-Y. Lueh, V. M. Parikh, and J. M. Stichnoth; "Fast, Effective Code Generation in a Just-In-Time Java Compiler", in *Proceedings of the 1998 ACM Sigplan Conference on Programming Language Design and Implementation (PLDI)*, published as *ACM Sigplan Notices*, 33:5, pp. 280–290; 1998.

[BCF95] M. Brandis, R. Crelier, M. Franz, and J. Templ; "The Oberon System Family"; *Software-Practice and Experience*, 25:12, pp. 1331–1366; 1995.

[Cha82] G. J. Chaitin; "Register Allocation & Spilling via Graph Coloring"; *Proceedings of the ACM Sigplan '82 Symposium on Compiler Construction*, published as *ACM Sigplan Notices*, 17:6, pp. 98–105; 1982.

[FK97] M. Franz and T. Kistler; "Slim Binaries"; *Communications of the ACM*, 40:12, pp. 87–94; 1997.

[FL91] M. Franz and S. Ludwig; "Portability Redefined"; in *Proceedings of the Second International Modula-2 Conference*, Loughborough, England, pp. 216–224; 1991.

[Fra93] M. Franz; "Emulating an Operating System on Top of Another"; *Software-Practice and Experience*, 23:6, pp. 677"692; 1993.

[Fra94a] M. Franz; *Code-Generation On-the-Fly: A Key to Portable Software* (Doctoral Dissertation No. 10497, ETH Zürich); Verlag der Fachvereine, Zürich; 1994.

[Fra94b] M. Franz; "Compiler Optimizations Should Pay for Themselves"; in P. Schulthess (Ed.), *Advances in Modular Languages: Proceedings of the Joint Modular Languages Conference*, Universitätsverlag Ulm, Germany, pp. 111–121; 1994.

[Fra97] M. Franz; "The Programming Language Lagoona: A Fresh Look at Object-Orientation"; *Software-Concepts and Tools*, 18:1, pp. 14–26; 1997.

[Fra98] M. Franz; "On the Architecture of Software Component Systems"; in R. Nigel Horspool (Ed.), *Systems Implementation 2000, (Proceedings of the IFIP TC2 WG2.4 Working Conference on Systems Implementation 2000: Languages, Methods and Tools, Berlin, Germany)*, Chapman & Hall, ISBN 0-412-83530-4, pp. 207–220; 1998.

[GHJ95] E. Gamma, R. Helm, R. Johnson, and J. Vlissides; *Design Patterns – Elements of Reusable Object-Oriented Software*; Addison Wesley; 1995.

[Gut94] J. Gutknecht; "Oberon System 3: Vision of a Future Software Technology"; *Software-Concepts and Tools*, 15:1, pp. 26–33; 1994.

[KP89] G. E. Krasner and S. T. Pope; "A Cookbook for using the Model-View-Controller User Interface Paradigm in Smalltalk-89"; *Journal of Object-Oriented Programming*, 1:3, 26–49; 1989.

[MTG89] H. Mössenböck, J. Templ, and R. Griesemer; *Object Oberon: An Object-Oriented Extension of Oberon*; Report No. 109, Department Informatik, ETH Zurich; 1989.

[MW92] H. Mössenböck and N. Wirth; "The Programming Language Oberon-2"; *Structured Programming*, 12:4; pp. 179–195; 1991

[PS94] D. Pountain and C. Szyperski; "Extensible Software Systems"; *BYTE*, 19:5; 1994.

[Szy92a] C. Szyperski; "Write-ing Applications: Designing an Extensible Text Editor as an Application Framework". In *Proceedings of the 7th International Conference on Technology of Object-Oriented Languages and Systems (TOOLS'92)*, Dortmund, Germany; Prentice Hall; 1992.

[Szy92b] C. Szyperski; *Insight Ethos: On Object Orientation in Operating Systems. Clemens Szyperski.* (Doctoral Dissertation No. 9884, ETH Zurich). Verlag der Fachvereine, Zürich; 1992.

[Szy98] C. Szyperski; *Component Software – Beyond Object-Oriented Programming*; Addison-Wesley; 1998.

[WG92] N. Wirth and J. Gutknecht; *Project Oberon: The Design of an Operating System and Compiler*; Addison-Wesley; 1992.

[Wir93] N. Wirth; "Recollections about the Development of Pascal", in T. J. Bergin and R. G. Gibson, *History of Programming Languages.* (Proceedings of the Second Conference on the History of Programming Languages, Cambridge, Massachusetts, April 1993). Addison-Wesley, pp. 97–120; 1996.

[Wir96] N. Wirth; *Theory and Techniques of Compiler Construction.* Addison-Wesley; 1996.

Compiler Construction
The Art of Niklaus Wirth

Hanspeter Mössenböck
University of Linz

Abstract

Niklaus Wirth is not only a master of language design but also a pioneer of compiler construction. For four decades he has refined his techniques for building simple, efficient and reliable compilers. This paper tries to collect some general principles behind his work. It is not a paper about new compilation techniques but a reflection about Wirth's way to write compilers.

1 Introduction

Among the numerous research topics that Niklaus Wirth approached during his professional career, programming languages and their compilers clearly was the dominating theme. There is hardly anybody in Computer Science who has such a deep insight into language design as Niklaus Wirth. Since the early sixties he has been active in this field and has contributed such seminal languages as Algol-W, Pascal, Modula-2 and Oberon. And being an engineer, he was always as much concerned about the simplicity and efficiency of his compilers as about the elegance of his languages.

In this paper I will try to summarize some principles of Wirth's art of compiler construction. Although I have no personal recollections from Wirth's early projects I have studied his compilers from the early eighties on and was lucky to have the chance to work with him for several years during the Oberon project. So this paper is more about what I learned from him and what I appreciate about his work. Wirth himself gave a much more thorough description of his compiler technology in his recent compiler book [22], in his Turing Award lecture [2] and in his recollections at the second conference on the History of Programming Languages [21].

When I write about Wirth's art of compiler construction I also want to honour the work of his colleagues and assistants [1, 3, 7, 9, 10, 11, 12]. However, although many of the well-known compilers from ETH Zurich were implemented by his bright PhD students, it was always Wirth who set the direction and determined the style of ETH compilers.

I will start this paper with some general principles that I learned from Wirth and then look at more detailed guidelines and techniques for the individual compilation phases.

2 Guiding Principles

Besides using specific techniques, data structures and algorithms it is also important that a compiler designer follows some general guidelines, which set the framework for the whole development. Here are a few principles, which I believe to be central in Wirth's compilers. The list is perhaps incomplete and somewhat arbitrary but hopefully still some food for thought.

- *Use straightforward techniques*
  Compiler technology is one of the most intensively researched fields in Computer Science. There are highly sophisticated algorithms for syntax analysis, semantic analysis, optimization and code generation. However, more sophisticated techniques do not necessarily lead to better compilers. Wirth's compilers use only the simplest techniques such as recursive descent parsing, context-free semantic analysis and single-pass code generation with only a few optimizations. Nevertheless these compilers generate sufficiently fast code and run much faster than most commercial compilers. A compiler writer should have the heart to refrain from using highly sophisticated algorithms if he can see that more straightforward techniques are perfectly sufficient. In his Turing Award lecture [2] Wirth wrote: "Within the Euler, Algol-W and PL360 projects, much consideration was given to the development of table-driven, bottom-up syntax analysis techniques. Later I switched back to the simple recursive-descent, top-down method, which is easily comprehensible and unquestionably sufficiently powerful, if the syntax of the language is wisely chosen."

- *Simple compilers are more reliable compilers*
  As in any software project it is essential that a single person can grasp the whole design of a compiler. This is what Brooks calls the *conceptional integrity* of a software system [6]. It can only be achieved if the compiler is simple enough. A compiler that cannot be understood as a whole by a single software engineer cannot be guaranteed to be correct and cannot be maintained without introducing new errors. In his Turing Award lecture Wirth confessed: "... that this Modula compiler is already at the limits of comprehensible complexity, and I would feel utterly incapable of constructing a good compiler for Ada."

- *Generate good code for the frequent case; don't optimize the exceptional case*
  It is much more important that frequent language constructs such as procedure calls, array accesses, or general control structures are compiled efficiently than to put too much effort into optimizations such as loop unrolling or induction vari-

able analysis that can only be exploited in rare cases. Wirth's compilers don't use any of the more advanced optimization techniques. Instead they generate good code for ordinary programs by fully exploiting the machine architecture and its addressing modes.

- *Generate good code from the beginning; don't generate bad code and optimize later*
  Some compilers first generate poor intermediate code because it is optimized later anyway. For such compilers it is often reported that optimizations achieve substantial speedups. However, this is not surprising since the unoptimized code was rather inefficient. If a compiler generates good code from the beginning there is much less room for speedups. Brandis and others [3] report that non-optimizing Oberon compilers for the Motorola 68020, for the Sun SPARC and for the DEC MIPS architectures generated code that was as efficient as the code generated by the standard C compiler with the optimization option switched on (cc -O). Only for the IBM RS/6000 was the optimizing C compiler able to generate more efficient code than the Oberon compiler.

- *Don't let the compiler repair poor programming style*
  Some people expect a compiler to smoothen inefficiencies caused by poor programming style. This includes some cases of common subexpression elimination, loop invariant code motion and copy propagation. It is, however, simpler and often also clearer if the programmer does these transformations in the source code instead of relying on the compiler to do them behind the scenes. Although not all of these transformations can be expressed in source code, most of them can and the remaining ones usually don't cause major inefficiencies, except in some frequently executed inner loops.

- *Generate predictable code*
  Optimizations often have the effect that minor changes in the source code cause major differences in the run time of the program, because a small change in the code may allow or disallow an optimization. Programmers feel uneasy if they cannot predict the behavior of the generated code. It impedes debugging and benchmarking.

- *What is difficult to compile is usually also difficult to understand*
  Like a programmer, a compiler has to analyze (i.e., to "understand") a program before it can translate it. If a language construct is difficult for a compiler to analyze, it is often difficult for a human to understand too. For example, in C the construct

  ```
  x (*y) ();
  ```

  declares a function pointer *y* whereas the syntactically similar construct

  ```
  x (*y);
  ```

denotes the call of a procedure x. Since both constructs can occur at the same place in a program, it is difficult to keep them apart syntactically, both for the compiler and for the programmer.

- *Instead of applying more sophisticated compilation techniques, simplify the language*
  Of course, this advice can only be followed if the compiler writer is at the same time also the language designer (as Wirth always was for his compilers). If the implementers of C did not rely on powerful compiler construction tools such as *Yacc*, the syntax of C would probably be simpler.

- *Strive for short compilation times*
  It is not only important that the compiler generates efficient code but that it also runs efficiently itself. These two goals are often in conflict and one has to find a reasonable trade-off. Unfortunately, many commercial compilers emphasize code efficiency and accept long compilation times. However, even a compilation time of 5 to 10 seconds per module can be perceived as unduly long, especially if several modules have to be recompiled after a program modification. During software development, the productivity of programmers can be boosted significantly if their work is not disrupted by unduly long compilation pauses.

- *A compiler is also an educational tool; it should inhibit bad programming style*
  Clearly a programming language can have an educational effect by providing only clean and structured language features. But a compiler can have a similar effect by introducing certain restrictions, which limit the size of a module, the number of imported modules, or the number of global variables to a reasonable maximum. It can also penalize questionable programming constructs such as the access to non-local variables by not optimizing such cases. Although these measures are not very popular with programmers they can have an educational value and may prevent major style deficiencies. Such restrictions are a problem, however, when source code is generated by a tool. In such a case the length of names or the size of modules cannot be influenced by the programmer.

- *Write the compiler in its own language*
  For Wirth, language design and compiler construction always went hand in hand. He writes [21]: "I never could separate the design of a language from its implementation, for a rigid definition without the feedback from the construction of its compiler would seem to me presumptuous and unprofessional." Writing a compiler in its own language not only proves that the language is powerful enough but it has also the advantage that any improvement to the generated code will make the compiler faster, too.

Other people will probably find even more principles. Wirth himself published some general compiler guidelines in an early paper [16] but I wish he would do it again today in the light of the Modula and Oberon projects.

In the remaining sections I will look at the individual compilation phases and try to extract some general principles from them.

3 Scanning

There is not much to say about scanning. Wirth's scanners are hand-crafted and optimized since the scanner is one of the most time consuming parts of a compiler. Token positions for error messages are recorded as character positions and not as line/column pairs, which simplifies book-keeping. Attributes and token positions are returned in global variables to avoid parameter overhead for information that is not needed with every token. The length of names is restricted to a reasonable amount (24 or 32 characters). This can be seen as an educational means since unduly long names can inhibit the readability of programs as much as cryptically short names do.

4 Parsing

The design of a parser is mainly determined by the selection of the parsing technique and the error recovering strategy. Since the times of Pascal, Wirth's compilers use top-down recursive descent parsing. Recursive descent is the simplest and fastest parsing technique. Although there are more powerful techniques, such as bottom-up LALR parsing, recursive descent is powerful enough if the syntax of the language is properly designed.

Recursive descent parsing requires the grammar of a language to be LL(1), that means it must be possible to analyze the language top-down from left to right with a single lookahead symbol. Whenever there is an alternative in the grammar, the lookahead symbol must lead the way and tell the compiler which alternative to select.

This is probably also the way in which humans read and analyze a program. Programmers read source code from left to right. Whenever they read a symbol (keyword, name, number, etc.) they want to know which language construct it belongs to. In contrast, bottom-up parsers read symbols without already deciding to which language construct they belong. They simply push the symbols on a stack. As soon as the end of the stack contains an appropriate right-hand side of a production they reduce this symbol sequence to the corresponding nonterminal symbol. Thus, bottom-up parsers delay the recognition of language constructs in a program for as long as possible, which makes them more powerful but also less natural for humans. Programmers don't have large stacks in their heads. They do not want to read many symbols ahead to know what a program construct means.

Programs are notations for humans and not so much for machines. They should be easy to read and therefore suitable for top-down parsing because it is more natural than bottom-up parsing.

Wirth always designed his languages so that recursive descent parsing could be applied. This did not compromise the flexibility or the power of the languages. I know of no language feature that must inherently be expressed in a way that is not amenable to recursive descent parsing. I even think that the availability of powerful bottom-up parser generators such as *Yacc* are responsible for the cryptic syntax of C. If the designers of C were forced to make their language LL(1) it would have probably become more readable.

Unfortunately even Wirth's languages contain a few constructs which are not LL(1). To analyze such constructs, it is not sufficient to rely on syntactic information. One must also take semantic information into account. For example, a type guard *x(T)* in Oberon cannot be distinguished from a procedure call syntactically. One has to consult the symbol table to find out if *x* is a procedure or a variable. This ambiguity could have easily been avoided, for example by using curly brackets instead of round brackets.

The second design decision in a parser is the selection of an appropriate error handling technique. Although good error recovery is more difficult for hand-coded recursive descent parsers than for table-driven parsers, there are a number of suitable standard techniques. The general goal of error handling is to find as many errors as possible in a single compilation and to avoid spurious errors. In addition, error recovery should not slow down error-free parsing and should not blur the parsing code with too many error handling statements.

The standard error recovery technique, which was also applied in the ETH Pascal and Modula-2 compilers, is to pass to every parsing procedure the set of follower symbols of the nonterminal that the procedure is to recognize. If an error is detected, the input is skipped until a symbol is found that is a legal follower of a currently active parsing procedure. The procedure stack is then unwound to the caller of this procedure and parsing can continue there.

Although this technique can be systematically applied, it requires a large amount of set operations and additional parameters of the parsing procedures. This slows down error-free parsing and tends to hide the parsing actions between the error recovery statements. Therefore, Wirth selected a different error recovery strategy for his Oberon compiler:

Given the fact that computers become faster and faster, it is not necessary any more to find *all* errors in a single compilation. If a compilation takes less than a second, it is acceptable to find just *some* errors, correct them, and then compile the program again to find the remaining errors. Thus the Oberon compiler does not synchronize with the followers of every nonterminal symbol but selects a few synchronization points in the grammar where recovery is particularly easy and safe. These synchronization points are the beginning of a statement, a declaration or a type where symbols such as "IF", "WHILE", "TYPE" or "RECORD" are expected. These symbols are considered particularly safe, because they are unlikely to be encountered in the wrong context. If the parser detects an error, it reports it and continues up to the next synchronization point (i.e., to the beginning of the next statement, declaration or type). There it skips input symbols until one of the expected safe symbols occurs. Parsing can be resumed with that symbol. To avoid spurious error messages, an error is only reported, if a certain number of tokens (e.g. three) has been recognized successfully since the last error.

This simple error recovery technique can be implemented in about ten lines of code. It does not slow down error-free parsing and does not burry the parsing statements between error recovery actions. It is another example of Wirth's search for simplicity and adequacy.

5 Symbol Table Handling

A symbol table maps the names in a program to their attributes such as their types and their addresses. It consists of several subtables (scopes), one for every module, procedure and record type. As a consequence of single pass compilation, which Wirth preferred in his later compilers, the scopes can be organized in a stack-like way. A new scope is opened at the top of the stack whenever the parser encounters a procedure, and it is closed when the parser has finished with this procedure. This has the advantage that most nodes of a scope can be discarded (or left for the garbage collector) after the corresponding procedure has been parsed. Only the nodes for the formal parameters have to be kept.

For the implementation of the symbol table, Wirth usually chose rather simple data structures such as binary search trees or even linear lists. Although a hash table would be more efficient for large scopes, it is more complicated to handle (e.g. to traverse, to enlarge or to shrink) and consumes more memory. Since too many names in a scope are often an indication of a questionable programming style, Wirth felt that large scopes should not be encouraged. Measurements showed that for procedure scopes, which usually don't contain more than ten names, a simple linear list is sufficient.

Symbol tables also store the types of objects. For type compatibility checks, Wirth again preferred the simpler technique (name equivalence) over the more powerful but also more complicated technique (structural equivalence). With name equivalence two types are the same if they are denoted by the same type name, i.e. by the same type node in the symbol table. This can be checked with a simple pointer comparison. In contrast, with structural equivalence (as it is used in Modula-3) two types are the same if they have the same structure, i.e. if they have the same components in the same order and if these components are structurally equivalent pairwise. This requires a recursive comparison of the type structures and is not only more complicated but also more time consuming.

A symbol table contains different kinds of objects (e.g., constants, variables, procedures, etc.) as well as different kinds of structures (e.g., basic types, arrays, records, etc.). With type extension, which was introduced in Oberon, it would seem natural to organize the objects and structures in type hierarchies, i.e. in an object-oriented way. There would be a base type with the common data of all object kinds as well as several extensions with the special data for constants, variables or procedures. Although this organization is elegant and is in fact recommended in some compiler books, it is complicated to handle in practice. Since a compiler often works with general objects, their actual extension types would have to be checked using run-time type tests, and their fields would have to be accessed with guarded type conversions. Alternatively, all operations on objects could be defined in terms of dynamically bound methods, but this would require a large number of methods and would compromise the efficiency of the compiler. Besides, there are some operations which depend on more than one operand. This would require methods that are dynamically bound depending on two or more objects (so-called multi methods). Thus, Wirth chose to represent the fields of all objects in a single flat record type and to use only those fields that belong to the respective object variant. Although less elegant, this technique makes the access to object fields simple and efficient. It is another example of an engineering trade-off, which can be found so often in Wirth's compilers.

6 Separate Compilation

A major achievement of Modula-2 was the concept of *separate compilation*, which emerged in the seventies in languages such as Mesa [13] and later also Ada. In contrast to independent compilation (e.g. as in Fortran and C), where subprograms can be compiled independently, separate compilation performs type checking across module boundaries, thus guaranteeing that separately compiled modules can be safely fit together by the linker. When a module is compiled the symbol tables of the imported modules have to be made available as well so that the compiler can access the types of the imported modules. In order to do that, the module interfaces have to be described in so-called definition modules, i.e. in files that contain the declarations of the exported objects.

Instead of recompiling the interface of a module every time this module is imported, Wirth chose to store the precompiled symbol tables in so-called symbol files [10]. Importing a module then simply requires the compiler to read the respective symbol file and to add the imported symbol table to the symbol table of the currently compiled module. Since symbol files are more compact than source files they usually fit into a single disk block and can be read with a single disk access.

A special problem is that the interface of a module can depend on the interfaces of other modules. This would require reading several symbol files when a module is imported. In order to avoid this, symbol files are made self-contained, i.e. they also contain parts of the symbol tables of those modules on which they depend. Thus every import requires just one symbol file to be read. However, it can happen now, that a partial symbol table of the same module gets imported twice from different symbol files. One has to make sure that these repeatedly imported symbol tables are consistent. This can be done by attaching a unique version number to every interface (either a time stamp derived from the compilation time of the interface or a fingerprint derived from the source code of the definition module). By comparing these version numbers, it can easily be checked, if repeatedly imported symbol tables are the same. The version numbers of the imported modules are also stored in the object file of the importing module so that the linker can check if the object files to be linked match the interfaces that were seen during compilation. Thus separate compilation not only performs type checking across module boundaries but also makes sure that consistent versions of modules get bound together by the linker.

In a recent dissertation [8], Régis Crelier refined the version checking between separately compiled modules and implemented it on a finer granularity. The problem with the basic version checking technique is that whenever the interface of a module is extended it gets a new version number. This invalidates all modules that import this interface, even if they use only features that did not change. The new idea is to provide distinct version numbers for all exported objects instead of a single version number for the whole interface. If an object is added to the interface or some exported object is changed, the version numbers of the other objects in the interface remain unchanged. This technique gives a programmer much more flexibility to change interfaces without having to recompile dependent modules. The implementation of this technique is non-trivial and is described in [8].

As a surprise to the software engineering community, Wirth abandoned the definition modules in Oberon. However, he did not abandon the concept of separate compilation, but only the necessity to write down a definition module explicitly. In Oberon, there are just implementation modules. The programmer simply marks those declarations that are to be exported in the source code, and the compiler generates a symbol file from them during the normal compilation. A definition module can still be generated from the symbol file of a module, but it is only documentation. A similar technique is also used in other modern languages such as Eiffel and Java.

The elimination of explicit definition modules caused much debate among Modula-2 enthusiasts. In fact there are good arguments in favour of definition modules, but there are also good arguments against them. A definition module is a clear description of a module interface. It forces a programmer to think about the design of a module first before starting its implementation. This is good software engineering practice. On the other hand, definition modules introduce redundancy into a language. For example, the interfaces of exported procedures have to be described both in the definition module and in the implementation module. Every time a procedure interface is modified, it has to be modified in two places, and the compiler has to check the consistency of these declarations. Definition modules also make it harder to selectively export record fields, because the record with the exported fields would have to be declared in the definition module and the rest of the record in the implementation module. Finally, explicit definition modules duplicate the number of source files and make it harder to maintain a large software system.

Personally, I think that the elimination of definition modules was a good decision, since it simplifies the language and its compiler. One can still start with designing the interface of a module by writing a skeleton of the implementation module that only contains the exported declarations. Later this skeleton can be filled with flesh by adding private declarations and code. Nevertheless, I must admit that it is tempting to mark the exported declarations only after the whole implementation module has been written.

7 Code Generation

The code generation phase is not as systematical to describe and to implement as the earlier compiler phases. It heavily depends on the peculiarities of the target machine, which is often irregular and full of machine-specific details. Nevertheless the code generators of Wirth's compilers show some common characteristics.

One principle that was already mentioned earlier is to generate reasonably good code from the beginning. This can be achieved by delayed code generation using the *Item technique* described below, by exploiting the special instructions and addressing modes of the target machine, and by applying simple optimizations such as constant folding and strength reduction.

The spine of Wirth's code generators is what I call the *Item technique*. It is described in Wirth's compiler book [22] although it is not given a specific name. The general idea is that every value that turns up during code generation is described by a structure that is called an *item*. Items can describe constants, variables, intermediate results, or condition codes resulting from compare instructions. Every parsing procedure processes a language construct and returns an item that describes the value of this construct. Items are thus the attributes of the imaginary syntax tree. While the parsing procedures move top-down, the resulting items are propagated bottom-up thus creating more complex items and generating code alongside.

For example, the code generation for the addition $x + y$ first leads to two items describing the variables x and y. In the next step, *load* instructions are generated for *x* and *y*, and the items describing the variables are transformed into items describing register contents, because the values of *x* and *y* are now in registers. Finally an *add* instruction is emitted and the two register items are combined into a single register item, which describes the result of the addition. If the target machine supports the addition of memory operands, only *x* has to be loaded into a register and *y* is still described by a variable item.

In many cases, items can be constructed without emitting code. For example, a record selection *r.f* results in an item describing the record variable *r* and an object describing the field *f*. In the next step, a new item is constructed that describes a memory cell with the base address of *r* and the offset of *f*. No code has to be emitted in this step. The transformation just leads to a compile-time addition of an offset. Using such compile-time operations, code generation is delayed as long as possible. An instruction is only generated if the result of the transformation cannot be produced at compile time.

The kinds of items depend both on the source language and on the target machine. For every object kind in the symbol table (i.e. for constants, variables, fields, procedures, etc.) an item kind has to be provided that describes that object. These are the *source level items*. Similarly, for every addressing mode of the target machine (i.e. for immediate, register, register relative, indexed, etc.) an item kind has to be provided that describes a value accessed by this addressing mode. These are the *machine level items*. Code generation proceeds by transforming source level items (e.g. variables) into machine level items accessed by a specific addressing mode (e.g. register relative). All items are implemented by a flat record that encodes the item kind and its attributes. Usually some source level items are identical to some machine level items (for example, a constant item corresponds to an immediate item, a variable item corresponds to a register relative item, etc). In this case the two item kinds can be combined into a single item kind.

Having identified the necessary item kinds, one has to implement three sets of procedures: (a) procedures that transform objects into source level items (e.g. variable objects into variable items), (b) procedures that transform one item kind into another (e.g. from register relative to register by loading the value into a register), and (c) procedures that generate the actual machine instructions: for every machine instruction *op a, b* one has to implement a procedure *Op(a, b)* where the parameters *a* and *b* are items. This procedure is implemented by a case statement considering all possible combinations of item kinds that *a* and *b* can assume. By applying these guidelines, item kinds and the corresponding code generation procedures can be developed systematically for any given machine.

Another important issue in code generation is register allocation. It is especially important for RISC machines where a large number of registers are available and should be exploited to have faster access to variables and intermediate values. Good register allocation, however, cannot be done in a single pass. It requires life range analysis of programs and a coverage of the life ranges by registers using a technique that is based on graph colouring. Since Wirth's compilers do code generation in a single pass a trade-off is used. The basic register allocation technique is quite simple. Whenever a new register is needed, the register allocator returns an arbitrary free register and marks it as used. At the end of every statement all registers are returned. This technique is simple and efficient but only exploits a small subset of the available registers.

As a simple optimization, a compiler can try to keep the first few variables of every procedure in registers. However, this can only be done if these variables are not accessed by nested procedures and if they are not passed to other procedures as reference parameters. Instead of allocating a memory cell for such register variables, the symbol table simply holds the register numbers where these variables are stored. Of course, register variables must not be marked as free at the end of every statement. One also has to save and restore register variables across procedure calls, since the called procedures will use the registers for their own variables. A detailed description of this technique can be found in [3].

8 Single Pass versus Multi Pass Compilers

Wirth designed his languages so that they can be compiled in a single pass: every name has to be declared before it is used; pointers and procedures can be forward declared in order to allow cyclic dependencies. If it was necessary a few years ago to decompose a compiler into several passes due to memory restrictions, this is not an argument any more. Current computers have enough memory to fit a whole compiler into it. The predominant reason for multi-pass compilers is optimization. Advanced optimization requires data flow analysis, which has to be performed on an intermediate program representation such as the control flow graph. Building this graph and analyzing it requires several passes. Wirth's compilers avoid sophisticated optimizations, thus no intermediate program representation is necessary and the code can be generated on the fly during parsing. Although the resulting code is not as efficient as it could be, it compares well with the code generated by optimizing C compilers on most platforms (measurements are given in [3]).

There is, however, another good reason to decompose a compiler into two passes: namely portability. If a compiler is decomposed in a language-dependent front end and a machine-dependent back end, porting the compiler to a new machine only requires rewriting the back end. This solution was chosen in the Oberon OP2 compiler [7], designed by Régis Crelier and ported to about 10 different platforms by various PhD students. All these compilers use the same front end, which contains the scanner, the parser and the symbol table handler. It generates an intermediate program representation in the form of an abstract syntax tree and a symbol table. These data structures are passed to the back end, which contains the code generator.

The syntax tree also allows for more optimizations in the back end such as the elimination of array index checks in certain situations. The back end for the IBM RS/6000 even applies heavy optimizations before code is generated [4]: it turned out that this multiscalar processor requires instruction scheduling to achieve a code quality comparable to the code generated by optimizing C compilers. Therefore the syntax tree is first transformed into a control flow graph using a simplified version of the static single assignment form [5]. Various optimizations such as common subexpression elimination, constant propagation, loop invariant code motion and instruction scheduling are applied to this graph before code is generated.

The intermediate program representation between front end and back end turned out to be of value for still another purpose: mobile code. Michael Franz found a compact encoding of the syntax tree and the symbol table, that can be transferred over a network to some target machine, where it is compiled to machine code by a code generating loader [9]. This is an alternative to the Java bytecodes and allows "write once run everywhere" software. It is interesting to note that this idea was published before the advent of Java.

9 Conclusion

This paper tried to highlight some principles that I believe are central in Wirth's compilers. Maybe my view is biased and incomplete, but I think that it reflects some valuable ideas. I always enjoyed studying Wirth's compilers. Although they contain hardly a line of comment, their structure is so clear, simple and elegant that they are a pleasure to read. The full source code of some of his compilers can be found in his books on compiler construction [22] and on the Oberon Project [20]. The source code of the OP2 compiler is also available online from ETH Zurich as part of the Oberon distribution.

For Wirth, compiler construction is an engineering discipline and not pure science. He prefers well-proven techniques to fashionable results. For him, a compiler is a tool that has to be as useful and practical as possible and not so much a piece of scientific experimentation.

I regard Wirth's way of compiler construction as an art, not in the sense of black magic but in the sense of a craft built on four decades of experience.

References

1. Amman U.: The Zurich Implementation, in "Pascal – The Language and its Implementation", Wiley 1978.
2. Ashenhurst R. L., Graham S.: ACM Turing Award Lectures – The First Twenty Years, 1966–1985. ACM Press 1987.
3. Brandis M., Crelier R., Franz M., Templ J.: The Oberon System Family. Software – Practice and Experience 25(12): 1331–1366, 1995.

4. Brandis M.: Optimizing Compilers for Structured Programming Languages. ETH dissertation, 1995.
5. Brandis M., Mössenböck H.: Single-Pass Generation of Static Single Assignment Form for Structured Languages. ACM Transactions on Programming Languages 16(6): 1684–1698, 1994.
6. Brooks F. P.: The Mythical Man-Month – Essays on Software Engineering. Addison-Wesley, 1975.
7. Crelier R.: OP2: A Portable Oberon-2 Compiler. Proceedings of the 2nd International Modula-2 Conference, Loughborough, 1991.
8. Crelier R.: Separate Compilation and Module Extension. ETH dissertation, 1994.
9. Franz M.: Code-Generation on the Fly – a Key to Portable Software. ETH dissertation, 1994.
10. Geissmann L.B.: Separate Compilation in Modula-2 and the Structure of the Modula-2 Compiler on the Personal Computer Lilith. ETH dissertation, 1983.
11. Jacobi C.: Code Generation and the Lilith Architecture, ETH dissertation, 1983.
12. Le V.K.: The Module: A Tool for Structured Programming, ETH dissertation, 1978.
13. Mitchell J.G., Maybury W., Sweet R.: Mesa Language Manual, CSL-79-3, Xerox PARC, 1979.
14. Wirth N.: The Programming Language Pascal. Acta Informatica 1: 35-63, 1971.
15. Wirth N.: The Design of a Pascal Compiler. Software – Practice and Experience 1: 309–333, 1971.
16. Wirth N.: Programming Languages: What to Demand and How to Assess Them. Symposium on Software Engineering, Belfast, April 1976.
17. Wirth N.: Design and Implementation of Modula. Software – Practice and Experience 7(1): 67–84, 1977.
18. Wirth N.: Programming in Modula-2. Springer-Verlag 1982.
19. Wirth N.: The Programming Language Oberon. Software – Practice and Experience 18(7): 671–690, 1985.
20. Wirth N., Gutknecht J.: Project Oberon. The Design of an Operating System and Compiler. Addison-Wesely 1992.
21. Wirth N.: Recollections about the Development of Pascal. Proceedings History of Programming Languages II, Sigplan Notices 28(3): 333–342, 1993.
22. Wirth N.: Compiler Construction

Medos in Retrospect

Svend Erik Knudsen
ETH Zurich, Switzerland

Abstract

The paper summarizes the target application areas planned for Wirth's single-user computer Lilith as well as its hardware, architecture, and main programming language. The objectives for Lilith's operating system Medos are also briefly outlined. Hereafter, I elaborate on the main principles and mechanisms which were instrumental in the design of Medos and list the main system components of Medos. I continue with a critical review of the advantages and disadvantages of Medos and conclude by hinting that operating system (and programming language) support of both latency- and throughput-critical applications should be improved – even for single-user systems.

1 Introduction

Professor Wirth started the project to develop a single-user computer in autumn 1977 when he came back to ETH Zurich from a sabbatical visit to Xerox's Palo Alto Research Center (PARC). Wirth was so impressed by the use of the then newly developed single-user computer Alto [TML79] that he could not imagine working again in the old fashioned way using a "tty" console connected to a computer in ETH's computer center. The subsequent development of "The Personal Computer" or the "PC", as it was called for the first few years, became a total workover: new hardware, a new instruction set, a new programming language, new utilities, new editors, etc. It did, at least, produce some new aspects, for example, of the "mouse". Consequently, the operating system also had to be something completely new, namely *Medos-2* or *Medos* for short [Knu83]. The writer of these lines "earned" the duty to develop the operating system, the often-hated "unwieldy beast" by experimental computer scientists (and by many others). Until then, it both isolated them from the harsh realities of simultaneous users and hardware, but also hindered them in performing many types of experiments.

The name of Lilith's operating system *Medos* (originally *Medos-2*) was taken from Greek mythology but here meant *Mein erstes Disk Operating System,* partly German, meaning *My First Disk Operating System.*[1]

The next section lists some of the operating systems' specific backgrounds. System objectives will also be described. Section three elaborates on principles and concepts applied during its design. Section four briefly describes the components of Medos and their functionalities. Section five is a review of the system's advantages and disadvantages as seen by its designer and programmer from a perspective of some 20 years after its initial construction. I conclude in the last section by mentioning some system objectives and qualities which are still missing in today's typical single-user computer systems and which are likely to remain missing for such systems in the near future.

2 Background

2.1 History

Professor Wirth initiated the the "PC"-project in autumn 1977. (I think that the "PC" was renamed "Lilith" as late as 1981, but for consistency, I will use the name Lilith.) Its main objective was the development of a (his own?) single-user computer. Those days, I had the feeling that Wirth also had an implicit wish or even research goal of showing what can happen when just a few software and hardware people work closely together on the development of a "small" computer.

Many aspects of the Lilith project are documented in papers and dissertations [e.g. Wir81, Wir82, Han82, Gei83, Hop83, Jac82, Knu83, Ohr84] and even in this book [e.g. Wag00]. I will therefore concentrate on some operating system (OS) peculiarities, which are relevant but often undocumented.

2.2 Some Lilith Details

The reader of the next few paragraphs must remember that the development of Lilith started more than two decades ago. In particular, processor clock rates were about two orders of magnitude slower and memory sizes were about three orders of magnitude smaller than today's standard.

Lilith's clock speed was around 7 MHz and enabled Lilith to execute between 1 and 2 million instructions (called M-code) per second. The M-code was designed to be compact and to support compilers in code generation. Some instructions require almost an unlimited number of micro-code steps for their interpretation, (e.g. M-code instructions for operations on bit maps). It is also important to know that Lilith's instruction execution was atomic (uninterruptible), as is typical today for RISC processors. (Or is it an axiom?) From an operating system designer's point

1. The "-2" is due to an experimental system called Medos. I considered to name the system *MSDOS* for *My Second Disk Operating System* but it didn't "sound" well!

of view – looking at Lilith's smallest guaranteed highest interrupt latency – there was nothing (good) to write home about!

Initially, the main memory was planned to have 65,536 16-bit words memory, but soon after its first version, it was enlarged to twice that capacity. For regular Modula-2 programs, however, only the initial 65,536 words were usable for storage of variables. The main cause for this memory "growth" was the refresh memory capacity required for the raster scan display (28 to 33 thousand words). Instructions, bit maps, and fonts were directly accessible anywhere in memory. Secondary storage was a disk drive for exchangeable media with about 9.8 MB capacity.

2.3 Some Modula-2 Details

Medos was programmed in Modula-2 [Wir82]. In comparison with its ancestors, for example Modula [Wir77], a Modula-2 program can be split into several separately compiled (and mutually type-checked) modules. Thus, a typical Modula-2 program consists of a main program module, which may import a collection of separately compiled library modules. A library module is split into a DEFINITION MODULE defining its signature (interface) and an IMPLEMENTATION MODULE being its realization.

Modula-2 also offers some basic facilities for specification of coroutines. A (single) processor executes coroutines one at a time. A new coroutine or *process,* as they are called in Modula-2, is set up by procedure *NEWPROCESS*. A transfer of control to another process is done by a *TRANSFER*-call. An interrupt (or a trap) initiates a TRANSFER-operation to a driver process referenced at a fixed memory location (interrupt vector).

2.4 Lilith's Target Use

Lilith was planned for two main application areas:

Office work. Lilith should assist office work such as preparing documents; writing letters, and sending messages to colleagues.

Advantages of a single-user computer for office work lies in its potentially better user interface compared to those provided by typical time-sharing systems of the time. Shorter response time, more information – including graphics – on the screen, response to each key-stroke, and the availability of a mouse as a pointing device were seen as key beneficial points. Editors could display formatted text as it will be when printed on a small – yet to be developed – laser printer.

In order to have even better tools at hand, it was also considered advantageous to connect the workstations to each other and to some dedicated server computers by a *local area network (LAN)*. Messages could be exchanged and expensive or noisy devices, like printers, high-capacity disk drives or tape units, could be shared and "hidden".

Workbench. Lilith was also intended to be a software-oriented computer scientist's own workbench. It should be a "program-friendly" test environment even for hardware-oriented software and useful in developing and testing new hardware. The computer scientists' students should also benefit from exercises with Lilith as a workbench.

Lilith's main advantage was seen in the potential freedom achievable in its use. The operating system should not hinder a scientist, engineer, or student to test a simple driver or even a new hardware interface. It should also not prescribe a certain layout in its display or fill most of the memory with resident programs. Virtual machine kernels [BH71, BDT84], which by their hardware-protected *virtual machines* enforce sandboxes with a fixed number of abstract resource types (e.g. process, file, signal or message) upon users, seemed to be both unnecessary and contradictory to the desire for system *openness*. The users also wanted to be able to make use of the *whole* and *real* Lilith computer. Simultaneous users got hardware-protection from each other by using separate *real* Lilith machines!

3 Principles and Mechanisms

Section 3.1 enumerates some attributes of good programs. These have significantly influenced the development of Medos. Medos presented itself to programmers as a collection of library modules. These modules were designed and implemented according to an object model or with an object-orientation, which is briefly presented in section 3.2. The next section explains the simple but powerful concept applied to execute user programs. Resource management mechanisms are explained in section 3.4, and section 3.5 summarizes principles, concepts, and mechanisms supporting system *openness*.

3.1. Attributes of Good Programs

Several objectives guided the design and implementation of Medos. It was certainly the intention to make a *good operating system* of *modest size*. However, which attributes of an OS or generally of any program qualify it to be called *good*? The answer differs from individual to individual.

The most important predicate for me is that the program is *reliable*. One cannot depend on an unreliable program. A reliable program must both be *understandable* and *correct* meaning that its "behavior" must be foreseeable for users. A reliable program must however also be *robust* to ward off commonly occurring errors. The correctness of a non-trivial program cannot be practically proven. But, by use of a high-level programming language, proofreading, run-time assertions and other techniques, one might later rather than sooner be convinced that a (certain piece of) program is correct (enough). Robustness is generally achieved by redundancy, in both data and code. Redundancy makes it possible to detect inconsistencies and consequently to prevent a single failure or error escalating to a "disaster".

A program should, however, also be *simple*, *adaptable* and whenever possible, *efficient*. Users (and implementers) need simplicity (not primitiveness) to understand the program. If programmers do not understand an algorithm to be programmed, they cannot be expected to deliver a correct and reliable program. Finding a simple solution to solve a huge number of complex problems is usually difficult. Most large programs should be usable over a period of several years and, therefore, be structured so that they can easily be adapted to "minor" changes in specification or run-time environment. A program should whenever possible also be efficient, if this does not conflict with being part of good programming as mentioned previoulsy. Fortunately, simple solutions are often also efficient and adaptable. If simplicity conflicts with robustness, pick robustness.

3.2 Medos Objectives

Professor Wirth wanted (among other OS specifics) a *small resident executive* permitting a user to initiate the execution of some standard utilities and applications as well as his (her) own programs. He (we) didn't want a multi-purpose OS structured with many "hard" protection layers, as taught in [BDT84] or provided by the T.H.E. multiprogramming system [Dij68], for example. Quite the opposite, the OS should be *open* according to the philosophy of the Xerox Corporation's Alto-computer [Lam74]. The following list summarizes the Medos objectives. It should:

- support the execution of Modula-2 programs
- itself be programmed in Modula-2
- include a file system
- be a single-user system
- be reliable, robust, convenient and efficient
- be *open*

In addition, it should *not* (necessarily) support:

- multi-programming
- real-time critical applications
- simultaneous users

3.3 Architecture

Programmers viewed Medos as a collection of separate Modula-2 (library) modules, which (mostly) provide abstract interfaces to object classes. One could also consider such modules as being managers of some kind of resources.

This design follows the *object model* [Jon78] by which an operating system can be described by a set of object types, each of which represents a *kind of* resource, either physical or artificial. In this model, an actual resource is represented by an *instance* (variable) of an object type (class). Each module (i.e. object manager) defines abstract operations to perform changes to the state of a resource. A user of a certain resource has only to understand the defined operations. Consider, for example, type *file* and operations on each instance of it: *Reset, Write, Read* as well as *Create* and *Destroy.* The view of an operating system as a collection of abstract types with instances can easily be expressed in high-level programming languages supporting abstract data types [Par72].

3.4 Programs

The resident part of Medos was the (resident part of the) default command interpreter. It was, of course, a Modula-2 program consisting of a main module importing separately compiled library modules needed for reading program names from a terminal, a "program executor", and for writing error messages to the terminal. The resident part of Medos was minimal in the sense that it included only the modules that are required by the command interpreter.

Before 1984, Medos did not support multi-programming, neither heavyweight (task) nor lightweight processes (threads). From an ordinary user or programmer's point of view, one process (task) was running. Initially, the process executed the resident program, which was the command interpreter. The command interpreter "interpreted" commands by *program calls*, which might be considered as a generalization of procedure calls. The program abstraction was mainly provided by the module *Program*, which provided routine *Call(programname, shared, status).* Medos's command interpreter called *Program.Call(commandname, FALSE, status)* to interpret the user's command by the execution of a program. During the execution of a called program, the program caller (e.g. the command interpreter) "waited" until the activated program finished and returned. Any running program could itself call a program; thus, all simultaneously activated programs formed a stack of activated programs. At the bottom of this stack was the resident part of Medos, i.e. the command interpreter, together with all modules used by it. The program at the top of the stack was the currently running program.

Some essential differences existed between this program abstraction and its *call*-mechanism compared to a Modula-2 procedure and its activation:

- A program was identified by a *computable program name* (a string).
- A caller was also resumed if the called program "crashes" (*exception handling*).
- Resources like memory and connected files were owned by programs and were retrieved again when the "owning" program returned (*resource management*).
- On activation of a program, its code was bound to imported modules. The program was bound to already loaded modules. Imported but not yet loaded

modules were of course loaded and linked. On program return it was unbound (and unloaded):

- The program level uniquely identified a called program. Program level 0 represented Medos. If the program on *level i* called a program, the called program was on *level i+1*. The running program was on *current level*. The caller could indicate that it wanted to share resources. The lowest program level sharing resources with current level was *shared level*.

The advantages of this program abstraction and its resource management mechanisms are found in the following three areas:

The stack of activated programs enables efficient memory use without any fragmentation.

Lilith's architecture did not support relocation of data in physical memory. More general memory allocation strategies than the stack seemed unable to guarantee comparably high memory utilization. From the very beginning, the small main memory (65,536 words) was very critical. By 1980, Medos occupied about 12 k words (including the default font (1.5 k words) and file buffers (2 k words)), the display bitmap used 28.5 k words. Only 23.5 k words remained for the execution of non-resident programs. This is somewhat more than required to execute the Modula-2 multi-pass compiler or the standard text editor.

The binding of an activated program to programs at lower activation levels is very desirable. This abstraction allows each user to dynamically expand the set of system-supported and managed resources and libraries. For example, calling another command interpreter were capable this by importing the modules providing the added resources were capable of this. Ordinary user-written programs may then be executed as programs on level 2. They can then make use of the extended set of supported resources.

The Modula-2 multi-pass compiler used this mechanism. The part common to all passes was the program (or actually command) *modula*. *modula* subsequently called the compiler passes one after another in *shared* mode. Shared mode guaranteed that shareable resources like those allocated from the heap were not freed (nor were the inter-pass files closed) when compiler passes terminated.

The program abstraction is convenient and easy for programmers used to high-level programming languages with nested procedure declarations. Letting activated programs be owners of resources (objects) is conceptually similar to procedures "owning" locally declared variables.

3.5 Resource Management

In sections 3.3, it was mentioned that separate modules manage resources. The resource managers provide routines for the creation and removal of objects (representing resources) as well as routines performing operations on these objects (resources). The instantiation strategy for objects as well as usage rules can be decided freely for each resource manager (module). Medos was in this respect an *open* system. Providing objects, however does not come for free. The resource manager must provide some memory space for the object to represent the state of the allocated resource. As a result, resource managers have to limit the "lifetime" of objects. Objects should exist only as long as they can legally be referenced and potentially used. Lifetime should be set to be as short as possible in order to eliminate the costs of no longer accessible (or "forgotten") objects and resources. If objects remain indefinitely, a system will eventually die due to lack of free resources for new objects.

In the module *Monitor*, placed lowest in the module hierarchy, Medos supported an *object ownership rule*: an activated program owned an object or resource. The module *Monitor* provided three routines to help resource management modules to enforce this ownership rule, namely *CurrentLevel()*, *SharedLevel()* and *TermProcedure(resetProc). CurrentLevel and SharedLevel* were functions that yielded the integer values, which identified the currently running program (*current level*) and the lowest level of a program (*shared level*) which could share objects with the currently running program. By a *TermProcedure* call, the body of a resource-managing module could "install" a parameter-free reset routine. Reset-routines would be called in the opposite order of their "installation" whenever a program terminated, provided the program resided on a higher level than the level containing the object-managing module.

3.6 Principles Providing Openness

Today, the attribute *open* is used in papers to characterize many different IT-related "things" like systems, protocols, busses, etc. *Open* seems also to mean *widely available*, *not proprietary* or *not a secret*. I will try to clarify which principles or mechanisms justify classifying Medos as *open*.

Extensibility. The freedom of any running program to activate other programs themselves makes the system *extensible*. A program may include a collection of "library" modules effectively providing a vastly enhanced environment for called programs currently running at higher program levels. The XS-1 system [BBF82] is implemented in this way. XS-1 is a single-user system providing an integrated user-interface and hierarchically structured files. The visibility and accessibility of *all* loaded modules including all those residing at lower levels is certainly part of the system's *openness*.

Abstract Interfaces. All resident modules (with two minor and unimportant exceptions: *DefaultFont* and *System*) have interfaces which only export Modula-2 types and procedures. From the specifications of these modules, programmers know very little about their implementation. This *protects* libraries and resource managers from being easily abused and *opens up* possible changes and module implementations for implementers. These will be invisible to users as long as interfaces remain unchanged. The quality and convenience of an abstraction and its implementation greatly influence the feasibility of a module to remain unchanged. Abstraction quality can partly be judged by its simplicity, cleanness, usage convenience, orthogonality to other provided abstractions, and completeness.

Plug-ins. Three resident modules (*Monitor*, *TerminalBase*, and *FileSystem*) also provide routines (one or two) which permit hierarchically higher-level (or even nonresident) modules to provide additional or alternative resource implementations. The modules that provide a mechanism to dynamically *plug-in* realizations of the abstractions can certainly be considered *extensible* and *open*. A plug-in installation is considered an object credited to and owned by the running program. It must be considered at the latest when the installing program is terminated.

- *Monitor* permits resource managers to install reset-routines (*TermProcedure*).
- *TerminalBase* permits programs to substitute implementations for the read- and write-routine in module *Terminal*.
- Before files residing on a specific *medium* can be accessed via module *FileSystem*, an implementation for files stored on the medium must be installed (plugged in). File system plug-ins were available for files stored on media accessed via the 3 Mb/s Ethernet-based local area network *Magnet* [Hop83], for example, to access the "standard" *Terminal* as a file(s), for memory resident files.

Unprotected hardware. Medos was also *open* in that it did not protect hardware.

4 Medos Versions

4.1 Medos V1 to Medos V 3

Medos V1 was the first experimental running release of Medos in April 1980. A lot of Medos testing and cross development software porting to Lilith took place during the summer of 1980. From the summer 1980, it was possible to maintain the system and all applications with Medos. Extensive use of the system and basic development tools from the developers themselves revealed deficiencies and motivated immediate corrections. The first official release of Medos V2 was in October 1980. It included some minor improvements, for example, in the module *FileSystem* interface. Medos V3 was a pure recompilation of Medos V2 in order to force Lilith-users (insiders might remember why!) to recompile their sources.

4.2 Medos V4

Medos V4 was released in mid-1982. This release was considered the reference version for this discussion. The resident part of Medos V4 consisted of 15 modules implemented by a total of 729 source lines for definition modules and 5,322 lines for module implementations, in all 6,049 lines of source code. Medos V4 required 14,768 words of memory to run, including 2,048 words of pure file buffer space and 1,439 words for the default font. These figures are microscopic compared to the tens of millions of source code lines and huge memory requirements of today's home or office computers.

Grouping the 15 modules according to their functions illustrates the main system components. The line numbers in the following group-descriptions are the sum of source code lines of the named module's definition and implementation.

Command Interpreter Module *SEK* (193 lines) was an abbreviation of *S*equential *E*xecution *K*ernel, but conveniently interpreted as *S*vend *E*rik *K*nudsen. The non-resident part of the command interpreter was program *Comint* (860 lines).

Program Linking-Loader and Executor The abstraction program provided by module *Program* (917 lines) and module *Monitor* (555 lines). These 555 lines in *Monitor* also included the system clock and keyboard driver.

File System The file abstraction and its implementation for Lilith's disk drive was provided by the following modules: *FileSystem* (805 lines), *DiskSystem* (2111 lines) and *D140Disk* (305 lines).

Terminal The "standard" terminal provided by the modules *Terminal* (76 lines), *TerminalBase* (109 lines), *DisplayDriver* (251 lines) and *DefaultFont* (43 lines). Module *CardinalIO* (61 lines) supported reading and writing of positive integers formatted as octal numbers via module *Terminal*. Module *FileMessage* (46 lines) helped display file system messages.

Memory Allocation Module *Frames* (260 lines) provided allocation and freeing of quad-word (64 bit) aligned memory segments.

User Authentication The module *UserIdentification* (91 lines) served the identification of the user (client) of the program on behalf of whom the process was running. This was particularly important when a user (client) made use of remotely provided resources or when Medos was used for the realization of servers (e.g. print or file server).

Modula-2 Runtime Module *System* (193 lines) was actually the Modula-2 runtime program needed by any Modula-2 program to be executed on Lilith. It mainly implemented the predefined procedure *SYSTEM.NEWPROCESS*.

The alert reader might have detected that the system "grew" (from 12.5 k words in the fall of 1980 to about 14.4 k word in the fall of 1982). People knowing Wirth know that he did not estimate unexplainable program "growth". So what caused the growth of Medos? In that period, the modules *Frames* and *UserIdentification* were added, and the implementation of module *DiskSystem* was greatly enhanced. (For example the usage of the fixed size buffer pool was changed from being a simple pool of read or write-through buffers into a pool of buffers for either read-ahead or file cache buffers. The read-ahead and caching strategy for a specific file depended on which fraction of the 16 most recent disk accesses performed for the file were sequential. [Knu83]) The slightly increased size of Medos was compensated by module *Frames*. This enabled the linking loader to store the code of loaded modules at addresses above the 64 k limit.

The interfaces (and symbol files) of the existing Medos modules remained unchanged from version 3. Only two additional modules were included. Existing abstractions continued to be stable!

4.3 Medos V5

Medos V5, released in January 1984, supported multi-programming. The module *Monitor* was "atomized" into four separate modules: *KernelBase, Programs, Processes* and *Clock*.

The main purpose of module Monitor was to hide driver processes from programmers. In Lilith's Handbook [Han82], it was stated that module *Monitor* was only to be used by Medos itself or by resource managing library modules.

Module *Programs* only provided those operations defining a low layer abstraction *program*. The possibility for resource managers to install plug-ins to be called at each program termination was complemented by plug-ins to be called at each program invocation.

Module *Processes* provided the abstraction *process* for all programmers. Both driver-processes optionally waiting on interrupts and simple processes (threads) could be instantiated by any program. The scheduling of processes was based on priorities and calls for blocking (or rescheduling) routines. In contrast to driver-processes, simple processes with lowest priority might also preempted and be scheduled in round-robin fashion. Processes could send and wait for signals, and all blocking routines could be issued with a time-out period. In order to support robustness to prevent incorrect or "crashing" programs, sent signals were defined as scheduling suggestions and not "transferred (firm) conditions". A process waiting on a signal for a sent "condition" had to (re-)assert the awaited condition after its resumption, and probably repeat the wait-operation if the check failed.

The *Clock* represented Lilith's hardware clock both as a system clock running in 1 ms steps and as a date and time indicator.

Programmers could get the impression that these three modules could be used independently of each other: the provided abstractions seemed to be mutually orthogonal ("clean"). One exception existed: only the process executing the body of a program's main module (and not all processes) was permitted to activate a program. Their implementations were, however, heavily dependent on each other. Module *KernelBase* existed to solve this problem. In some sense, the "to be considered hidden" attribute of module *Monitor* was now instantiated in module *KernelBase*.

Medos V5 included a few new interface changes such as the inclusion of a new module *Heap* for memory allocation. Memory allocation was removed from module *Program*. Module *UserIdentification* was renamed *Users*. Medos's openly usable process abstraction increased its capabilities to support programming of drivers and servers.

Splitting module Monitor into four modules representing three separate abstractions (*Programs, Processes* and *Clock*) as well as slightly adapting the program abstraction could be seen as an indication of some arising abstraction stability problems. Medos V5 was the last version of Medos.

4.4 Port of Medos V5 onto the Ceres Workstation

During the period December 1984 to July 1985, Frank Peschel and Matthias Wille ported Medos V5 to the Ceres computer [Ebe87, PW87]. Ceres was an ETH-design for a simple and yet powerful workstation based on a National Semiconductor's NS32016 microprocessor. After the port, the conclusions were "that it was possible to transport most of the utility programs and the whole cross-development software with a minimal effort". [PW87]

Hereafter, Peschel and Wille decided to design and implement Vamos [Pes88], a new operating system for the Ceres computer. The goal was to provide better support for the modern Ceres computer. Many aspects of Vamos can be seen as a big version-step after Medos V5 or a generalization of Medos.

The much bigger uniformly addressable memory of the Ceres computer together with its support of virtual addresses and hardware protection suggested that more general and advantageous memory allocation schemes could be realized than Medos's stack of activated programs. Vamos [Pes88] supported concurrent execution of programs in one global address-space. Each running program was executed in optionally hardware-protected memory segments associated with a so-called *Domain*. All managed objects are credited to a specific Domain, itself an abstract object.

5 System Advantages and Disadvantages

I will not end this chapter dealing with aspects of the Medos system without mentioning some of its advantages and shortcomings as seen in retrospect.

5.1 System Advantages

Well-defined Objectives. The few well-defined objectives for Medos did in essence enable a single person to design and to program more than 90% of its implementation.

Reliability and Robustness. The system was virtually error-free from its first official release-date in October 1980. Its robustness against erroneous user-programs remained quite high, considering that no hardware-supported protection mechanism was used. The use of Modula-2 with its type checks, even across module boundaries, helped to reduce protection violations. Medos' reliability and robustness in deterring parameter value errors, inconsistent internal states, "soft" peripheral device failures and "crashing" programs had a price, however. This "battle" cost about 70% of all source code! High system reliability, however, is considered a prerequisite for providing a good human interface.

Simple Structure. Medos V4 consisted of 15 modules. Ordinary programmers needed only to be familiar with two, namely, *FileSystem* and *Terminal*. They could be used like other non-resident library modules and remained *stable* through different public versions of Medos.

Abstract Programming Interface. All module interfaces (apart from *DefaultFont* and *DisplayDriver*) represented a purely abstract programming interface. The abstraction causes a separation of concerns between its users and its implementers. The abstraction is a vertical separation of concerns between users and implementers. Stability of an abstraction is of course important for its users.

Openness. Openness was achieved, to a great extent, by separating concerns horizontally. Clean, simple and stable abstractions (module definitions) provide openness if such abstractions can be used by a "take it or leave it" method. This can be considered as breaking up a conventional monolithic (and protected) OS kernel into many independently usable resource managers, i.e. modules, one for each supported resource type.

Extensibility. Medos supported extensions by two methods: Installation of procedures providing additional or alternative abstraction implementations (i.e. plug-ins) and by calling programs, which extended the resident operating system with additional importable modules. Programs could even load, link, and initialize modules when using Medos V5.

Programs. Running programs were considered activated "super-procedures", an abstraction suggesting sequential execution. It was also well understood that resource management was related to a "super-procedure" – all well-known aspects from ALGOL-like programming languages. Medos separated the abstractions for concurrency (process) and for resource allocation (program). In retrospect, this seems to have been a good decision.

Modest size. A resident operating system requiring less than 30,000 bytes of memory for execution was of modest size – even in 1980.

Efficiency. Both program execution time and average I/O transfer rates compared favorably against other mini-computer systems in 1982 [Jac82 App. 5]. Short and consistent response times to trivial actions, reliability and robustness are necessary for a good human interface.

5.2 System Disadvantages

Module *DiskSystem*. The implementation of files on disk packs for Lilith's disk drive was highly optimized for robustness, compactness, high transfer rates and many small files for the given hardware. *DiskSystem* was hard to adapt to other disk media, however. The decision to make a hardware-specific design derived from the feeling that *DiskSystem* would be replaced by a generally better adaptable version. Such developments were made when F. Ostler built the file server Maple [Ost85] for LAN-connected Liliths, and with the port of Medos V5 to the Ceres computer [PW87]. The maximal supported file-size (192 k bytes, later 3.072 MB) was much too small for many "real" applications.

File name directories. Module *FileSystem's* support for the abstraction of files and file names did not initially include operations for the inspection of file name directories. As soon as files could be accessed on other machines via a LAN, the fact that this feature was missing became evident to most Lilith users.

Module *FileSystem*. Module *FileSystem* does not have a small, simple and easily understood interface. In retrospect, it would have been better to split this module in two: a module *FileBase* providing the abstraction between file implementing plug-ins and a simple-to-use module *Files*.

All these disadvantages were, however, clear to the keen reader of the Lilith Handbook [Han82] and were not hidden as undocumented implementation details. In a comparison of five workstation computer systems (UNIX, Medos, Cedar, Taos and Oberon) [Pes88, pp. 23–25] F. Peschel wrote that Medos distinguished itself by being robust, compact, flexible, and efficient at file accesses.

6 Functions Missing Today or which may be Important for Single-User Computers

Bill Joy, cofounder of Sun Microsystems, wrote in [Joy00] that "..., we should be able to meet or exceed the Moore's law rate of progress for another 30 years. By 2030, we are likely to be able to build machines, in quantity, a million times as powerful as the personal computer of today – sufficient to implement the dreams of ... (SEK-deleted)".

In spite of such prognoses for an exponential rate of technological progress, it is obvious that we in the next few years we will see even more desktop and portable general purpose single-user computers. We will also see small, cheap and specialized computers (PDAs, mobile phones, set-top boxes, etc.) everywhere.

What is missing today? It was mentioned above that reliability and, for simple functions, short response times, are to be considered part of a good human – yes *human* – interface.

Lilith with its Medos was ready to be used less than 30 seconds after power up. Current PDAs are virtually "instantly-up" devices after power-up. Is there a good reason why modern personal computer operating systems force us to wait minutes during a boot or restart operation?

The following concluding remarks on missing or soon likely to be missed functions in operating systems for "single-user" systems are pointing in three directions: Latency control, multi-processing and ubiquitous information:

Real-time critical applications. The support of real-time critical program sections is an important missing function or system quality. *No* widely sold operating system for workstations provides support for *real-time critical applications*. None! See for example [CRH99]. Nevertheless, video-conferencing, voice-over-IP (VoIP), audio and video servers (even for broadcast stations), on-location recording equipment, etc., all based on workstations, are sold today. How are the latency problems, which the lack of support for real-time critical applications causes, typically solved? By a best-effort see-what-happens method! If this doesn't work: add hardware and repeat! This solution is not elegant and the design method guarantees nothing for the user of the system. Another method is to buy a specialized box to solve the scheduling problem. This latter solution "sounds" sub-optimal. A scheduler supporting real-time critical applications is simply a common, serious and apparently also implementable [BH99] requirement today.

Multi-processing for transformations. Propagation delays cause headaches to computer architects. Extensive use of simultaneous executing (virtual) processors (multi-processing) seems unavoidable to hide memory access latencies caused by the distance between memories and processors. Technological progress suggests that a single chip is going to contain many (possibly) multi-threaded processors, for example [Tul95]. Therefore, both programming languages and the operating system must be able to, or help to, apply multi-processing to individual programs (in a machine independent way). Algol 68's collateral clauses [Tan76, pp. 188–189] or statement-sets [Knu96] may be an orthogonal (complementing) approach to support programmed simultaneous execution. Only mutually independent program parts should be executed simultaneously. I once suggested [Knu96, Appendix] that it is a *bad idea* to let people hope that mutual independence of program parts is generally going to be something that can be decided automatically.

Ubiquitous computing. Ubiquitous computing is causing many questions. What degree of accessibility and consistency of, in particular, local or private data is going to be required in an environment with many poorly or unreliably connected small computers? What degree of inconsistency among replicated data is tolerable? Which principles and mechanisms guarantee reduction of inconsistencies among distributed data repositories over time and according the needs of its users? These questions are only some of those raised by the immediate future's portable "intelligent" devices.

Acknowledgements

I have to thank Prof. N. Wirth for giving me the opportunity to develop what became Medos. Søren Lauesen, one of the three RC 4000 monitor designers, motivated me in few sentences not to condemn "unusual", but in my opinion convincing, OS designs on a visit in Copenhagen, Easter 1979. I also thank all my colleagues in the Lilith-project.

I would also like to thank László Böszörményi. Without his almost endless motivation (and remarks) this Medos retrospect would hardly have been written. I also thank the other two reviewers (J. Gutknecht and J. Sametinger) and the three proofreaders (D. McLaughlin, P. Muller and W. Petersen). The highly improved quality of the paper is due to their comments on earlier versions of this paper.

References

[BBF82] G. Beretta, et al., XS-1: An integrated interactive System and its Kernel, Proc. 6th International Conference on Software Engineering, Tokyo, Sept. 1982, pp. 340–349.

[BDT84] R. L. Brown et al., Advanced Operating Systems, IEEE Computer, pp. 173, Oct. 1984.

[BH71] P. Brinch Hansen, RC 4000 Software: Multiprogramming System, a/s Regnecentralen, Copenhagen, April 1969.

[BH99] M. Baker-Harvey, ETI Resource Distributor: Guaranteed Resource Allocation and Scheduling in Multimedia Systems, Proc. of the Third Symposium on Operating Systems Design and Implementation, New Orleans, Feb. 1999.

[CRH99] E. Cota-Robles, J. P. Held, A Comparison of Windows Driver Model Latency Performances on Windows NT and Windows 98, Proc. of the Third Symposium on Operating Systems Design and Implementation, New Orleans, Feb. 1999.

[Dij68] E. W. Dijkstra, The Structure of the T.H.E. Multiprogramming System, CACM 11, No. 5, pp. 341-346.

[Ebe87] J. J. Eberle, Development and Analysis of a Workstation Computer, Diss. No. 8431, ETH Zürich, 1987.

[Gei83] L. Geissmann, Separate Compilation in Modula-2 and the structure of the Personal Computer Lilith, Diss. 7286, ETH Zurich, 1983.

[Han82] L. Geissmann et al., Lilith Handbook, Institut für Informatik, ETH, Zurich, 1982.

[Hop83] J. Hoppe, Magnet: A Local Area Network for Lilith Computers, Institut für Informatik, ETH, Zurich, Dec. 1983.

[Jac82] C. Jacobi, Code Generation and the Lilith Architecture, Diss. ETH No. 7195, ETH Zürich 1982.

[Jon78] A. K. Jones, The Object Model: A Conceptual Tool for Structuring Software, Operating Systems, An Advanced Course, Lecture Notes in Computer Science 60, 1978, pp. 7–16.

[Joy00] B. Joy, Why the future doesn't need us, Wired, April 2000, pp. 238–262.

[Knu83] S. E. Knudsen, Medos-2: A Modula-2 Oriented Operating System for the Personal Computer Lilith, Diss. 7346, ETH, Zurich, 1983.

[Knu96] S. E. Knudsen, Statement-Sets, In: Proc. of the Third International ACAP Conference, Ed. by Laszlo Böszörmenyi, Lecture Notes in Computer Science 1127, Springer-Verlag, 1996, pp. 161-173.

[Lam74] B. W. Lampson, An Operating System For a Single-User Machine, Lecture Notes in Comp. Sc., Vol. 16, Springer-Verlag, 1974, pp 208–217.

[Ohr84] R. Ohran, Lilith: A Workstation Computer for Modula-2, Diss. 7646, ETH, Zurich, 1984.

[Ost85] F. L. Ostler, Maple: A Modula-2 File Server for the Lilith Environment, Diss. ETH No. 7936, ETH Zürich.

[Par72] D. Parnas, A Technique for Software Module Specification with Examples, CACM, Vol 15 No 5, May 1972, pp. 330–336.

[Pes88] F. Peschel, Vamos – Entwurf und Realisierung eines erweiterbaren Betriebssystems für Arbeitsplatzrechner, Diss. ETH No. 8713, ETH Zürich, 1988.

[PW87] F. Peschel, M. Wille, Porting Medos-2 onto the Ceres Workstation, Institut für Informatik, ETH Zürich, Report No. 78, April 1987.

[Tan76] A. S. Tannenbaum, A Tutorial on Algol 68, ACM computing surveys, Vol. 8, No. 2, June 1976, pp. 155–190.

[TML79] C. Thacker et al., Alto: A personal computer, Xerox Corp. Palo Alto Research Center, 1979, technical report CSL-79-11.

[Tul95] D. M. Tullsen et al., Simultaneous multithreading: Maximizing on-chip parallelism, International Symposium on Computer Architecture, 1995.

[Wag00] B. Wagner, Lilith Meets the World of Business, In: The School of Wirth, <this book>, 2000.
[Wir77] N. Wirth, Modula – A language for Modular Multiprogramming, Software – Practice and Experience, 7, 3–35, 1977.
[Wir81] N. Wirth, The Personal Computer Lilith, A. I. Wassermann Ed., Software Development Environments, IEEE Computer Society Press, 1981.
[Wir82] N. Wirth, Programming in Modula-2, Springer

Lean Systems in an Intrinsically Complex World

Peter Schulthess
University of Ulm

Abstract

Whereas chaos and complexity seems to be the natural state of the world and of software systems in particular - the challenge re-mains to design lean and elegant systems similar to the examples given by Niklaus Wirth as a teacher and as a software engi-neer. One of the interesting examples we like to dis-cuss is the design and the history of Pascal P-code and the lessons we have learnt from it. – Our suggestion is that lean systems will open a "window of simplicity" and free additional resources to attack first-hand problems outside of the inner realm of computer science.

1 Introduction

In their exciting book about "The Collapse of Chaos: Discovering Simplicity in a Complex World" [2] the authors Jack Cohen and Ian Stewart point out that the world as such is exceedingly complex and largely inaccessible to simple and unified theory. This seems true for the world in general but even more so in the realm of software systems. In recognition of this fact, the faculty of computer science in Karlsruhe installed a graduate college in 1995 with the title "Management of Complex Systems" [4]. A multitude of factors contribute to the complexity of contemporary software systems:

- the use of inadequate development tools and programming languages very often leads to products of exaggerated size and to unexplained system behavior.
- Commercial products try to retain or even to expand their customer base by supporting a wide spectrum of new and old document formats and by including all the functions and commands which are offered by its competitors.
- Software companies will occupy a market segment by establishing a de facto standard which is complex enough to scare away potential competitors.

A university teacher must prepare his students for a business career in the real world and he might be inclined to accept software complexity as an inevitable fact of life and as a special educational challenge. However, from an engineering perspective accepting complexity as a natural fact is unsatisfactory (no pun intended).

The goal should not only be to master the complexity of existing systems but rather to construct lean and elegant systems which are reliable, inexpensive, understandable and functionally adequate. Engineering lean and elegant systems as it has been practiced by Niklaus Wirth will imply:

- identifying important, unimportant and hideous features
- focussing on the problem rather than on the tools
- not to design for universal applicability
- intellectual modesty and restraint
- superior professional skills
- using the right tools.

2 The Pascal P-Code Example

Selecting from the multitude of examples given by Niklaus Wirth we would like to discuss the concept of Pascal P-code. P-code was first introduced by Wirth as a source program in 1973 [14] and then in the German version of his book on Algorithms and Data structures [15]. P-code is a "reduced complexity" instruction set for a virtual machine – or as it was called in the old days – for a hypothetical stack computer (HSC). Writing an interpreter for P-code is easy because there are only about fifty simple stack instructions and the instruction semantics are straight forward. Zero address instructions or one-address instructions operate on a single run-time stack. Tag fields are used to indicate the operand type where applicable. Source text and P-code for the corresponding Pascal P-compiler were available from ETH and could be used in unmodified form to compile student programs or it could be used as the starting point for developing native Pascal compilers. Many institutions implemented their own P-code interpreter in order to run the Pascal P-compiler on their local machines and operating systems. It was both easy and fascinating to bootstrap the P-compiler on a new machine using a P-code interpreter. In this way the P-compiler and its associated hypothetical stack computer were instrumental for the world-wide success of the Pascal language.

Designing a simple P-code machine was important so that even a programmer without experience in code generation and machine architecture could write an emulator for it in some language available on the target computer. On the other hand compiling to P-code was easy because the target was a virtual stack machine with only a minimal set of registers. The stack machine required no register allocation strategy, memory addressing was strictly linear and a simple loader for symbolic P-code was already included in the P-code interpreter. As a consequence, a light-weight Pascal compiler could be built which would compile itself to approximately 13000 P-code instructions – easily fitting on a deck of punched cards for transportation across machines. Other Pascal compilers developed later for Control Data machines, for IBM System/370 and other sophisticated architectures were substantially larger and labored much harder because they had to generate native machine code.

Many variants and refinements of the original P-code instruction-set were created all over the world. P-code served in the UCSD Pascal system which was the first viable software development environment on the famous Apple II machines. A P-code variant was used for years in the Microsoft Word program before native code was installed and the volume of MS-Word increased beyond expectations.

More recently the Java language owed part of its sweeping success to Java byte-code and the underlying Java Virtual Machine (JVM). Byte-code and JVM bear an obvious resemblance to good old P-code or some descendant of it [5]. Again just like in the old Pascal days the virtual machine approach made it possible to port Java language execution to many different platforms in a short time. In the context of the world-wide web it was important to guarantee safe execution in any browser and the required "sandbox" is more readily built into an interpreter. Only gradually, high-performance just-in-time compilers are becoming available which eliminate the speed disadvantage of byte code interpretation. The JVM instruction set is combined with a sophisticated class file format to support the class oriented language paradigm, exception handling, late binding and separate compilation. A portable Java compiler was less important because Java applets might be compiled anywhere and would then be distributed across the network

A microprogrammed instruction-set with very dense code representation was designed by Wirth and Jacobi [3] for the Lilith personal computer. The Lilith instruction-set was another offspring of Pascal P-code and was called M-code. It could support the module structure of Modula-2 and access variables or procedures in external modules. The path of simplicity was left for the sake of performance and the Lilith computer used two stacks: a firmware stack for lexical recursion and a hardware stack for expression evaluation. The separate evaluation stack was implied by the AMD2901/3 bit sliced CPU and provided a significant speed-up.

3 Doing our Own Virtual Machine Project

As a Ph.D. student I had the privilege to build on P-code research done at ETH by Wirth, Amman and Nägeli [1], [6], [7], [14]. My task was to implement the Pascal language for Burroughs B1770 machines [8] and thereby to explore the microprogrammable virtual machine facilities [12]. The architecture of the B1700 offered tailored instruction-sets for the operating system and potentially for each programming language. The operating system was written in a Pascal-like high-level language called SDL and used a descriptor-oriented instruction set. The SDL virtual machine used seven different stacks (name, value, program, blocks, display ...) and was able to address and to manipulate variable-length bit-fields. Instructions and operands were Huffmann encoded in odd container sizes [13]. SDL-code was very compact and the challenge was to use it to implement "lean" Pascal. The resulting compiler was able to recompile itself within 10 minutes in a memory partition of 50 Kbytes (Operating system included). In hindsight the SDL instruction-set and the associated virtual machine was very efficient but exceedingly complicated. Code generation for the machine proved to be difficult because the variable-length formats were hard to handle and the multiple stacks created a memory management problem at run-time. From the perspective of lean systems design the SDL machine yielded very compact programs but the complex instruction formats created substantially more overhead in the compiler and in the subsequent assembler/linker/loader than original P-code. Today a memory requirement of 50 Kbyte is almost negligible but compilers still struggle to generate good code for complex architectures.

In a subsequent project we explored the virtual machine option further and designed OPA, an Object Pascal Architecture [9] [10] [11]. The idea was to design a semantically rich instruction set with superior code density, to narrow the semantic gap between programming language and machine architecture and eventually to implement the Object Pascal Architecture in VLSI hardware. We were always concerned about simplicity and elegance of the design but we were fighting a loosing battle. A new generation of Reduced Instruction-Set Complexity machine architectures was emerging which achieved, at the expense of increasing code size, better execution speed than any high-level language instruction set. Simplicity of the instruction set at the time was more important than efficient compilation and code density.

4 Compiler complexity

With the advent of RISC machines the volume and the complexity of compilers increased but the new machines were able to take the load and to compile even large systems components if the user was prepared to wait. Sophisticated modern compilers have taken the same avenue as modern operating systems and will often comprise 20 000 to 500 000 lines of code. It seems that eventually the lean and elegant recursive descent compilers for the Pascal family languages which were designed at ETH will stand as some kind of historic monument in a future land of semi-automatic hyperoptimizing multifaceted high-performance compilers and project development studios.

As the art of compiler construction developed further it appeared that even carefully handcrafted RISC compilers would turn into hideous beasts it they were to exploit the full optimization potential inherent in the new CPU architectures and in the object oriented programming style. Compiler construction toolkits relieve language implementors from simple tasks such as parsing and lexical analysis but tend to make code generation and optimization even harder. It may well be that Wirth finally turned to FPGA programming and hardware description languages because he felt that the art of compiler construction was no longer elegant and lean. Hopefully the next generation of compiler writers will find new and elegant ways to write or – if it really can be done – to generate sophisticated optimizing compilers and code generators.

5 Opening a window of simplicity

Most systems found in real life tend to increase their complexity over time. This is true for nations, societies, legal frameworks, tax systems, marriages and for software systems. Historically a system grows until it is no longer manageable by current technology. With the advent of a new technology a system can grow larger and still be manageable. The limit of complexity to which a system can grow is pushed further up, but ironically most of the additional performance and capacity will be spent on managing added complexity. We sadly acknowledge that computers have not made our life easier or more relaxed.

To make our life easier and to free our mental capacity for practical problems we must deliberately build simple systems which remain below the limit of complexity achievable by current technology. If we do this a window of opportunity will open which we like to call the "window of simplicity" as depicted in figure 1.

Figure 1 presents the progress of technology as an idealized staircase function. Systems development will attempt to follow this staircase function and approach the limit of manageable complexity as time proceeds. We suggest now according to master Wirth that the full range of technological opportunities should not be exploited and that whenever possible software systems should be kept simple and lean. If we do this well a window of simplicity will open and we can decide ourselves where to focus the extra capacity available in the window.

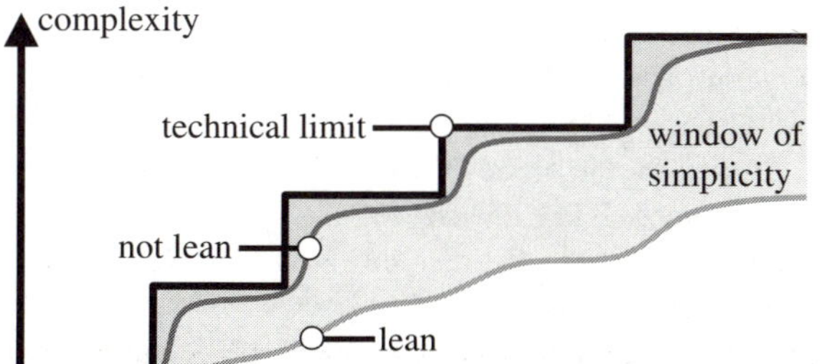

Figure 1: Opening the window of simplicity

From a practical perspective, working with functionally rich and complicated systems is an integral part of our professional experience every day. The rich functionality may be required to solve some external first-hand problem like writing a letter, printing a photograph, booking a flight or designing a piece of furniture. More often, however, the problem at hand is installing a printer driver or configuring the network connection and as such some indirect consequence of the original task. Solving all these second-hand problems takes most of our time and intellectual capacity. We should whenever possible insist on lean systems which open the mentioned window of simplicity and enable us and the computer users at large to focus on relevant problems extrinsic to the realm of computer science

6 Conclusion

The various projects of Niklaus Wirth are practical examples and experiments in the area of lean systems design. As a Swiss citizen, economy and simplicity came to him more naturally than to other nationals and it might have been against his upbringing and against his deeper motivation to give in to external demands for more functionality and therefore increased complexity. Good engineering in his sense is finding simplicity and elegance in a world of overcomplication and to continue in spite of the fact that disorder and nondeterminism is the natural state of things [2] and of software in particular.

References

[1] Urs Amman: "Entwicklung eines Pascal Compilers nach der Methode des Strukturierten Programmierens"; ETHZ Dissertation #5456.

[2] Jack Cohen, Ian Stewart: "The Collapse of Chaos: Simplicity in a Complex World", Taschenbuch (April 1995) Penguin Books; ISBN: 0140178740

[3] Christian Jacobi: "Code generation and the Lilith architecture"; Zürich 1982, ETHZ Dissertation #7195.

[4] http://www.uni-karlsruhe.de/~presse/Veroeffentlichungen/Graduier-tenkollegs/index.html#beherrschbarkeit

[5] http://www.cabot.co.uk, (distributing modern UCSD-Pascal)

[6] Hans-Heinrich Nägeli: "Der Stammcompiler: ein Beitrag zum Uebertragungsproblem"; Zürich 1978, ETHZ Dissertation. #6095.

[7] Nori K. V., Amman U., Jensen K., Nägeli H. H.: "The Pascal P-Compiler Implementation Notes"; Report, Institute for Informatik ETH Zürich, 1974.

[8] Peter Schulthess: "Ein Pascal-System basierend auf einer interpretierten Deskriptorarchitektur"; Zürich 1978, ETHZ Dissertation #6099.

[9] Peter Schulthess: "A Reduced High-Level Language Instruction Set"; IEEE Micro, June 1984, pp. 55–67, adapted for NIKKEI Electronics, Jan. 1985.

[10] Peter Schulthess, Christian Jacobi: "Anatomy of a small Pascal Compiler"; IEEE Transactions on Software Engineering, March 1983, pp. 185–191.

[11] Peter Schulthess, F. Vonaesch: "OPA – A New Architecture for Pascal-like Languages"; ACM comp. arch. news, Vol. 10, No. 6, Dec. 1982, pp. 9–20.

[12] Wayne Wilner: "Design of the B1700"; AFIPS Conference Proceedings, vol. 41, FJCC 1972.

[13] Wayne Wilner: "B1700 memory utilization"; AFIPS Conference Proceedings, vol. 41, FJCC 1972.

[14] Niklaus Wirth: "Quellprogrammliste des HSC Interpreter-Assemblers"; Institut für Informatik der ETH Zürich, 1973.

[15] Niklaus Wirth: "Algorithms + Data Structures = Programs", Prentice-Hall, 1986, ISBN: 0-13-022418

Learning the Value of Simplicity

Stephan W. Gehring
Interval Research Corporation

Abstract

Change for the better in hardware and software construction starts with the realization that powerful and flexible does not necessarily equate to complex. The digital laboratory created at the ETH is a prime example of how Niklaus Wirth's deliberate decision to simplify the existing leads to novel and flexible solutions.

1 The Moment of Surprise

Niklaus Wirth loves the moment of surprise. The first time I witnessed this was during my undergraduate studies at ETH in Zürich. There had been rumors about a new computer being developed at the Institute for Computer Systems and in late 1988 my classmates and I crammed into a small lecture hall where the system was to be demonstrated for the first time. Niklaus Wirth introduced the goals of the project and explained that not only had they developed a new computer, but also an operating system and a new programming language named Oberon. He placed a slide on Oberon onto the slide projector, exposed the top four lines and said: "These are the features that we added to Modula-2." He then uncovered the rest of the slide, about a dozen more lines, and said with a triumphant smile: "And these are the features that we removed from Modula-2!"

I was struck. How could one possibly create a more powerful programming language by adding a few features to an existing one, but removing a host of others? And why was simplicity such a central aspect of the project?

2 Simplifying the Hardware Laboratory

For Niklaus Wirth, striving for simplicity is more than just a means of problem solving; it is the core of engineering, a way of life. A teacher at heart, it is also dear to him to pass on his knowledge and insights gained through a life of building elegant software and hardware systems.

I realized this soon after I joined his group as a Ph.D. student in late 1992. Wirth had been giving an introductory course in digital circuit design for Computer Science students. The course was accompanied by a laboratory where the students could deepen their acquired knowledge by building circuits from discrete components plugged together with wires. Wirth was not satisfied with this solution because the time-consuming and error-prone process of wiring components distracted the students from solving the actual problem. The laboratory was also costly as the components often failed and needed to be replaced.

When he became involved with Field-Programmable Gate Arrays (FPGAs)[1], Wirth recognized their great potential in the field of education: the ability to be instantly reconfigured to perform a different circuit made FPGAs ideally suited for the digital circuit laboratory. A single FPGA chip could replace a whole catalog of discrete components!

Thus we set out to build an FPGA extension board for the Ceres computers that the students were already using for their programming classes. Along with the hardware, we developed a suite of software tools consisting of a compiler for the hardware specification language Lola, a graphical circuit editor, a circuit checker, and a circuit loader to configure the FPGA. The students would use the system in the following way to complete an exercise:

1. Specify the circuit using the Lola hardware description language and compile it into an intermediate form
2. Enter the circuit using the graphical circuit editor
3. Verify that the entered circuit conforms to the Lola specification using the circuit checker
4. Download the circuit onto the FPGA
5. Test the correct functioning of the circuit with a test program written in Oberon

The new digital laboratory proved an immediate success because of the simplicity of its approach: students were familiar with the Ceres workstations and thus quickly learned how to operate the tools. The new laboratory allowed them to concentrate on the problem at hand and, as a result, they were able to successfully complete far more challenging exercises than ever possible with the previous laboratory. In contrast to the old laboratory, where finding mistakes in the wiring could be very time-consuming, the circuit checker enabled students to quickly and mechanically find inconsistencies between the circuit specification and its implementation. Finally, the new laboratory offered substantial cost savings compared to the previous old solution due to very low maintenance costs.

The project was completed by three people within three months. Wirth designed the Lola language and implemented its compiler while closely monitoring our progress on the graphical editor (Stefan Ludwig) and the circuit checker and

1. Field-Programmable Gate Arrays are chips that consist of configurable logic blocks, a configurable interconnect, and input/output blocks. By altering the configuration of the logic blocks and of the interconnect, an FPGA can implement a large variety of digital circuits.

loader (myself), reminding us to focus on the essential when we deviated too far from the path of simplicity. With only incremental enhancements, this laboratory was used for over five years in education and research.

3 Teaching Simplicity

FPGAs not only greatly simplified the laboratory but also proved valuable to Niklaus Wirth in achieving his didactic goals. In a world where computing power and memory were quickly becoming abundant, the limited size and capabilities of FPGAs at the time offered a refreshing contrast. Students and teachers alike were challenged to map elaborate digital circuits onto the scarce resources provided by the FPGAs. In preparation for the course, Wirth therefore demanded that all of us teaching assistants complete the exercises ourselves. During the group meetings, we would then discuss and compare our solutions in terms of simplicity, size, and performance. It was always a moment of personal victory when our solution to the problem came close to, or even outperformed, his!

Niklaus Wirth didn't demand this from the teaching assistants by coincidence. Knowing that only solving a problem by oneself provided ultimate insight, he challenged us for our own good. The limitations imposed by the FPGAs really forced us to carefully plan and lay out the circuits and thus sharpened our skills to concentrate on the essential.

Teaching students to strive for simplicity is a formidable task. How can a life's worth of experience conquering complexity be communicated to an aspiring engineer within a short time? The obvious answer is: it cannot. But what can be conveyed is the necessary mind-set, a first step on the right path. Niklaus Wirth accomplishes this task by serving as a role model. During talks and lectures, he emphasizes the need to systematically simplify problems to a manageable size and, unlike most lecturers, also provides supporting evidence, such as the implementation size of his own solutions. True to his principles, he also practices simplicity and frugality in everyday life demonstrating that outstanding technical solutions can often be accomplished without the latest and greatest computer hardware.

I am very grateful to have had the opportunity to work with Niklaus Wirth. What I have learned from him about the importance of striving for clarity and simplicity and how to systematically tackle complex problems has had implications reaching far beyond my professional life.

References

1. Gehring, Ludwig, Wirth: "A Laboratory for a Digital Design Course Using FPGAs", 4th International Workshop on Field-Programmable Logic and Applications, 1994.

Part IV
New Ways in Education and Research

Compiler Construction versus Lotus Notes ™: A Strange Battle

Jürg Gutknecht
ETH Zentrum

Abstract

A recent discussion at the local Technopark about computer science education versus industrial needs culminated in a curious question: Compiler construction or Lotus Notes- what should be taught? As the discussion went on, the two terms gradually mutated from harmless topics to concepts of enemies named no-demand and ephemeral respectively, and the controversy remained largely unresolved. I learnt from this discussion that the level of general misunderstanding with regard to compiler construction could not be greater, and that clarification is badly needed.

Having had the privilege of a decade-long close collaboration with Niklaus Wirth, the grand master of programming languages and compiler construction, I feel both obliged and authorized to dare an attempt. With a short tutorial case study and three non-standard examples I will try in this essay to unlock the reader's rigid association of compiler construction with general programming languages and machine-code generation, and to advertise small, special-purpose languages as a powerful problem-solving tool.

The Power of Recursive Descent

Perhaps the most important practical result of formal language research in the 1960s was a clear definition of the notion of *syntax* or grammar, together with a concise notation called BNF (Backus-Naur-Form). The essential benefit of this notation is its capability to express grammars of a large class of languages in a precise textual form that can easily be mapped (either manually or automatically) to a *compiler*, i. e. to a program that reliably recognizes and processes any syntactically correct construct.

A simple case study may clarify this. Assume that we are asked to develop a *query-machine* for some existing object database, and that we decide in favor of a language-oriented approach. Further assume that the database is able to handle

Boolean *method queries* and *property queries*. Then the syntax description of a suitable *query-language*, expressed in Wirth's streamlined version of BNF called EBNF (Extended BNF), could look like this:

```
Expression = Term { OR Term }.
Term = Factor { AND Factor }.
Factor = "(" Expression ")" | name [ relop value ].
```

This syntax description consists of three *production rules*, each defining a syntactical construct together with a substituting identifier. By convention, words in upper case denote *keywords*, quoted characters or strings denote *literals*, curly braces "{" and "}" stand for arbitrary textual *repetition* (including 0 times) of their contents, brackets "[" and "]" stand for *optional* occurrence of their contents, and the vertical bar "|" means *alternative* occurrence of the parts separated by it. Keywords, literals, names, relops (relational operators), and values are considered *symbols* that are delivered to the parser as atomic units one by one by the underlying scanner of the source text. Here is an example of a syntactically legal query expression, consisting of 19 symbols:

NewRelease OR topic = "Adventure" OR topic = "Fiction" AND (author = "Hubbard" OR date >= 1970)

NewRelease is a method query, while *topic = "Adventure", date >= 1970* etc. are property queries.

It is worth noting that the mapping of any syntax description in EBNF to a compiler is now a purely mechanical endeavor, guided by the following laws, given in tabular form:

EBNF Construct	Program Construct
Identifier id	Procedure call id(..)
Repetition { .. }	WHILE statement
Alternative .. | ..	IF/ELSE statement
Option [..]	IF statement
Symbol s	Symbol s

Assuming that procedure *GetSym* reads the next symbol and deposits it in the global variable *cursym*, then, after successive application of the above laws, we get to the following parser program (in Oberon):

```
PROCEDURE Expression;
BEGIN Term;
  WHILE cursym = OR DO GetSym; Term END
END Expression;
PROCEDURE Term;
BEGIN Factor;
  WHILE cursym = AND DO GetSym; Factor END
END Term;
PROCEDURE Factor;
BEGIN
  IF cursym = leftpar THEN GetSym; Expression; GetSym
  ELSE GetSym;
    IF cursym = relop THEN GetSym; GetSym END
  END
END Factor;
```

Obviously, this program drives the scanner by invariantly letting it "look one symbol ahead" in the source text, and it parses the source text according to the underlying syntax. Otherwise it performs no semantic action, nor does it rigorously reject syntactically invalid constructs. However, it shows two undeniable qualities:

– It is able to handle arbitrarily complex, nested queries
– It provides a template that can be gradually extended to a fully-grown compiler

It should be pointed out that the power of the program lies in a fortunate combination of its top-down parsing strategy with recursion, together called *recursive descent*. It is fair to mention at this point that not every language qualifies for the recursive descent strategy. As can easily be seen from the above code, the crucial criterion is the "one symbol look-ahead" property, requesting that a one-symbol look-ahead in the source text suffices to decide the path of descent. It turns out that this property can most often be complied with in practice, once the language designer is consciously aware of it in advance.

Trying now to upgrade the template to a compiler, we should remember its original purpose of querying an object database. In particular, we should notice that one and the same query has to be applied repetitively to a potentially large set of objects. From this perspective, it makes sense to apply a general two-phase procedure:

1. Compile the query, i. e. parse it and generate an internal representation.
2. Repetitively evaluate the query for objects by traversing the internal representation.

In our case, the internal data structures are *expression trees*. For their implementation, we use a summary type *Node*, suitable for representing nodes of all types, i. e.

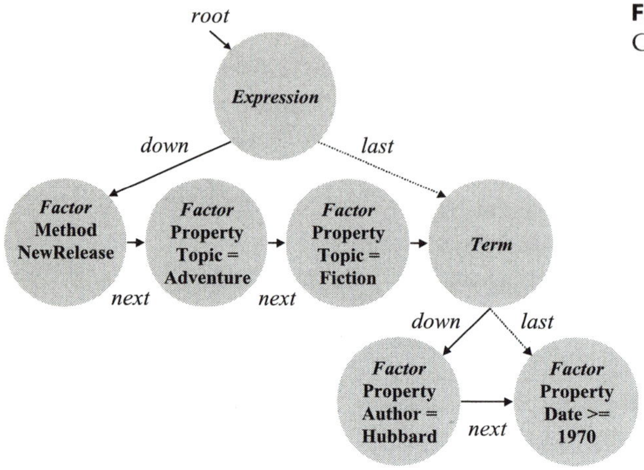

Figure 1: Expression Tree Corresponding to Sample Query

expression-nodes, *term-nodes*, and *factor-nodes*. The *next* field points to the next node on the same hierarchical level, while the *down* and *last* fields are references to the first and last node on the next lower level. As an illustration, Figure 1 depicts the expression tree corresponding to our sample query.

```
TYPE
  Node = POINTER TO RECORD
    next, down, last: Node;
    queryType: QueryType;
    name: Name; relop: Relop; value: Value
  END;
```

The following code fragment is a compiler, implementing phase 1 of our two-phase process. It has emerged from the mechanically created template by adding error recognition code and semantic actions generating the expression tree. The code assumes the existence of a global Boolean variable *error*.

```
PROCEDURE Expression (VAR f: Node);
  VAR q: Node;
BEGIN
  NEW(q); q.last := NIL;
  f.last := q; Term(q);
  WHILE cursym = OR DO GetSym; Term(q) END
END Expression;
PROCEDURE Term (q: Node);
  VAR t; Node;
BEGIN
  NEW(t); t.last := NIL;
  IF q.last # NIL THEN q.last.next := t ELSE q.down := t END;
```

```
  q.last := t; Factor(t);
  WHILE cursym = AND DO GetSym; Factor(t) END
END Term;
PROCEDURE Factor (t: Node);
  VAR f: Node;
BEGIN
  NEW(f); f.last := NIL;
  IF t.last # NIL THEN t.last.next := f ELSE t.down := f END;
  t.last := f;
  IF cursym = leftpar THEN GetSym; Expression(f); GetSym;
    IF cursym # rightpar THEN error := TRUE END
  ELSIF cursym = name THEN f.name := name; GetSym;
    IF cursym = relop THEN f.queryType := range; f.relop := relop; GetSym;
      IF cursym = value THEN f.value := value; GetSym
        ELSE error := TRUE
      END
    ELSE f.queryType := method
    END
  ELSE error := TRUE
  END
END Factor;
```

Next, we need to develop process phase 2, an evaluator of expression trees. The following code is a straightforward derivation from the hierarchical tree structure. It makes use of two procedures *MethodQuery* and *PropertyQuery* that are assumed to be exported by the database interface.

```
PROCEDURE EvalExpression (q: Node; VAR matching: BOOLEAN);
  VAR t: Node;
BEGIN t := q.down; EvalTerm(t, res);
  WHILE ~matching & (t # q.last) DO t := t.next; EvalTerm(t, matching) END
END EvalExpression;

PROCEDURE EvalTerm (t: Node; VAR matching: BOOLEAN);
  VAR f: Node;
BEGIN f := t.down; EvalFactor(f, matching);
  WHILE matching & (f # t.last) DO f := f.next; EvalFactor(f, matching) END
END EvalTerm;

PROCEDURE EvalFactor (f: Node; VAR matching: BOOLEAN);
BEGIN
  IF f.down # NIL THEN EvalExpression(f.down, matching)
    ELSIF f.queryType = method THEN MethodQuery(curobj, f.name, matching)
    ELSE PropertyQuery(curobj, f.name, f.relop, f.value, matching)
  END
END EvalFactor;
```

The only program component still missing is a controller for the whole querying process. In our implementation, we postulate the existence of an abstract interface *{ GetObj, curobj }* for the database iterator. In analogy to the abstract scanner interface *{ GetSym, cursym }*, we assume *GetObj* to deliver the next object according to some enumeration, and to deposit it in variable *curobj*. Finally, we assume procedure *Register* registering matching objects, and variable *root* representing the root of the expression tree of the current query.

```
error := FALSE; NEW(root); GetSym; Expression(root);
IF ~error THEN GetObj;
WHILE curobj # NIL DO EvalExpression(root, matching);
  IF matching  THEN Register(curobj) END;
  GetObj
END
```

To summarize the procedure, we had first chosen a language-oriented approach in our hypothetical database querying project, and then followed an archetypal recipe:

1. Define a small, special-purpose language with the "one symbol look-ahead" property and specify its syntax in EBNF.
2. Using a fixed set of transformation rules, map the EBNF description to a program template.
3. Upgrade the template to a compiler by adding error detection code and actions for generating an internal data structure.
4. Develop an evaluator, operating on the internal data structures.
5. Write a two-phase controller, making appropriate use of the compiler and evaluator.

Our endeavor not only resulted in an ultra-compact program but it is also unbeatably flexible. Having the full power of "software" at our disposal, we can easily extend the query-machine or change it in other ways. For example, if we would like to add introspective queries like "IS class" and "IMPLEMENTS interface", we could simply extend the syntax description accordingly, and then carry the changes through the different steps. If *introp* denotes either one of the keywords ISCLASS or IMPLEMENTS, this would be the new syntax:

```
Expression = Term { OR Term }.
Term = Factor { AND Factor }.
Factor = "(" Expression ")" | name [ relop value ] | introp name.
```

Be Wise- Generalize

The scope of application of EBNF is by no means restricted to "ordinary" languages. So EBNF is a perfect tool to express the formal specification of virtual code formats like the *Pascal p-code* or its rebirth, the *Java byte-code*. Perhaps even more surprisingly, Wirth applies EBNF in [1] to the specification of *file formats* and *network protocols*. The following two examples illustrate convincingly that a few lines of formal text, in combination with expressive names, are worth more than a thousand pages of verbose and lengthy explanations. Notice that, in both examples, the EBNF syntax itself has been tuned-up slightly but effectively by Wirth.

Use of EBNF to specify the original Oberon object file format

```
ObjectFile = HeaderBlock EntryBlock CommandBlock PointerBlock ImportBlock
LinkBlock
    DataBlock CodeBlock TypeBlock [ ReferenceBlock ].
HeaderBlock = 0F8X versionCode refBlkPos:4 nofEntries:2 comSize:2 nofPtrs:2
nofImps:2 nofLinks:2
    varSize:4 codeSize:2 key:4 Name.
EntryBlock = 82X { entryAdr:2 }.
CommandBlock = 83X { Name entryAdr:2 }.
PointerBlock = 84X { pointerOffset:2 }.
ImportBlock = 85X { key:4 Name 0X }.
LinkBlock = 86X { procNumber moduleNumber }.
DataBlock = 87X { byte }.
CodeBlock = 88X { byte }.
TypeBlock = 89X { tdsize:2 tdadr:2 { byte }}.
ReferenceBlock = 8AX { ProcRef }.
ProcRef = 0F8X entryAdr:2 Name { LocalRef }.
LocalRef = mode form adr:4 Name.
Name = { byte } 0X.
```

The notation "item:n" is an ad hoc extension to EBNF, specifying the number *n* of bytes used to represent the entity *item* on file. Omission of ":n" is equivalent to ":1".

Use of EBNF to specify the Oberon file transfer protocol

```
Protocol = { request }.
Request = ReceiveFile | SendFile | SendMsg | NameRequest.
ReceiveFile = SND username password filename ( datastream | NAK | NPR ).
datastream = DAT0 data ACK1 { DATi data ACKi+1 }.
SendFile = REC username password filename (ACK0 datastream | NAK | NPR ).
datastream = DAT0 data ACK1 { DATi data ACKi+1 }.
SendMsg = MSG message ACK.
NameRequest = NRQ partnername [ NRS ].
```

This example is interesting because it cleverly combines two different streams or processes in one coherent description. Normal letters are used to denote message traffic from the client to the server, while *italics* are used to denote counter traffic.

The reader may wonder about the corresponding compilers in the previous two examples. In the case of the file format description, the compiler is simply an *internalizer*, mapping the serial representation onto an internal data structure. The case of the network protocol is more intricate, because two processes are involved. Instead of just one mechanical mapping from the EBNF representation to a program, there are now two projections, one to the client process and one to the server process. Obviously, the set of transformation laws introduced in the previous section can easily be adjusted to produce appropriate communicating sequential programs by replacing the transformation from *identifier* to *procedure call* by two analogous transformations from *identifier* to *rendez-vous*:

EBNF Construct	Program Construct
Identifier in home font	Rendez-vous of write type
Identifier in foreign font	Rendez-vous of read type

Small Languages are Great

The previous decade of computing could roughly be characterized as the decade of "visual interactivity". WYSIWYG document-editors, CAD systems, CASE tools, GUIs, and visual programming languages are witnesses to an era of glorified visual approaches. Undoubtedly, visually interactive user interfaces are "friendly" and convenient, and they have made computers a useful tool for many. However, it should not be overlooked that, in countless cases, language-based, descriptive methods are superior in at least three respects: They are (1.) far more terse and resource-efficient, (2.) more precise, and (3.) accessible to processing by programs.

Prominent representatives of the language-based category are Knuth's typography systems METAFONT and TEX, and the Internet markup languages HTML and XML. It is the goal of the following examples to propagate the small language approach for the areas of graphics, layout design, and object composition respectively.

A Simple Graphics Description Language

Our first example takes up the topic of graphics design. Surprisingly little effort has been invested so far in the development of graphics description languages. For example, there is no standard way at present to integrate line graphics into a HTML page descriptively.

Here is our own proposal of a simple graphics language. It supports open and closed polygons and circles, unfilled or filled. The underlying imaging model is a

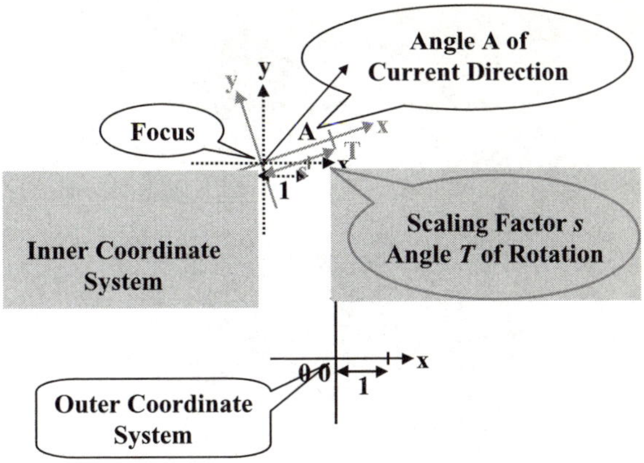

Figure 2: Imaging Model of Scripted Graphics

nested hierarchy of *scenes*, each of them optionally attributed with a local coordinate system (see Figure 2). Scenes can be defined in advance and named for reuse.

```
graphic = { declaration | scene }.
declaration = name "=" scene.
scene = name | "{" { attribute } { scene | command } "}".
attribute = coord [ rot T ] [ scale s ] | linew w | linecol c | fillcol c.
command = go d | goto pos | turn a | turnto A | line d | lineto pos | circle r | close | fill.
pos = X Y | polar a d.
```

A compiler in this case is a program translating graphics from their descriptive form into some form of visual representation. Unlike in the previous examples, the compiler in this case needs to build up and maintain a register of declarations, sometimes called "symbol table". Also, a simple *graphics API* along the lines of the following module definition is clearly necessary:

```
DEFINITION SimpleGraphics;
  CONST close = 1; fill = 2; stroke = 0;
  PROCEDURE Open;
  PROCEDURE SetWidth (w: REAL);
  PROCEDURE SetLineCol (col: LONGINT);
  PROCEDURE SetFillCol (col: LONGINT);
  PROCEDURE BeginPoly (x, y: REAL; mode: INTEGER);
  PROCEDURE LineTo (x, y: REAL);
  PROCEDURE EndPoly;
  PROCEDURE Circle (x, y, r: REAL; mode: INTEGER);
END SimpleGraphics.
```

Note in particular that this API needs to deal with absolute coordinates only because the hierarchy of nested coordinate systems can be resolved easily by the compiler while descending recursively.

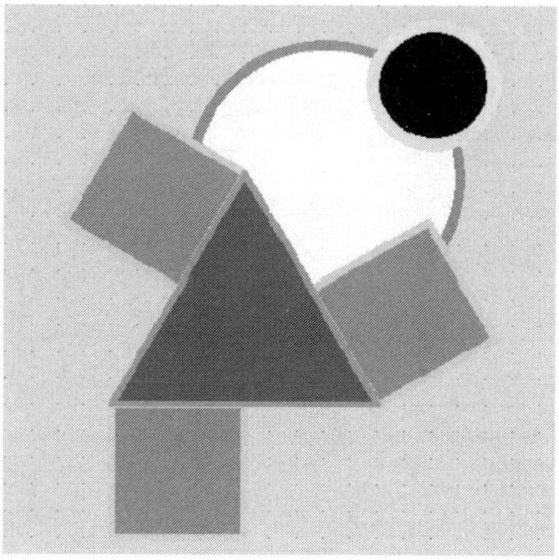

Figure 3: "Raven Stealing Sun"

In spite of its caricatural simplicity, our small graphics system consisting of language, API, and compiler is remarkably powerful, as the following examples "Raven Stealing Sun" and "Twinkling Stars" may indicate. We should clarify that the recursion in the second example is stopped by a built-in size check.

Script for "Raven Stealing Sun"

```
quad = {coord linew 6 linecol 10 fillcol 1 lineto 100 0 lineto 100 -100
lineto 0 -100 lineto 0 0 fill}{coord linew 8 linecol 1 fillcol 5 goto 360
370 circle 100 fill
  {linew 10 linecol 2 fillcol 15 goto 440 440 circle 45 fill}}
{coord linew 5 linecol 4 fillcol 3 goto 200 200 line 200 turn 120 quad line
200 turn 120 quad line 200 turn 120 quad fill}
```

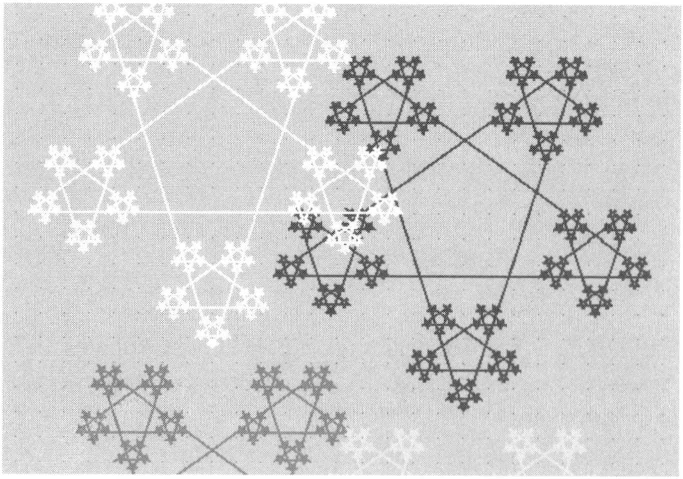

Figure 4: "Twinkling Stars"

Script for "Twinkling Stars"

```
star = {coord scale 0.3 line 300 turn 144 star line 300 turn 144 star line
300 turn 144 star line 300 turn 144 star line 300 turn 144 star}
{ coord linew 2 linecol 1 goto 50 200 star }
{ coord linew 2 linecol 6 goto 250 150 star }
{ coord linew 2 linecol 3 goto 250 450 star }
{ coord linew 2 linecol 5 goto 50 500 star }
```

An Artwork Layout Generator

Our next example has emerged from collaboration with Peter Schweri, an artist who had developed *Artcode 86*, a code system that is visualized by a set of regularly tiled, bi-colored double-squares. The idea in this project was to provide a computer aided design tool for the support of hierarchical constructions based on Artcode 86. We eventually decided in favor of a descriptive approach, mainly because of the systematic nature of the constructions and the possibility to develop the tool quickly. The decision turned out beneficial in all respects but in particular regarding the flexibility of the tool and the effectiveness of its use. Referring to a famous step-shaped Egyptian pyramid, we called the tool *Sakkara*. We first implemented Sakkara in Oberon, continuously fine-tuned it, gradually optimized it, and finally ported it from Oberon to a Java applet (where it happily lives ever since).

The Sakkara Syntax

```
artwork = declarations { layout [ title ] }.
declarations = { name "=" (color | layout) }.
layout = "[" { layer } "]".
layer = "#" number texture { field }.
field = number [ "*" number ] "|" number [ "*" number ].
texture = name | color | layout.
color = "(" number number number ")".
```

A layout is a sequence of congruent layers lying on top of each other. A layer is a textured and grid-structured double-square. The grid is regular n by n, where n is given by the number following the "#" sign. Fields are located via chess-board notation A1, A2, .., B1, B2, .. Recursion enters through textures that are allowed to be full layouts. Colors are specified in RGB notation. Again, the syntax enables reusable declarations that can be cascaded when required.

The following example does not nearly exhaust the potential of the Sakkara formalism. However, it may give a quick impression of its use and in particular of the varied options of reuse of a layout pattern.

Artcode 86 System 080400 a Sakkara Description

```
white = ( 1 1 1 )
gray = ( 0.666 0.666 0.666 )
black = ( 0 0 0 )
pat = [ #1 white A1 #4 gray B1 D1 A2 B2 A3 C3 A4 D4 ]
pat4 = [ #4 pat A1 A2 A3 A4 B1 B2 B3 B4 C1 C2 C3 C4 D1 D2 D3 D4 ]
pat16 = [ #4 pat4 A1 A2 A3 A4 B1 B2 B3 B4 C1 C2 C3 C4 D1 D2 D3 D4 ]
texture = [ #1 pat16 A1 #4 black B1 D1 A2 B2 A3 C3 A4 D4 ]
[ #1 texture A1 #3 pat A3 B2 C1 ]
```

The result of a compilation of this description by the Sakkara compiler is a layout in Postscript form (another special purpose language). Figure 5 shows a print out.

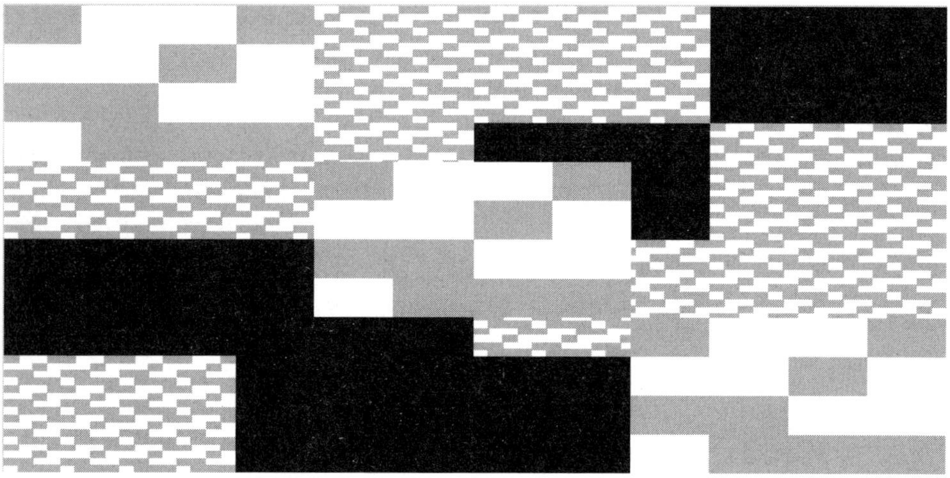

Figure 5: The Artcode 86 System 080400

Scripted Component Composition

The next and concluding example is devoted to *components*. Components are the latest trend in software engineering [2, 3]. Even though no commonly accepted definition of the term *component* exists to date, and Wirth in [4] wisely recommends ignoring it for the time being, component technology is a reality. Its essence manifests in a two-stage software development process as summarized by the following table:

Stage	**Developed Entities**	**Tools**
1	Specialized software components that are detachable from their original development context and deployable in a multitude of runtime environments	Programming language ● Class library ● Template library
2	Composites composed from components	● Visual builder ● Scripting language

PowerDoc is a scripting language and document-oriented runtime framework for active document pages that essentially (1.) supports the second stage of the two-stage software development process tabulated above and (2.) provides a runtime infrastructure for viable groups of logically connected components. Although its concepts are independent of the underlying runtime environment in principle, we shall occasionally implicitly or explicitly refer to its implementation on the basis of the Oberon system with Gadgets [5].

The underlying PowerDoc architecture is based on the notion of *frames*, where a frame is a rectangular area within the display space of the document that is able to consume arbitrary contents, including other frames. Typical frame contents are pictures and objects. However, frames can also consume parts of text streams or, more generally, parts of object streams. The PowerDoc language comprises constructs to

- define hierarchies of nested frames
- define frame attributes and contents
- dispatch and render text streams into frames

Its syntax description is amazingly compact:

```
CompilationUnit = { Lib | Doc }.
  Lib = "(" LIB name { Frame } ")" [ comment ].
  Doc = "(" DOC [ name ] { DocSpecs } ") [ comment ].
  DocSpecs = Meta | Frame | StreamDef.
  Meta = "(" META string ")" [ comment ].
  Frame = "(" FRAME [ name ] { FrameSpecs } ")" [ comment ].
  FrameSpecs =
    Position | Size | BG | Object |
    Grid | Padding | Boundary | Separators |
    Frame | StreamDef | StreamImp |
    Declaration.
  Position = "(" POS num "@" num ")" [ comment ].
  Size = "(" SIZE num "@" num ")" [ comment ].
  Grid = "(" GRID { Extent } "@" { Extent } ")" [ comment ].
  Extent = num ":" ( num [ "%" ] | "*" ) [ comment ].
  Padding = "(" PAD num [ "@" num ] ")" [ comment ].
  Boundary = "(" BND num [ "@" num ] ")" [ comment ].
```

```
Separators = "(" SEP num [ "@" num ] ")" [ comment ].
BG = "(" BG name ")" [ comment ].
Object = "(" OBJ name { Declaration } ")" [ comment ].
StreamDef = "(" STD name Dest ")" [ comment ].
StreamImp = "(" STI name Dest ")" [ comment ].
Dest = "(" DST { name } ")" | "(" DSP [ num "@" num" ] ")" [ comment ].
Declaration = "(" name Object ")" [ comment ].
```

The following comments may clarify and help the reader to understand the comprehensive concept of the PowerDoc architecture.

1. The outermost two levels of the frame hierarchy are *document frame* and *page frame* respectively.
2. Two layout strategies are supported: Bottom-up and top-down. While the former strategy proceeds by successively composing frames of a given size to a "parent" frame, the latter strategy continuously fits sub-frames into a parent frame.
3. The following kinds of frame contents are possible: Visual containers and components, pictures, and running text. Colored and pictured backdrops are also supported.
4. If the content of a frame is a *container*, components in its sub-frames are automatically considered to be contents.
5. PowerDoc text is scope structured. A set of attribute values is associated with each scope. Unspecified attributes in nested scopes inherit their values from outer scopes. There is a command attribute determining the reaction to a mouse click within its scope.

So far we have emphasized the ability of PowerDoc to manage the graphical layout of document pages and composite objects. However, PowerDoc additionally provides a powerful framework for connecting and "wiring" components, and for specifying their intercommunication. The first step when trying to establish a connection with a partner component is to locate the partner component by name within the hierarchical name space defined by the hierarchy of frames. The second step comprises the actual exchange of data or, to be more specific, of attribute values.

Every component culture relies on the existence of a "component market", or at least on an arsenal of pre-fabricated components. In our case, two different forms of object repositories corresponding to two different ways of representing pre-fabricated components exist: Modules and object libraries. Modules correspond to the "class" representation of "fresh" components, i. e. of components in their initial state immediately after compilation. Object libraries correspond to serialized representations of components (and composites) at a certain moment of their existence. Furthermore, there are two different ways of reusing pre-fabricated components: Reuse by value and reuse by reference or, in other words, reuse by cloning and reuse by generating a new view. The following table summarizes:

Representation	**Repository**	**Kind of Reuse**	**Method of Creation**
Class	Module	By Value	Instantiation
Serialized	Object Library	By Value	Cloning
		By Reference	Generation of View

The Powerdoc language construct for (re)using an existing component is

```
"(" OBJ repName "." objName { " (" attrName attrValue ")" } ")"
```

The method of creation is selected implicitly by Powerdoc. By default, *repName* is taken as a module name and *objName* as a generator corresponding to the class of the object. If no module of name *repName* exists, a serialized representation is assumed, and *objName* is interpreted as a symbolic identifying index. The current version of Powerdoc supports reuse by value only and allows a series of initial assignments of attribute values. Because links are considered as component-valued attributes by Powerdoc, an initial specification of links (for example with MVC models) is also possible.

The development of the PowerDoc compiler followed exactly the lines propagated in the first section of this article, applied to the PowerDoc syntax. The result is a lean five-page Oberon program, making essential use of the basic component API provided by the Oberon kernel. In spite of its compact size, the PowerDoc compiler is amazingly versatile. For example, it allows compiled component descriptions to be stored persistently in object libraries, and thereby upgrades PowerDoc from a pure consumer to a consumer and producer in the component market.

It is now time for an example to clarify PowerDoc. Figure 6 displays the first page of a document about the magic crop circles ("Kornkreise" in German). The document features a non-symmetric two-column design, three integrated pictures, two integrated "interactive" composite objects, and running text.

Here is its formal description in PowerDoc notation:

```
PowerDoc.Open
(DOC (META "Kornkreise/JG, 21.3.00")
  (FRAME ENV (BG "6")
    (GRID 2:* @ 2:*)
    (FRAME FILLER (POS 1 @ 1) (SIZE 50 @ 50))
    (FRAME PAGE1 (POS 2 @ 2)
      (SIZE 500 @ 700) (BG "10") (PAD 20) (SEP 1)
```

```
      (GRID 10:10% @ 1:40% 1:60%)
      (FRAME TITLE (POS 10 @ 1:2) (BG "3") (STI Kornkreise.Title (DSP)))
      (FRAME PICT1 (POS 1:3 @ 2:1) (OBJ Kornkreise.Bild1))
      (FRAME PICT2 (POS 6:4 @ 2) (OBJ Kornkreise.Bild2))
      (FRAME PICT3 (POS 4:4 @ 1) (OBJ Kornkreise.Bild3))
      (FRAME PANEL (POS 1:2 @ 1) (OBJ Kornkreise.RefPanel))
      (FRAME CONTROL (POS 3:1 @ 1)
        (PAD 4) (OBJ Panels.NewPanel)
        (GRID 1 @ 3:33.3%)
        (FRAME (POS 1 @ 1) (OBJ BasicGadgets.NewButton
          (Color 4) (Caption "Pause") (Cmd "SaveScreen.Run")))
        (FRAME (POS 1 @ 2) (OBJ BasicGadgets.Checkbox))
        (FRAME (POS 1 @ 3) (OBJ BasicGadgets.NewButton
          (Color 11) (Caption "Time") (Cmd "System.Time"))))
      (FRAME TEXT1 (POS 8:2 @ 1) (STI Kornkreise.Text (DSP)))
      (FRAME TEXT2 (POS 4:2 @ 2) (STI Kornkreise.Text (DSP)))
      (STI Kornkreise.Text (DST TEXT1 TEXT2))
      (STD Kornkreise.Title (DST TITLE))
    )PAGE1
   (STD Kornkreise.Text (DST PAGE1))
  )ENV
)DOC
```

This script directly reflects the nested frame structure. It shows how the contents of the page frame is deployed to sub-frames under control of a 10 by 2 grid. Among the sub-frames are: One title frame, three picture frames, one frame containing a pre-fabricated panel, one frame containing an inline control panel, and two frames containing running text, dispatched appropriately by the STI (text import) clauses. The pictures and the pre-fabricated panel are assumed to be retrieved from an object library called *Kornkreise.Lib* under the name *Bild1*, *Bild2*, *Bild3*, and *RefPanel* respectively.

The control panel is an inline construction that is further subdivided into three frames, each containing a basic component. The basic components are generated by the specified generator at document compile time and initialized with the desired attribute values. Note that the command attribute specifies a method that comes into effect whenever the button is pressed.

All that still remains is a preliminary compilation of the following Powerdoc program to fabricate and register the *RefPanel* in the *Kornkreise.Lib* object library:

```
PowerDoc.Compile
(LIB Kornkreise.Lib
  (FRAME RefPanel
    (OBJ Panels.NewPanel)
    (GRID 1 @ 3:33.3%) (PAD 4)
    (FRAME (POS 1 @ 1:2) (OBJ Kornkreise.List (Name "itemList")))
    (FRAME (POS 1 @ 3) (OBJ BasicGadgets.NewButton
      (Color 13) (Caption "Get") (Cmd "Desktops.OpenDoc &itemList.Sel")))))
```

The *RefPanel* is made up of two components: A list and a button. While the button is generated "on-the-fly", the list was filled in advance and was stored in the *Kornkreise.Lib* interactively. The interesting aspect of this panel is the "wiring" of the two components. As can be seen in the above specification, the value of the attribute *Sel* (for *selected entry*) of the list named *itemList* (within the scope of the panel) is used as a parameter of the *Desktops.OpenDoc* command associated with the button.

Conclusion

Using a variety of examples from different areas we have demonstrated the scope and effectiveness of the language-oriented, descriptive approach to computer aided design in its broadest sense. In particular, we have tried to convince the reader that this approach is an interesting alternative to the visual, interactive method predominantly used today. Small languages, customized for certain topics provide a highly effective, flexible, and resource-efficient alternative to graphical user interfaces. However, competence, skill, and experience in the discipline of compiler construction is indispensable to be able to fully exploit the possibility of constructing customized language-tools. Basic concepts like "syntax", "EBNF", "one-symbol look-ahead", "recursive descent", and "symbol table" must be understood thoroughly by the tool-smith. These concepts have not only been taught but also substantially co-developed and refined by Wirth over the past three decades.

Recursive descent has always been both Wirth's preferred approach to the discipline of compiler construction in his lectures and books [6, 7], and his favorite tool for actually constructing compilers. This is more than pure coincidence, it is witness to an admirable congruence of teaching and research, based on the pillars of clarity, simplicity, effectiveness, and elegance, often cited but seldom practiced.

Unfortunately, bare recursive descent is no longer a popular approach to compiler construction today. It has been replaced gradually by far more pompous but far less effective table-driven, semi-automated algorithms, often hidden behind some compiler-generating wizard. If today's designers and implementors of multivendor languages like HTML, Postscript etc. were to remember Wirth's principles and take them to heart, the behavior of Internet browsers, printers etc. would at least be far more predictable.

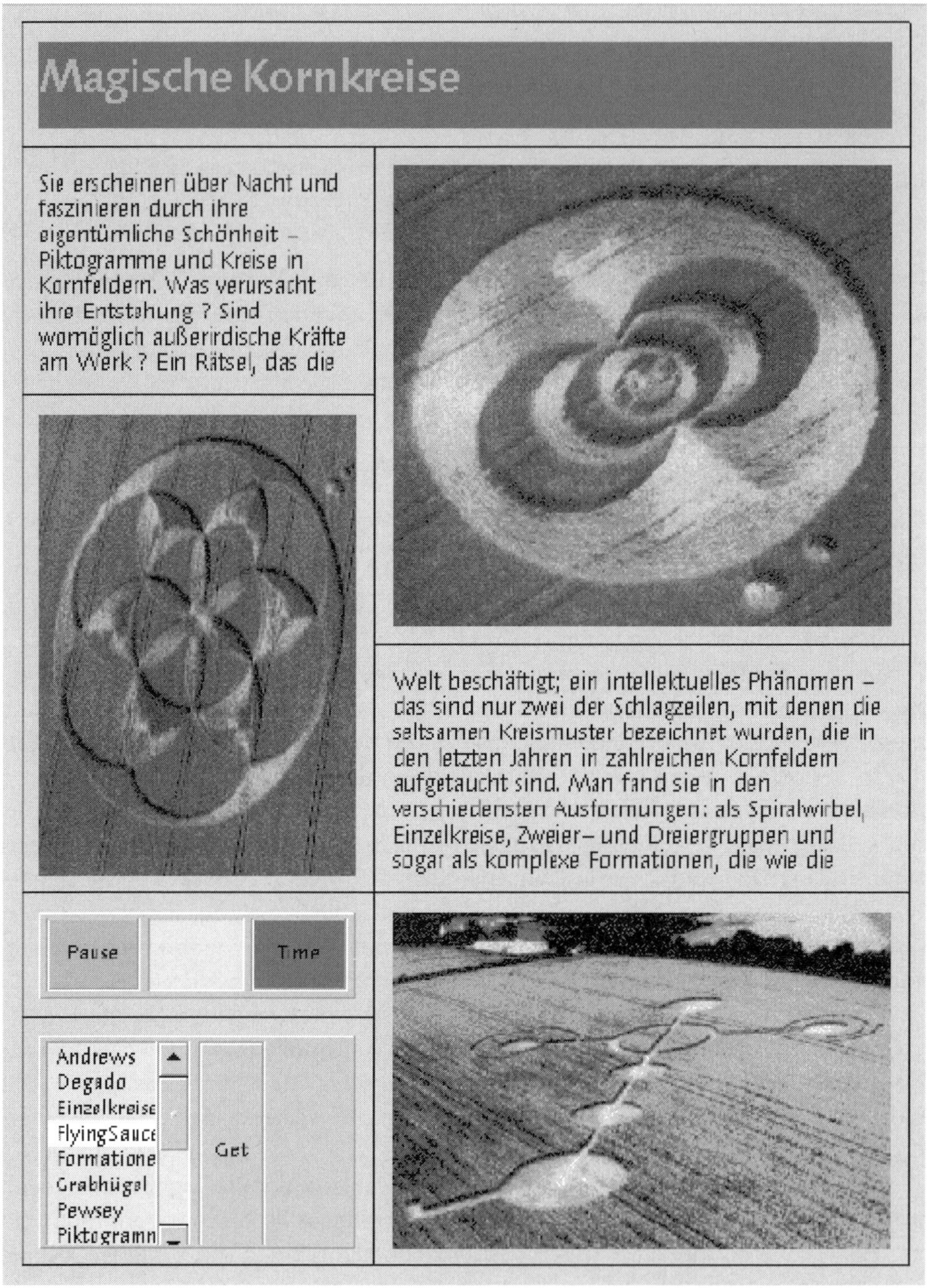

Figure 6: The "Crop Circles" Power Document

Referring to our initial controversy, I must confess that I am definitely unable to present an even slightly analogous set of *generic* capabilities that could emerge from lectures on Lotus Notes. This should not be interpreted as a devaluation of Lotus Notes. It is in fact the development of professional high-quality products like Lotus Notes that relies upon generic skills like compiler construction. The opposite, however, is false.

Acknowledgement

I owe a great debt of gratitude to Niklaus Wirth, not just because he taught me all of this via his superbly written books and excellent live examples, but because he taught it only after a radical liberation from all the unessential. In a world of blown-up details and forgotten substance, such an effort appears as a true blessing.

I am also deeply grateful for the high-class contributions of my former and current collaborators. In particular, I should mention Hannes Marais (co-architect of the Gadgets component framework), Pieter Muller (author of Native Oberon), and Erich Oswald (designer of the graphics API). Last but certainly not least I express my warmest thanks to my friend and artist Peter Schweri for the development of the Artwork Code and its evolution. Thanks to his high level of intelligence coupled with ultimate scrutiny, working with him has always been both a challenge and sheer pleasure and satisfaction.

Bibliography

[1] N. Wirth and J. Gutknecht, Project Oberon, Addison-Wesley, 1990.

[2] B. Cox, Object-Oriented Programming, An Evolutionary Approach, Addison-Wesley, 1986.

[3] C. Szyperski, Component Software, Beyond Object-Oriented Programming, Addison-Wesley, 1998.

[4] N. Wirth, Invited Lecture, In Honor of C. A. R. Hoare's Retirement, Oxford, October 1999.

[5] A. Fischer and H. Marais, The Oberon Companion, vdf, 1998.

[6] N. Wirth, Grundlagen und Techniken des Compilerbaus, Addison-Wesley, 1996.

[7] N. Wirth, Digital Circuit Design, An Introductionary Textbook, Springer, 1995.

Modules and Components – Rivals or Partners?

Clemens Szyperski
Microsoft Research

Abstract

Component software sets out to address some of the fundamental problems separating software construction as executed today from a long-held vision of reuse, extensibility, and evolvability. At the same time, programming languages began to explicitly support modular programming already in the late 1970's. In this chapter these efforts are summarized and related to the goals of component software. As it turns out, modularization is a necessary condition for component software; language support is thus clearly a good idea. However, modularization is not sufficient for component software and components are not just modules. This observation opens new avenues for programming language innovation. Some of the interesting dimensions are explored in this chapter. Since composability is at the heart of component software, language features that improve the degree of composability are particularly important. Examples from spaces as diverse as exception handling and type systems are examined to illustrate this point.

Motivation

Battling over the meaning of terms that escape unanimously accepted mathematical definitions has a tendency to border on taste. However, *de gustibus non est disputandum*, as Jürg Gutknecht liked to remark while I was still working as a PhD student at ETH – right in the middle of the fascinating Oberon days. Why would one set out to discuss the differences and similarities between the module and component concepts? My motivation is quite plain. Modules ought to be one of the most fundamental building blocks in programming languages and components ought to be one of the most fundamental building blocks of software systems. I say *ought to be* rather than *are*, because far too many designs of contemporary programming languages and software systems do not follow these ideals – often offering no clear structural building blocks at all. Fortunately, complaining or lamenting about the odd shape that software "engineering" tends to take today is beyond the scope of this short chapter.

Back to the point, ignoring popular disagreement in practice, and exaggerating just a little bit: Modules are the most fundamental building block in programming languages and components are the most fundamental building block of software systems. Programming languages are used to express the construction details of software systems. Could it thus be that modules and components simply align, covering the same notion at the levels of system description and system realization? In other words, does a module translate into a component, provided we subject it to proper compilation and packaging technology?

As demonstrated so convincingly by the Oberon system (Wirth and Gutknecht 1992) and its commercial offspring, the BlackBox Component Builder and Framework (Oberon 1997), it is quite feasible to take an Oberon module and compile and package it into a deployable unit. Wait – what is a deployable unit? Well, that is lingo from the component software world, but the key idea is that such a unit can be installed and dynamically loaded on its own. (Of course, this may trigger the loading of other units that the newly loaded unit statically depends on – more on this later.)

A one-to-one mapping of modules at the language level to what could be rightfully called dynamic link libraries (DLLs) at the deployment level seems to resolve the matter at hand. Modules are the language-level equivalent of components. Or are they? As we journey deeper into the fascinating universes of modules and components we discover that such a simple resolution tends to do neither of these powerful concepts full justice. To begin this journey, the following sections first explore the history of modules and then, more briefly, that of components. In a final section we then attempt a richer and hopefully insight-inspiring correlation of the module and component concepts.

A little history of modules

An exact historic account on how modules came about should be left to those at the helm at the time. While there is an abundance of literature on this topic, the cross-references tend to be surprisingly circular. All major players knew each other and all seemed to have known about some of their ongoing work while pushing their own research. The result is an often puzzling co-publication of similar work—accompanied either by mutual references or by shared common genes: seminal work that bore fruit on both branches. Besides the slippery slope of historic inaccuracy, the following account also suffers from *information overload* – only those readers already familiar with the mentioned concepts will appreciate some of the details. The details are nevertheless mentioned to document how intertwined modules and other language-level concepts are. Indeed, it is fair to observe that one person's module isn't normally another person's module …

Recognizing a link between structured programming and systematic ways to modularize systems, David Parnas was probably the first to promote modular programming (1972a, 1972b). In a way, Parnas' ideas were well ahead of their time and in many ways can be seen as precursors to component software (covered in the next section).

Starting in the early days: A concept that could be seen as the grandfather of all static scoping constructs is the Algol *block*: a construct that defines a scope for definitions and an opportunity for the *import* of further definitions from the environment. Algol blocks do not export anything – separate compilation of blocks was thus not meaningful (and, in the case of Algol 68, outright impossible). Both C and Pascal followed Algol's block structure; modern followers include C++ and Java.

Driven by a clear need to support separate compilation, Pascal was augmented by a *unit system* around 1975 as part of the UCSD Pascal development (Clark 1982). Units provided a simple top-level partitioning of programs into early modules. A unit is split into an interface and an implementation section, each of which can contain a uses clause to import the interfaces of other units. The interface section defines what is visible to importing units. Supporting separate compilation addressed one of the key shortcomings of Pascal when applied to serious software development. Brian Kernighan published an influential and detailed list of problems with Pascal (1981).

Roughly in parallel with UCSD Pascal, CLU (Liskov et al. 1981) introduced *clusters*, a construct to package abstract data types (ADTs). Predating many other efforts, clusters already supported constrained parametric polymorphism (genericity). The focus of a cluster on a single ADT can be seen as a continuation from the Simula class concept.

While the UCSD units point into the direction of soon-to-be modules, there was another key concept that vied for the attention of language designers: *monitors*. First proposed by Dijkstra, Hoare and Brinch Hansen in 1971, monitors were soon presented in the form of a language construct (Brinch Hansen 1973, 1993; Hoare 1974). In 1975, Per Brinch Hansen introduced Concurrent Pascal, where monitors are shared classes based on Simula 67 classes (Dahl and Nygaard 1970). In Mesa (Mitchell et al. 1976), monitors got unified with units rather than classes.

As early as in 1977, the ideas from Mesa got cast into fresh shape, leading to a first cut at Modula (Wirth 1977, 1995). As refined in Modula-2 (Wirth 1982), modules arguably developed into their most well known form. A Modula-2 module unites in itself all of the following:

- A *namespace*, with the ability to use qualified names to access names from imported modules. Qualified naming avoids polluting the importing namespace with all the names exported by the imported modules. Unqualified imports are also supported if so desired. (It took several revisions of Modula-2 to arrive at the final form of qualified and unqualified imports and exports.)

- A *scope for declarations*, split into local and exported ones. Unlike ADT-centric languages like CLU, Modula-2 modules can implement multiple related ADTs. The CLU successor Theta (Liskov et al. 1995) adds modules containing multiple classes, but limits cross-ADT implementation dependencies: unlike Modula-2, Theta modules cannot expose (export) most of the implementation details they contain. Even instantiation is encapsulated: a class can only be instantiated from outside its defining module, if that module exports a constructor routine.
- A *scope for state*: global variables turn a module into a classless singleton object.
- An optional *priority monitor*: An entire module can be declared to be a priority monitor: a monitor variation that allows entrance by higher-priority threads while the monitor is locked by a lower-priority thread. Modula-2 does not support the Mesa notion of marking exported procedures as *mutex* to selectively specify which entry points require mutual exclusion. (A recent rebirth of this Mesa concept is Java's *synchronized* attribute on methods.)

In addition, Modula-2 modules can be nested in two ways: modules can be placed either directly within other modules or indirectly within the declaration section of procedures. The latter possibility has dramatic consequences: modules nested within procedures get "instantiated" (as far as their global variables go) and initialized each time the enclosing procedure is entered.

Outermost modules in Modula-2 are special for two reasons. First, they correspond most closely to older unit concepts in forming units of compilation. Second, they cannot refer to the context established by some enclosing module. In particular, imports and exports among outermost modules are special in that they are coupled through a "universal" outermost namespace. All modules at this level have to have unique names in order to coexist in a single project, although there is no established naming authority that could prevent clashes.

Java (Arnold et al. 1997) attempts to clean up the flat universal namespace at the outermost level by using structured package names, using a conventional approach to the avoidance of name clashes. (Initially, the proposal was to use reversed Internet domain names to form unique package names: *com.barcorp.baz-package*... Since such names quickly become quite unwieldy, the current trend is to use trademarks instead.) As an aside, it is worth noting that Java actually does not support modules: Java packages are an *open* namespace construct, quite similar to much simpler namespace constructs as found in, for example, C++ (Ellis and Stroustrup 1990). Like Eiffel (Meyer 1988) and CLU before it, Java relies on classes to model the closed nature of modules. By supporting nested classes in the style of Beta's nested patterns (Kristensen et al. 1983), Java goes beyond Eiffel. However, since visibility/accessibility constraints remain half bound to the package construct, Java classes form only partially useful modules.

Modula-3 (Cardelli et al. 1989) drops the Modula-2 notion of nested modules. However, it introduces the interesting concept of incremental revelation. Interfaces and implementations of modules can incrementally reveal more and more implementation detail of a type; effectively creating a layered structure where clients can commit to the least revealing layer they can do with. Since incremental revelation relies on a linear chain of revelations from the most abstract to the most concrete, it tends to interfere with separate compilation. Indeed, Modula-3's problems with true separate compilation never got resolved completely.

Both Ada (DOD 1980) and Modula-3 go beyond Modula-2 and Mesa modules by adding support for generic modules (generic packages in Ada), following the lead of CLU. Unfortunately, both languages do not require compilers to type check a generic module before instantiation, leaving these extensions in the same space as C++ templates: that of glorified macros (Roe and Szyperski 1997). Even several of the most advanced higher-order module systems, such as the one found in the original Standard ML (Harper et al. 1986), often suffer from an inability to support separate compilation. For ML this has been fixed in a relatively recent revision (Harper et al. 1997), while most other languages with parametric module systems retain the flaw of not actually supporting separate compilation.

Oberon (Reiser and Wirth 1992) is most interesting in that in its design Wirth went full circle. Oberon is close to the spirit of simplicity of Pascal and much simpler than any of the Modula-derived languages. However, despite this striking simplicity, Oberon addresses all the concerns Kernighan (as a particularly outspoken Pascal critic) had. The module system of Oberon is no exception. An Oberon module is quite close to the UCSD Pascal unit: there are no separate definition files, there is no commingling of module and monitor functions, and there is no notion of nesting. Unlike units, Oberon modules are based on qualified import only. Local aliasing of imported module names allows for compact qualified names where this is desirable.

Adding features to a language with modules in the spirit of Oberon usually amounts to adding to constructs placed within modules and not to adding features to the module construct itself. For example, parametric polymorphism is added to types and typed entities defined within modules (Roe and Szyperski 1997) and not to modules themselves, as the tradition from CLU to Modula-3 would suggest. Oberon-style modules thus retain their slim and elegant nature.

Software components

While the roots of module concepts can be traced back to the early 1970's, the roots of software component concepts predate even that and go back to the mid 1960's. Software components where alluded to at least as early as 1968 (McIlroy).

Software components from their inception were meant to be the software analogy of components in established engineering disciplines. In contrast, modules were meant to be structuring means in programming languages. As argued elsewhere (Szyperski 1998), the analogies with other disciplines, such as civil, mechanical, or electrical engineering, don't do software engineering full justice. Could it be that the module concept, with its strong roots in core computing, is an artifact that was always meant to technically fill the role ascribed by the non-technical analogy-driven vision of software components? In order to answer this question, it is useful to first rehash what we mean by software component.

For starters, components are elements of some composition theory: based on rules of composability, components are composed into composites. If that sounds like music to some, then that's not a bad analogy. Unfortunately, this definition of component is extremely broad. For example, reusable fragments of human-digestible documents can be seen as 'document components' (Sametinger 1997).

In engineering disciplines components are used to construct (compose) products out of smaller units whose manufacturing can be outsourced or delegated. Importantly, to be able to exist at all, components in engineering need to exist consistently in all viewpoints of an engineered system using them. (Viewpoints are also called projections or design dimensions.) For example, consider an alleged component that appears as one entity in the functional viewpoint of a system while it appears as an aspect spread across all entities in the performance viewpoint of that same system. Clearly, this 'thing' is not a component, as it cannot be uniquely identified in the system. Thus, engineering components differ from abstract components in that they "cut through" all viewpoints of an engineering system, while abstract components merely partition one viewpoint. For a discussion of aspects in programming, see *Aspect-Oriented Programming* (Kiczales et al. 1997).

Software components are intended to play that same role for software systems that mechanical components play for mechanical systems, or that electronic components play for electronic systems, etc. In fact, modern engineered systems typically span most known aspects of engineering from mechanical via electronic to software and still have a requirement for identifiable components. For software components, this leads to a first defining property: software components are binary units. "Binary" in this context refers to the machine-digestible form required to blend into an engineering system. For example, a software component implemented using some untyped interpreted scripting language (oh my!) is shipped in what very much looks like "source code." However, while source code needs to be human-digestible but not fully self-contained (since a developer can provide additional information to fit the source fragment into some context), binary code needs to be machine-digestible and self-contained. Whether such binary code takes the form of a processor-specific dynamic load library, or whether it takes the form of a text file containing a script is rather irrelevant as far as the notion of software components goes. (For a public exchange on these issues see the Beyond Objects column in the Software Development magazine at http://www.sdmagazine.com/.)

Since software, unlike other engineering substrates, is not physical, there is no need to use components to gain advantages of economies of scale when casting shapes into atoms. Instances (objects, values, etc.) are created by executing software and there is no need to aim at "reusing" such instances. The reusable essence of software is not the dynamic instances, but the static "factories" (classes, functions, etc.) that are used to create the required instances automatically. Software components thus have to capture the isolatable essence of such static factory abstractions. Static is important in this context: if a component can morph itself, then it really escapes isolation. (It is better to view such a self-modifying artifact as creating a series of new components along the trajectory of self-inflicted changes.) A separate procedure (as in CLU) or a separate class (as in Eiffel) could thus be seen as a software component. However, there are a few further requirements to be met for something to be a (useful) software component and many self-standing procedures or classes turn out to not qualify as software components in the end.

For an engineering component to be deployable in the context of some engineering system, the component needs to be well specified in all relevant viewpoints. For a software component, such a specification has to include all execution environment dependencies (also called platforms), be it virtual or physical. Clearly, it is highly desirable to minimize such built-in dependencies and replace them instead by mechanisms that allow for the dynamic establishment of dependencies between instances (a form of composition that is sometimes called "wiring" or "assembling"). However, it is impossible to completely eliminate dependencies on an execution context. (Consider parameterizing at the level of the used instruction set – and then consider in what terms to express the parametric form.)

To make the world of composition rich enough to be useful, components should adhere to some component composition standard (a.k.a. component model) that, at some level, specifies protocols of interoperation, establishes common ontology, and does all this relative to at least one but possibly several execution environments. JavaBeans (JavaSoft 1996) and Enterprise JavaBeans (JavaSoft 1998) are such component models relative to the Java VM and base library platform. COM (Microsoft 1995) and COM+ (Microsoft 1999) are such component models relative to the Pentium/Windows platform. The new CORBA Component Model (OMG 1999) is actually not a component model, but rather a parametric schema that leaves the concrete platform open; multiple component models can be derives by substituting in some concrete platforms.

Components are static entities that should not have observable state. To manage stateful abstractions, a component can create instances (objects). This separation of stateless components from stateful instances is crucially important. Consider repeated deployment of the same component. Such copying of the component must not lead to observable differences that would expose which copy is servicing a request. State held by a component is permissible provided it is not observable. The canonical example here is cache structures used transparently to tune performance.

Finally, to create a sufficiently general model, it is useful – but not strictly necessary – to allow for constant (immutable) data to form part of a component. The important observation here is the code-data duality that underlies universal computing as exemplified by the Universal Turing Machine (Turing 1936). Put simply, data can be replaced by code that computes that data and code can be replaced by data that, if interpreted by some other ("universal") code, yields the same computational effect. It is possible to replace all data by code (the resulting coding of basic concepts like integers gets rather esoteric); however, it is impossible to replace all code by data – some fundamental interpreter needs to be left in place.

Exploiting the code-data duality of Turing machines for the definition of components yields substantial flexibility. For example, the result of an instance-level composition operation can either be described by generating code to perform the required instance composition or by generating data that, if interpreted, reconstructs the composition. Hence, a tool implementing some composition paradigm – such as visual wiring – is free to either generate code or to persist prototype objects. At runtime, the desired composition is then established by either executing the generated code or by cloning the persistent prototype objects, yielding the exact same result in both cases.

To summarize: a software component needs to be a binary unit (an immutable collection of code and data bits) that is well specified, has no observable state, has known context dependencies only, and follows a composition standard. There are many other characterizations of similar effect possible (Szyperski 1998), but that is not the focus of this chapter.

Synthesis: modules in a world of components

Modules and components are related concepts in that both are about partitioning of software. Where modules partition the implementation description of software systems, components partition the systems themselves. It is clear that the independent existence of a component implies the existence of an independent description of its implementation. That is, componentizing a system naturally leads to modularized implementation descriptions. The inverse does not generally hold, though. Quite to the contrary, most traditional software construction approaches fuse the results of compilation steps in a linking step, yielding a monolithic *blob of bits*. Whether the source used at construction time was modular or not is relevant for many reasons, but it has no impact on the fact that the resulting blob is, at best, just a single component. In other words, modularization does not necessarily lead to componentization.

One could argue that the fusing of multiple modules into a single component is a mere packaging aspect and not very interesting. If such fusing were fully optional, then that would be true. However, as pointed out in the above section on actual module systems, there are many seemingly harmless or even useful features to module systems that effectively prevent true separate compilation. A common example is type-parametric modules that cannot be compiled separately. In such module systems, the fusing is not optional. Indeed, the production of any component using such systems can be a challenge.

Since modular programming is still not ubiquitously accepted or practiced – and since modularity is a necessary though insufficient condition for component production – it is useful to move from traditional to modular programming before considering a second step towards components. However, to make that second step reasonably feasible, it is important to stay away from those "modular" constructs that do clash with the notion of components. For example, it is advisable to introduce conventions that restrict those language features that lead to undesirable degrees of coupling at any stage between construction and deployment.

A mundane example is the coupling caused by import relations, where two modules import a shared third that maintains some global state. However, things can be far subtler. An otherwise impressively powerful language feature may well introduce stealth coupling. Generic constructs have been in this category for many languages: while they promise to enable rapid production of a whole family of components, generic constructs also often preclude actual production of components unless all genericity is eliminated by full instantiation. As pointed out earlier, many languages do not even type-check a generic construct until it is fully instantiated. Such languages exclude some of the most promising applications of parametric polymorphism: those that safely compose components based on parametric typing (Szyperski 1998).

Clearly, modules can be constrained to always yield components. Given such suitably constrained modules, *components can be defined as sets of compiled modules and immutable resources*. Requiring compilation ensures that an explicit mapping from source to binary code exists, regardless of the complexity of that mapping. In the case of script code, compilation degrades to mere consistency checking or even to nothing.

This definition nicely links modules and components and also yields an astoundingly trivial low-level composition operator: the composition of any two components is the set union of their (compiled) modules and resources. Since under such composition suitable code may come from another component, it is useful to allow components that contain resources only. Resource-only components could, for example, be the result of visual assembly as advocated by approaches such as JavaBeans.

Beyond constraints on module and type systems that ease the construction of components, programming languages could and should evolve to cater for more of the genuine needs of component software. By following this path, programming languages will finally mature from a myopic focus on details in the small to a holistic view of programming across a spectrum from the very small to the very large. Intentionally non-Turing-complete composition operators seem to be one useful step in this direction. Such operators, when applied in the large, retain properties such as verifiability that computationally complete operators cannot maintain when moving from the small to the large. The key problem here is not one of absolute decidability, a property that matters only marginally in practice. The key problem is one of scalable efficient decidability: how does the cost of analysis/verification grow with the size of the composed artifacts.

Another promising line is research into type-system support for system-level properties. For example, even quite simple type system enhancements can yield effects such as statically guaranteed avoidance of resource-bound deadlocks, as they commonly occur in systems communicating over bounded-capacity channels (Roe and Szyperski 2000). To illustrate the importance: every single application using something like TCP is in danger of running into such deadlocks! Besides deadlocks caused by communication, similar resource pressure can lead to denial of service – whether part of an intentional attack or not.

Finally, since component composition may happen as late as on demand at runtime (as is the case with today's applets), it seems useful to explore the potential of proof-carrying code (Necula 1997) to its fullest. The idea is simple: while it is hard to establish a proof that some given code meets some given specification property, it is usually efficient and simple to check that a proof exists for some given code, provided the code comes with useful hints. The checking process doesn't need to trust the hints: if they don't point the checker in the right direction, the checker will simply fail to reconstruct the proof and thus reject the checked code.

The list of interesting open problems that can be targeted at the language level – while keeping the goal of component software in mind – is quite substantial. To a degree, it is again early days – this time for programming in the large. Our good old modules are only a first step – an important one, though!

References

Arnold K. and Gosling J. (1997) *The Java Programming Language.* Java Series, Addison-Wesley, Reading, Mass., 2nd edition.

Brinch Hansen P. (1975) The Programming Language Concurrent Pascal. *IEEE Trans. Softw. Eng.* **1**(2), pp. 199–207, June.

Brinch Hansen P. (1973) *Operating System Principles.* Prentice-Hall, Englewood Cliffs, NJ.

Brinch Hansen P. (1993) Monitors and Concurrent Pascal: a personal history. *The second ACM SIGPLAN conference on History of programming languages*, pp. 1–35, ACM Press, New York.
(http://www.acm.org/pubs/citations/proceedings/plan/154766/p1-hansen/).

Cardelli L., Donahue J., Glassman L., Jordan M., Kalsow B., and Nelson G. (1989) The Modula-3 report (revised). *Technical report.* DEC Systems Research Center and Olivetti Research Center, November.

Clark R. (1982) *UCSD Pascal Handbook : A Reference Guidebook for Programmers.* Simon & Schuster.

Dahl O.-J. and Nygaard K. (1970) *Simula-67 Common Base Language.* Publication S-22, Norwegian Computing Centre, Oslo. (Current version: Data Processing – Programming Languages – SIMULA, Swedish Standard SS.63.61.14, SIS.)

DOD (1980) *Ada Reference manual.* Military Standard 1815, Dep. of Defense, July. (Approved 10 December 1980: Augusta Ada Bryon was born 10 December 1815.)

Ellis M.A. and Stroustrup B. (1990) *The Annotated C++ Reference Manual.* Addison-Wesley, Reading, Mass.

Geschke C.M., Morris J.H., and Satterthwaite E.H. (1977) Early Experience with Mesa. *CACM* **20**(8), pp. 540–552, August.

Harper R., MacQueen D., and Milner R. (1986) Standard ML. Technical Report ECS-LFCS-86-2, University of Edinburgh, Laboratory for Foundations of Computer Science, March.

Milner R., Tofte M., Harper R., MacQueen D. (1997) The Definition of Standard ML. Revised edition, MIT Press, Boston, Mass., October.

Hoare C.A.R. (1974) Monitors: an operating system structuring concept. *CACM* **17**(10), pp. 549–557, October. (Erratum in *CACM* **18**(2), p. 95, February 1975.)

JavaSoft (1996) *JavaBeans.* (http://java.sun.com/beans/).

JavaSoft (1998) *Enterprise JavaBeans.* (http://java.sun.com/products/ejb/).

Kernighan B.W. (1981) Why Pascal is not my favorite programming language. *Technical Report.* AT&T Bell Laboratories, Murray Hill, New Jersey, April 2. (http://www.threedee.com/jcm/psystem/whypascal.html)

Kiczales G., Lamping J., Mendhekar A., Maeda C., Lopes C.V., Loingtier J.-M., Irwin J. (1997) Aspect-Oriented Programming. *Proceedings, European Conference on Object-Oriented Programming* (ECOOP). *Lecture Notes in Computer Science*, No. 1241, Springer-Verlag, Berlin.

Kristensen B.B., Lehrmann Madsen O., Møller-Pedersen B., and Nygaard K. (1983) Abstraction Mechanisms in the BETA Programming Language. *Proceedings, 10th ACM Symposium on Principles of Programming Languages*, January 24-26, Austin, Texas.

Lampson B. (1983) A description of the Cedar language. *Technical Report* CSL-83-15, Xerox PARC, Palo Alto, California.

Liskov B., Atkinson R.R., Bloom T., Moss J.E.B., Schaffert C., Scheifler R., and Snyder A. (1981) CLU Reference Manual. *Lecture Notes in Computer Science*, No. 114, Springer-Verlag, New York.

Liskov B., Curtis D., Day M., Ghemawat S., Gruber R., Johnson P., and Myers A.C. (1995) Theta Reference Manual (Preliminary Version). *Programming Methodology Group Memo*, No. 88, MIT Laboratory for Computer Science, Cambridge, MA.

McIlroy M.D. (1968) Mass produced software components. In: Naur P. and Randell B. (eds.), *Proceedings, NATO Conference on Software Engineering*, Garmisch, Germany, October 1968. NATO Science Committee, Brussels (published as a book in 1976).

Meyer B. (1988) *Object-Oriented Software Construction.* Prentice-Hall, Englewood Cliffs, NJ.

Microsoft (1992) The Component Object Model specification. In: *Object Linking and Embedding 2.01.* (http://www.microsoft.com/com/).

Microsoft (1999) *COM+ extensions to the Component Object Model (COM).* (http://www.microsoft.com/com/tech/complus.asp).

Mitchell J.G., Maybury W., and Sweet R. (1979) The Mesa Programming Language, Version 5.0. *Technical Report* CSL-79-3. Xerox PARC, Palo Alto, California, April.

Necula G.C. (1997) Proof-Carrying Code. *Proceedings, ACM Conference on Principles of Programming Languages* (POPL97), January.

OMG (1999) *CORBA Component Model.* (Work in progress as of April 2000). Object Management Group, (http://www.omg.org/).

Parnas D. (1972a) A Technique for Software Module Specification with Examples. *CACM* **15**(5), pp. 330–336, May.

Parnas D. (1972b) On the Criteria To Be Used in Decomposing Systems into Modules. *CACM* **15**(12), pp. 1053–1058, December.

Roe P. and Szyperski C. (1997) Lightweight parametric polymorphism for Oberon. In Mössenböck H. (ed.) *Proceedings, 4th Joint Modular Languages Conference* (JMLC97), Lecture Notes in Computer Science, No. 1204, pp. 140–154. Springer-Verlag, Berlin.

Roe P. and Szyperski C. (2000) Mianjin: A Parallel Language with a Type System that Governs Global System Behaviour. *Proceedings, 5th Joint Modular Languages Conference.* Lecture Notes in Computer Science, No. *tba*, Springer-Verlag, Berlin.

Sametinger J. (1997) *Software Engineering with Reusable Components.* Springer-Verlag, New York.

Szyperski C. (1992) Import is not inheritance – why we need both: modules and classes. In Lehrmann Madsen O. (ed.) *Proceedings, 6th European Conference on Object-Oriented Programming* (ECOOP92). Lecture Notes in Computer Science, No. 615, pp. 19–32, Springer-Verlag, Berlin.

Szyperski C. (1996) Independently extensible systems – software engineering potential and challenge. *Proceedings, 19th Australasian Computer Science Conference*, Australian Computer Science Communications, 18(1), pp. 203–212.

Szyperski C. (1998) *Component Software – Beyond Object-Oriented Programming.* Addison-Wesley, Harlow, UK.

Turing A.M. (1936) On computable numbers, with an application to the Entscheidungsproblem. *Proceedings of the London Mathematical Society*, Series 2, Vol. 42, pp. 230–265. (Correction published 1937 in Vol. 43, pp. 544–546.)

Wirth N. (1971) The programming language Pascal. *Acta Informatica* **1**, pp. 35–63.

Wirth N. (1977) Modula: a programming language for modular multiprogramming. *Software – Practice and Experience* 7(1), pp. 37–52, January.

Wirth N. (1980) Modula-2. *Technical Report* 36, ETH Zürich, March.

Wirth N. (1982) *Programming in Modula-2.* Springer-Verlag, Berlin.

Wirth N. and Gutknecht J. (1992) *Project Oberon – The Design of an Operating System and Compiler.* Addison-Wesley, Reading, Mass.

Wirth N. (1995) A brief history of Modula and Lilith. *The ModulaTor*, No. 0, January, (http://www.modulaware.com/mdlt52.htm).

A Compiler for the Java HotSpot™ Virtual Machine

Robert Griesemer, Srdjan Mitrovic
Sun Microsystems, Inc.

Abstract

This paper documents the design and implementation decisions chosen for the Java HotSpot™ Client Compiler. Its code generator was strongly influenced by the design of Niklaus Wirth's Modula-2 and Oberon compilers. The client compiler is part of the Java HotSpot Client VM, which is the default virtual machine delivered with the Java 2 Runtime Environment, Standard Edition 1.3.0, by Sun Microsystems. The client virtual machine exhibits excellent performance for client applications.

1 Introduction

The performance of a statically compiled program depends largely on the quality of the compiled code. Consequently, static compilers aim at the generation of excellent code, usually at the expense of compilation time. In the context of virtual machines and dynamic compilers, i.e., compilers compiling at run time of the virtual machine, compilation time impacts the perceived overall performance. The performance gain of highly optimized code may be easily destroyed by the extra time needed for its generation. Thus, a dynamic compiler must strike a delicate balance between adequate code quality and short compilation times. Also, some code optimizations slow down other virtual machine operations, such as garbage collection. Thus, cooperation of compiler and virtual machine is essential.

Originally, the Java HotSpot™ Virtual Machine [Sun 99] was delivered with a highly optimizing, but relatively slow compiler, called the server compiler. This compiler provides peak performance for long running server applications. In the server environment, compilation time is usually irrelevant since it impacts the system only during its warmup phase. Furthermore, large server systems employ several processors and compilation can be done "in the background".

On the client side, i.e., for interactive applications, slow compilations may lead to noticeable "compilation pauses" that affect the perceived system performance negatively (e.g., see [Hölzle 94]). The goal of the client compiler is to provide significantly higher compilation speed possibly at cost of peak performance. In particular, it needs to fulfill the following criteria:

- Compilation speed: ~ 80 Kbytes/s of bytecodes on a 400 MHz Pentium® II
- Code quality: ~ 80% of server VM peak-performance
- Complexity: simple but sufficiently powerful
- Modularity: de-coupled from the core VM via compiler interface
- Extensibility: optimizations can be added easily if desired

Simply put, the client compiler is supposed to follow the "80/20" or "skim the cream" principle (e.g., see [Koch 98]) applied to compiler optimizations: achieve 80% of the performance of the server VM with 20% of the effort.

Not coincidentally, the compilers developed by Niklaus Wirth for Modula-2 and Oberon [Wirth 85][Wirth 92][Wirth 96] followed a similar guideline. We have studied those compilers extensively and have borrowed ideas liberally.

In the following, we will refer to the client compiler as *C1* or just *compiler*, and to the server compiler as *C2*[1]. The Java HotSpot Virtual Machine is referred to as the VM.

2 Overall System Structure

The VM can be built in three different configurations:

- Core VM (interpreter only)
- Client VM (Core VM + C1)
- Server VM (Core VM + C2)

The Core VM is a complete Java™ virtual machine implementation using an interpreter for the execution of programs. It features:

- accurate generational and compacting garbage collection
- pre-emptive multithreading based on native threads
- mixed-mode native stacks (all code running on one stack per thread)
- uniform object model
- system-specific runtime routines generated at VM startup time
- compiler interface supporting parallel compilations
- extensive support for pre-emptive debugging

When configured with a compiler, the VM profiles a Java™ program at run time and invokes the compiler if necessary. The compilation unit is a method and the compiler translates the method's bytecodes into native machine code. In particular, the VM counts method invocations and loop iterations. If a method's invocation counter reaches a certain threshold, the method is scheduled for compilation. At every method activation, the interpreter tests if the method has a compiled form. If so, the compiled form is executed instead. Thus, once a method is compiled, the

1. The names C1 and C2 are used because of historical reasons.

next time the method is invoked its compiled form will be executed. Consequently, the execution stack contains interpreter activation frames corresponding to interpreted methods, and "compiled" activation frames corresponding to compiled methods.

The VM also supports a mechanism called *On-Stack-Replacement* or *OSR*, which allows switching from interpreted to compiled code in the middle of method interpretation as opposed to at method entry only. OSR is used to switch to compiled code if the interpreter spends too much time interpreting a long-running loop. For this purpose, the interpreter counts backward branches (as an estimate for the number of loop iterations). When a threshold is reached, interpretation is suspended and the method is compiled with a so-called *OSR entry point*, corresponding to the beginning of the loop body (i.e., the backward branch's destination). Then, control is transferred from the interpreter to the OSR entry point. The code at the OSR entry point will set up a new compiled activation frame and initialize it such that its state corresponds exactly to the corresponding (and still suspended) interpreter activation. Afterwards, execution of the loop (and the rest of the method) continues in compiled code. Upon method return, the compiled activation frame and the suspended interpreted activation frame are removed at once.

At compile time, the compiler interacts with the core VM via the *Compiler Interface*. It summarizes all the VM functionality needed by a compiler and provides a clean separation between the two components. Also, it decouples the compiler from the garbage collector (GC): since the system uses a compacting GC, objects may move around. The compiler refers to VM objects via *handles* (i.e. an extra indirection) at compile time, so both the compiler and the GC can run simultaneously[2]. This is important if compilations are scheduled as background tasks, potentially running on a different processor. The compiler interface provides functionality to inspect the class hierarchy (used to perform class hierarchy dependent optimizations) and functions to "install" compiled code in the VM, among other things.

At run time, the compiled code interacts with the VM via the *Runtime Interface*. This interface is a set of assembly code stubs that are called from compiled code and which interface with the VM.

C1 itself consists of two main components: the machine-independent front end, and the machine-dependent back end. The front end constructs an *Intermediate Representation* (IR) from the bytecodes. Emphasis is placed on extracting and preserving as much information as possible from the bytecode level (e.g., locality information, initial control flow graph) which directly translates into reduced compilation time. The back end uses the IR for code generation.

Note that it is possible to generate code directly from the bytecodes without constructing an IR. Unfortunately, some of the information needed by the back end

2. Note that interpreted and compiled Java™ code do not use handles, but direct pointers.

cannot easily be determined with a single pass over the bytecodes (these details are beyond the scope of this paper). Iterating multiple times over the code is more cumbersome than building an IR once, which then can be used for all further analysis. An earlier version of C1 used an IR-less approach. The IR-based solution has proven to be simpler, faster, and more reliable.

3 Front end

The front end is responsible for initializing the compiler, parsing bytecodes, and building and optimizing the IR. The JVM bytecodes are based on a stack machine architecture [Lindholm 99]. Control flow is expressed via branches, switch bytecodes, and some special bytecodes for exception handling. The IR contains a control flow graph (CFG) representing the basic blocks of a method. Within a basic block, individual bytecodes are represented via a sequential list of instruction nodes.

3.1 Intermediate Representation

To build the IR, the bytecodes are read twice. In the first pass, the starts of all basic blocks are determined. This pass is very fast. Subroutine calls (jsr)[3] and exception paths[4] do not terminate a basic block but are handled separately. In the second pass, the gaps between the basic block starts are filled with IR instructions by parsing and performing abstract interpretation of the bytecodes. A BlockBegin node represents the start of a basic block and a sequential list of *Instruction* nodes forms the basic block body, which is terminated by a *BlockEnd* node. BlockEnd nodes represent control flow and contain a possibly empty list of successors, which are just other BlockBegin nodes. A (BlockBegin, BlockEnd) pair[5] represents a basic block, and all these pairs represent the CFG within the IR. This graph can be traversed quickly without the need to traverse every single instruction. Instructions refer to their arguments via pointers, and in turn the arguments themselves are instructions. Thus, an instruction represents both a computation and its result, or *value*, if any. This IR form is also called *triples representation* (see e.g. [Muchnik 97]). Additionally, instructions are linked together sequentially in the bytecode's original order. Note that sequentially executing (or generating code for) the instructions is correct but not necessarily required.

Within a basic block, instructions that must be executed in the original order are marked as *pinned*. Thus, the execution order of pinned instructions is defined

3. In retrospect it may have been better if subroutine calls terminated a basic block. The subroutine analysis may have turned out simpler.
4. Many bytecodes can throw exceptions. If the exception path is modeled as a branch, basic blocks become very small. Large basic blocks are desirable for better code quality.
5. Having a pair of nodes to represent a basic block seemed to simplify our particular implementation somewhat; but this design decision is not crucial for the system.

by the order of the corresponding bytecodes. The execution order of all other instructions is only constrained by their data dependencies. In this scheme, pinned instructions and instructions that are referred to more than once[6] are defined as *roots* of *instruction trees*. By marking instructions that are referred to more than once as roots, directed acyclic graphs are broken into trees. Code generation proceeds from root instruction to root instruction, and then generates code by recursively traversing the trees[7].

Basic blocks are independent, in the sense that none of the instructions of one basic block refer directly to values in another basic block, but only to *Phi* instructions[8] representing them. This significantly simplifies register allocation and code generation. The following figure illustrates the relationships between CFG, basic blocks, and individual instructions:

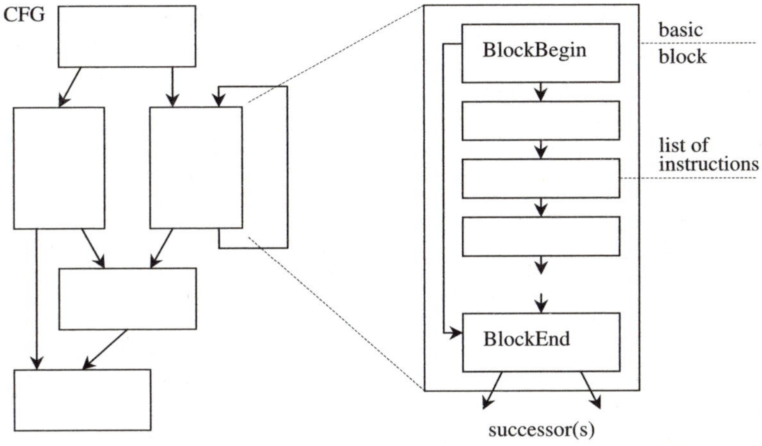

All IR nodes are subclasses of the *Instruction* class. Some of them hold extra information such as operand stack and monitor information. This is the case for the *BlockBegin* and *BlockEnd* nodes but also for instructions that potentially call other methods or the runtime system. The operand stack information is needed to generate correct debug information (see section 4.5), and the monitor information is used for *MonitorEnter/Exit* instructions. In the Instruction class hierarchy

6. The JVM specification defines bytecodes that copy expression stack entries. During abstract interpretation, this yields values that can be referenced more than once. Also, if value numbering is enabled, values may be referenced multiple times.
7. The sequential ordering enforced via pinning is overly restrictive. We may relax this constraint in the future in order to generate better code.
8. Our Phi nodes are simply placeholders representing an expression stack value. The name is borrowed from SSA phi nodes since the concept is closely related.

below, only the BlockBegin and leaf classes are concrete classes (i.e., are actually instantiated). All other classes are abstract and serve for factoring.

```
class Instruction;
class   HiWord;
class   Phi;
class   Constant;
class   AccessLocal;
class     LoadLocal;
class     StoreLocal;
class   AccessField;
class     LoadField;
class     StoreField;
class   AccessArray;
class     ArrayLength;
class     AccessIndexed;
class       LoadIndexed;
class       StoreIndexed;
class   AccessLoop;
class     LoopEnter;
class     LoopExit;
class   NegateOp;
class   Op2;
class     ArithmeticOp;
class     ShiftOp;
class     LogicOp;
class     CompareOp;
class     IfOp;
class   Convert;
class   NullCheck;
class Instruction;
class   JsrContinuation;
class   StateSplit;
class     Jsr;
class     Invoke;
class     NewInstance;
class     NewArray;
class       NewTypeArray;
class       NewObjectArray;
class       NewMultiArray;
class     TypeCheck;
class       CheckCast;
class       InstanceOf;
class     AccessMonitor;
class       MonitorEnter;
class       MonitorExit;
class     Intrinsic;
class     BlockBegin;
class     BlockEnd;
class       Goto;
class       If;
class       Switch;
class         TableSwitch;
class         LookupSwitch;
class       Ret;
class       Return;
class       Throw;
class       Base;
```

Some of these instructions appear only after optimizations (e.g., *IfOp*, *Intrinsic*, *LoopEnter*, and *LoopExit*), and some are specific to the way the IR is built. The root of the IR is an empty basic block that ends with a *Base* node. The *HiWord* node is used to fill the second word slot of two-word entities on the operand stack during abstract interpretation. Phi nodes are placeholders on the initial operand stack of BlockBegin nodes. A Phi node stands for the corresponding operand stack value of any predecessor block (stored in its BlockEnd node), if the stack is not empty. The purpose of the other instructions corresponds directly to the bytecodes with related names. The following illustration shows the relationships between a small Java program example, its bytecodes, and the corresponding IR graph:

Java Program

```
int x, y, z;
z = x + y;
```

Bytecode Form

```
local 0: x
local 1: y
local 2: z

iload_0
iload_1
iadd
istore_2
```

IR (Instruction) Form

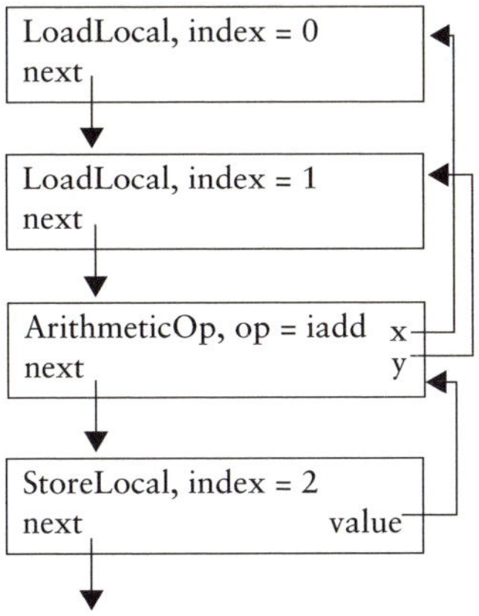

Each Instruction class contains only a minimum of data and functionality. Compiler phase-specific functionality (e.g. for IR printing, register allocation, code generation, etc.) is factored out by means of a *visitor scheme* [Gamma 95]. *InstructionVisitors* provide type-based dispatch for instructions. For each concrete Instruction class X, a virtual function *do_X* is provided in InstructionVisitor. Compiler functionality that needs to be implemented for all classes (printing, code generation) is factored out into a specialized visitor instead of being added to the instruction classes themselves.

```
class InstructionVisitor: StackObj {
 public:
  virtual void do_Phi         (Phi*         x) = 0;
  virtual void do_Constant    (Constant*    x) = 0;
  virtual void do_LoadLocal   (LoadLocal*   x) = 0;
  virtual void do_StoreLocal  (StoreLocal*  x) = 0;
  virtual void do_LoadField   (LoadField*   x) = 0;
  // etc. ...
  virtual void do_Return      (Return*      x) = 0;
  virtual void do_Throw       (Throw*       x) = 0;
  virtual void do_Base        (Base*        x) = 0;
};
```

The visitor scheme allows the concentration of all compiler phase-specific data and functionality into the corresponding InstructionVisitor subclass. As such, an object-oriented programming style can be used without cluttering all instructions with phase-specific code. Each Instruction class needs to provide only a visit function, which implements the dispatch:

```
virtual void visit(InstructionVisitor* v);
```

C1 uses several InstructionVisitor subclasses, ranging from the *InstructionPrinter* class (responsible for IR printing used for debugging) to the *ValueGen* class (responsible for code generation).

3.2 An Example: Factorial

The following example may help to give a better understanding of an actual IR built by the compiler. Compilation of the method

```
static long factorial(int n) {
  long p = 1;
  while (n > 0) {
    p = p * n;
    n = n - 1;
  }
  return p;
}
```

will lead to the CFG and instructions shown in the figure below. Each rectangle represents a basic block. Basic blocks are numbered B0, B1, B2, and so forth. They span a bytecode range [begin, end[and may have successors (e.g., -> B1, B2). Within a basic block, there is a line for each instruction. Each instruction has a corresponding bytecode index (bci), a use count (use), an instruction type and id (tid), and an instruction description (instr). The use count is only determined before code generation, and thus always zero here. The instruction type is one of int (i), long (l), float (f), double (d), object (a), or void (no letter); the instruction id is a unique number. Pinned instructions are marked with a "." in the first column. Locals are named L0, L1, L2, and so forth. Instruction descriptions are more or less self-explanatory. An instruction refers to other instructions via their tid's.

```
B4 [0, 0] -> B5
__bci__use__tid___instr__________
. 0    0     33   std entry B5
```

```
B5 [0, 0] -> B3
__bci__use__tid___instr__________
. 0    0     32   goto B3
```

```
B3 [0, 2] -> B0
__bci__use__tid___instr__________
  0    0    14    1L
. 1    0    17    L1 := 14
. 2    0     8    goto B0
```

```
B0 [14, 15] -> B1 B2
__bci__use__tid____instr______________________
  14   0    i9     L0
  15   0    i10    0
. 15   0     11    if i9 > i10 then B1 else B2
```

```
B1 [5, 13] -> B0
__bci__use__tid____instr______________________
  5    0    l16    L1
  6    0    i19    L0
  7    0    l20    i21(i19)
  8    0    l22    l16 * l20
. 9    0    l25    L1 := l22
  11   0    i26    1
  12   0    i27    i19 - i26
. 13   0    i28    L0 := i27
. 13   0     29    goto B0
```

```
B2 [18, 19]
__bci__use__tid____instr______________________
  18   0    l12    L1
. 19   0    l15    lreturn l12
```

Note that this is the IR immediately after parsing. The blocks B4 and B5 are automatically introduced for technical reasons and have no equivalent in the source (i.e., the bytecodes of the method).

3.3 Focus on the Common Case

The *Focus on the Common Case* principle is one of the most important design guidelines used in the VM: this principle demands that if an operation's implementation can be split into a common and an uncommon case, the focus should be on the common case. For example, the VM's GC algorithm permits extremely fast memory allocation. Allocating an object *obj* of size *s* essentially requires 3 steps[9]:

```
allocate:  obj = top
           top = top + s;
           if top > limit then goto slowcase; // alloc failed
```

The common case is that allocation succeeds. If allocation fails, GC is invoked.

---

9. The VM supports thread-local and shared allocation spaces. The latter requires an atomic compare-and-swap instruction since several threads may compete for allocation. If allocation fails because another thread succeeded first, allocation is retried. On multiprocessor systems, thread local allocation is preferred.

Since the common case is so much more frequent than the uncommon case, the common case should be the fast path for performance reasons even at the cost of a more complicated slow path.

In practice, many of the complex bytecodes can be split into a common and an uncommon case. In our example, the compiler inlines the common case directly into the generated code since it is only a couple of machine instructions, making object allocation extremely fast. If allocation fails, a branch leads to the slow case, eventually calling the runtime and invoking GC. Upon return, the code jumps back to the original allocation site:

```
slowcase:  save registers if any
           call GC
           restore registers if any
           goto allocate
```

A similar pattern is used for many other instructions. Since the slow case is uncommon, its code should be outside the method's regular code, e.g. at the end. This will improve instruction cache usage for the common case.

In the IR, we only focus on the common case. No provisions are made to express the control flow and instructions necessary for the slow paths. This greatly reduces IR size and speeds up operations on it. For example, object allocation is simply represented by a single *NewInstance* instruction. It is very easy to keep track of instructions with uncommon cases *when* they occur during code generation. The necessary information is simply collected in a linked list. At the end, this list is traversed and the slow case stubs are emitted.

3.4 Optimizations

Currently only a few straightforward optimizations are performed by the compiler. Among them are constant folding, the removal or merge of basic blocks, and some dead code elimination (which is a side effect of parsing and other optimizations). A simple form of value numbering is used on the basic block level. Very short methods[10] are inlined if no restrictions apply. A standard loop-detection algorithm based on dominator trees is used to determine innermost loops (e.g., see [Muchnik 97]). This information may be used by the back end for better register allocation. Note that these optimizations are not crucial to avoid obviously bad code generation. But they have shown a good price/performance ratio, and that is why they were included.

10. In the Java™ programming language, object allocation is followed by an implicit call of the object constructor, which in turn calls the superclass constructor. The constructor of the root class Object and of many other classes is empty. Calls to empty methods are trivially inlined by eliminating them.

4 Back end

The back end is mostly machine-specific. It has been implemented for the IA32 and the SPARC™ architecture. It is responsible for register allocation, code generation, and the construction of compiled methods, i.e., the VM structures holding compiled code. Code generation consists of two passes: a register allocation pass and a code generation pass. The two passes use exactly the same framework, except that code emission is disabled in the first pass. In both passes, the IR is traversed, basic block by basic block, in an order determined after IR building. For each basic block, all root instructions are traversed sequentially. For each root instruction, the corresponding tree is traversed recursively.

4.1 Register Allocation

The explicit register allocation pass is not strictly necessary. Code generation is correct even without this pass. However, the gain in code quality justifies the extra complexity.

The IR distinguishes between local variables (including parameters) and temporary values. Local variables are referred to explicitly in the bytecodes and the IR. Their number is known at the beginning and they can be allocated directly. In C1, this mapping is represented by the *FrameMap*, a data structure that maps local variables to stack or register locations. The FrameMap provides the context for code generation, very much like a symbol table.

Temporaries correspond to the intermediate values occuring during expression tree evaluation. Register allocation for expression trees is straightforward and has been discussed extensively in the literature. In particular, it can be closely coupled with code generation.

If it occurs that after code generation some registers have not been used, it may be possible to generate better code by using these registers to hold local variables instead of keeping them on the stack. This is where our register allocator enters the game: in a first pass, the back end's code generator is invoked with code emission disabled. At the same time it keeps track of all registers used. If some registers remained unused, they are assigned to hold local variables. Then, the process is repeated, this time with code emission enabled. Since the allocation of locals to registers eliminates the need for load and store operations, the code quality is guaranteed to improve. Note that after one such iteration, even more registers may have freed up. However, we refrain from running the iteration until a fixpoint is reached.

If there are not enough registers available during code generation, some values must be spilled on the stack. Spilling occurs rarely as it is only operand stack temporaries that can be spilled. The amount of spill space required is computed as a welcome side effect of the register allocation pre-pass. It simplifies code generation since all stack offsets are known at that time.

4.2 Code Generation

The compiler's code generator is strongly influenced by the design of Niklaus Wirth's Modula-2 and Oberon compilers [Wirth 85][Wirth 92][Wirth 96] and their successors [Templ 90]. The recursive, item-based code generation allows for good local code quality and is systematic, efficient, and very flexible. It produces predictable code quality ("linear" behavior; i.e. a localized source code change results in a localized compiled code change). Using the same notation as in [Wirth 85], and omitting the influence of the context for clarity, code generation for instruction trees can be described as follows: let T be an (instruction) tree of the form

$$T = N(T_1, T_2, \ldots T_n)$$

with N corresponding to T's root node, and the T_i's corresponding to T's subtrees. Obviously, our Instruction classes correspond to the nodes N. Each N has an evaluation function F_N of the form

$$A(T) = F_N(A(T_1), A(T_2), \ldots A(T_n))$$

and a code generator G_N of the form

$$P_N = G_N(A(T_1), A(T_2), \ldots A(T_n))$$

associated with it. F_N and G_N are determined by the root node N, and depend on the result of the subtree's evaluation functions. $A(T)$ is called the attributes of T. P_N is the code pattern for the node N, dependent on the subtree's attributes. The code for the whole tree T, $C(T)$, is the concatenation of the individual P_N's:

$$C(T) = P_{N1}, P_{N2} \ldots P_{Nn}, \; P_N$$

The order of the P_i's in $C(T)$ depends on the tree traversal order. Like in [Wirth 85], the attributes $A(T)$ are represented by *items* in the compiler. An item is a descriptor of a *value* during code generation; it is the equivalent of an attribute in attribute grammars [Knuth 68]. A value can be a constant, or it can be in a register, on the stack, in memory, etc. The item describes the value's location and its access mode (e.g., "register indirect"). Typically, the set of access modes corresponds to the set of addressing modes supported by the platform's machine instructions. When generating code for an instruction $N(T_1, T_2, \ldots T_n)$, first code is generated for its "input values" $T_1, T_2, \ldots T_n$. The location of each T_i is described by a corresponding item. Then, code is generated for N under consideration of the individual T_i's. If N generates a result value, a result item describing the location of that value is produced by the code generator.

4.3 Hint Items

The problem with this scheme is that the attributes *A(T)* for a tree *T* depend on *T* (and the omitted context) only. In particular, they cannot directly be influenced by the tree's parent node, if there is one. For example, in case of the assignment

```
x = a + b
```

it would be nice to be able to influence the evaluation function F_+ and the code generator G_+ associated with the +-node such that the code *C(a+b)* generated for *a+b* is storing the result of the addition directly into the location of *x* instead of a freshly allocated register. Templ extended the simple item-based code generation scheme for the SPARC™ implementation of Oberon-2 by *hint items* [Templ 91]. Hint items represent attributes flowing "down" during evaluation as opposed to "up" towards the root of the tree (see also attribute grammars). This extension corresponds to evaluation functions and code generators of the form

$$A(T, H) = F_N(A(T_1, H_1), A(T_2, H_2), \ldots A(T_n, H_n))$$

and

$$P_{NH} = G_N(A(T_1, H_1), A(T_2, H_2), \ldots A(T_n, H_n))$$

with *H* representing the hint, and the individual H_I's denoting hints for the subtrees (the hints H_i can be derived from *H* and $A(T_j, H_j)$ for $j < i$).

With the code generator being a subclass of InstructionVisitor, the evaluation functions F_N correspond directly to the individual visitor functions *do_N*. For a given instruction N, *do_N* computes a new hint *A(T, H)* by recursively calling the visitor for N's subtrees. The corresponding G_N are implemented as code emission routines called by *do_N*.

4.4 Basic Block Boundaries

At the end of basic blocks, occasionally the JVM operand stack is not empty, which means that intermediate operand values are still in registers. In order to avoid a more complicated register allocator to handle control flow merges of basic blocks with non-empty operand stacks, we employ an *operand stack passing convention.* Considering only the types of the values on an operand stack, each operand stack defines a unique *signature*, very much like the signature of a function. Since the signatures of operand stacks of merging blocks must match (otherwise the code could not be executed properly to begin with), mapping each unique signature to a corresponding register/spill location set is a simple solution to this problem. In most cases where the operand stack is not empty, only one operand stack element is alive anyway, which means only one register needs to be dedicated to operand stack passing. Hint items can be used to direct code generation such that the operand stack elements end up in the right registers without extra moves.

4.5 Debug Information

The back end generates *debug information*[11] as a side effect of code generation. Debug information includes a mapping of program counter offsets to bytecode indices, so-called *pc-maps*. It also includes *oop*[12] *maps* (i.e., pointer maps), specifying the exact stack location of all oops for all pc's where GC can occur. Finally, it includes *safepoint information*, which is used for GC as well.

Pc-maps are required for exception handling: if a runtime exception occurs, the pc where the exception occurred is mapped to the corresponding bytecode index (bci). This bci is used to look up the exception handler.

Oop maps are bit maps specifying which stack and register locations hold oops for a given pc. During GC, these locations need to be visited since they represent roots for GC. Also, if GC moves objects, pointers must be updated.

GC cannot happen at arbitrary places, but only at *safepoints*. Safepoints are designated places in the code, usually function calls, backward branches, and return instructions. All threads running code (interpreted or compiled) must be suspended at a safepoint before GC is executed. At a safepoint, the location of all oops on all stacks is known. The safepoint suspension mechanism is independent of the compiler. Its discussion is beyond the scope of this paper.

Debug information is stored in a compressed form together with the generated code in *native method objects*. They reside in the *code cache* managed by the VM.

5 Implementation Issues

Both the VM and the compiler are implemented in C++. Many of the more advanced features of C++ have been carefully avoided. In particular, no multiple inheritence and no C++ exceptions have been used. Selected features are used where they improve safety or readability: a template definition provides the equivalent of arrays with bounds checks; this template is used rigorously for arrays. Operator overloading is used for handles, allowing them to be dereferenced as if they were direct pointers. Otherwise, overloading is generally avoided. With a handful of exceptions, all code resides within the scope of classes. Static classes substitute the missing modules. No instance variables are accessed directly; accessor functions are used instead. For efficiency, the code relies heavily on (C++)

11. The term *debug information* is borrowed from C2, which generates a mapping from compiled code to interpreted code that could be used for bytecode-level debugging. It is required for deoptimization [Hölzle 92]. C1 does not currently implement this feature.
12. The term *oop* is historical. It stands for *Ordinary Object Pointer.* The notion is commonly used in the Smalltalk VM community and denotes pointers to "ordinary objects," as opposed to "immediate objects," which are represented by the pointer itself (e.g., tagged integers) [Miranda].

inlining. Assertions are sprinkled liberally throughout the code. Generally, a defensive and factored coding style is employed.

The system contains a significant amount of code for self-verification and printing of data structures. It has proven invaluable in the presence of bugs. For example, more complicated data structures implement a verify function that checks the data structures' invariants. In debug mode, these verify functions are called frequently and help expose damaged data structures (and thus buggy code). Also, since all compiler optimizations can be disabled, bugs related to optimizations are fairly easy to track down.

Besides these more passive precautions, the system contains active stress testing code for *pre-emptive debugging*. Features such as "GC-A-Lot" and "OSR-A-Lot" stress test GC and OSR functionality by causing a GC or OSR at every possible location. Obviously they cause the VM to run extremely slowly but they have been invaluable in determining the empirical absence of bugs that might show up in rare circumstances.

6 Performance

The benchmark commonly used to assess Java™ runtime environment performance is the SPEC JVM Client98 benchmark. It includes seven programs derived from real-life applications which are run repeatedly and measured for slowest and fastest runs. A score is associated with each run. The score is the quotient of the execution time for the run on the measured platform and the execution time for the same run on a reference platform. The geometric mean of the scores represents the SPEC performance, with higher means being better. For a detailed description of the individual benchmark programs and the exact benchmarking rules, see [Spec].

We have measured the SPEC performance of the Java HotSpot VM with the client (C1) and the server (C2) compiler[13]. The machine is a Dell Dimension XPS B866r, containing an 866MHz Intel Pentium® III and 256MB of memory, running Windows NT 4.0. To measure C1, we used the Java 2 Runtime Environment, Standard Edition 1.3.0, Java HotSpot Client VM, which includes C1. To measure C2, we used the Java 2 Runtime Environment, Standard Edition 1.3.0, Java HotSpot Server VM 2.0, which includes C2.

13. At the time of this writing, these numbers have been submitted to SPEC for review. They also have been announced by Sun Microsystems at the JavaOne conference in San Francisco, June 5–9, 2000. Note that the detailed measurement setup also includes tuning flags that have been omitted here for brevity.

SPEC JVM98	*C1*		*C2*		*C1/C2*	
program	*slowest*	*fastest*	*slowest*	*fastest*	*slowest*	*fastest*
_227_mtrt	61.8	63.3	61.5	165.0	1.00	0.38
_202_jess	66.1	74.0	35.4	93.0	1.87	0.80
_201_compress	66.9	67.4	77.8	79.2	0.86	0.85
_209_db	22.4	27.6	24.2	29.8	0.93	0.93
_222_mpegaudio	85.8	89.7	87.5	111.0	0.98	0.81
_228_jack	92.0	105.0	36.5	139.0	2.52	0.76
_213_javac	32.5	37.9	11.3	42.5	2.88	0.89
geometric mean	**55.2**	**60.9**	**39.4**	**81.4**	**1.40**	**0.75**
w/o _227_mtrt	54.2	60.5	36.6	72.4	1.48	0.84

The slowest runs are an indication of the VM's startup speed. The higher the score for the slowest runs, the faster the VM is at starting the program. This number is heavily influenced by the compilation speed of the compiler. With a slow compiler, much of the time is spent compiling methods instead of executing them. The fastest runs are an indication of the VM's peak performance. If the VM is doing a good job of compiling the relevant methods, only compiled code is executed during this run, and no new compilations occur (i.e., the system has reached a fixpoint). Thus, the fastest run is an indicator of the quality of the generated code.

For the slowest runs, C1 outperforms C2 by 40%; i.e., the client system has significantly better startup performance than the server system, as expected. For the fastest runs, C1 is about 25% slower than C2.

The biggest difference for the fastest runs is found for _227_mtrt, a ray-tracing algorithm that makes heavy use of floating-point operations. C1 is sub-optimal for floating-point-intensive code. This is also an area where highly optimizing compilers traditionally perform well. Without _227_mtrt, the slowest run of C1 is 48% faster than C2, and the fastest run only 16% slower than C2.

Another under-performer is _228_jack. This program makes heavy use of exception handling. In particular, it throws an exception in one method that is caught by a caller. With inlining, the method throwing the exception and the method catching it become one compiled method. Therefore, much of the functionality required for exception handling and forwarding can be eliminated (throwing an exception becomes an unconditional branch). C2 does this optimization while C1 does not.

For this benchmark, C1 generates 1298 compiled methods and consumes 1654KB of memory to cache them. C2 generates 1184 compiled methods and consumes 3373KB of memory. Thus, C2 needs roughly twice as much code cache memory as C1. Note that in both cases, currently only about 35% of that space is used for machine instructions. The rest is used for debugging information.

The comparison of C1 with C2 is relevant since the Java HotSpot Server VM 2.0 is the world's best-performing Java virtual machine for this benchmark at the time of this writing. Among the closest competitors is IBM's Java virtual machine (J2RE V1.3.0 for Windows) which produces a SPEC score of 79.1 for the fastest run on the same machine [Spec].

Not surprisingly, C1 compiles much faster then C2 (by a factor of about 10). Given SPEC scores and memory consumption, we conclude that C1 is indeed a very good 80/20 solution.

7 Related Work

Dynamic code generation has enjoyed renewed interest in recent years. It is a relatively old idea and has been employed before in a variety of systems for a variety of reasons. Applications range from speeding up interpreters [Mitchel 70][Bell 73][Johnston 80], achieving platform independence through compilation at load time [Franz 94], and debugging support [Kessler 90], to improving graphics primitives [Pike 85], to mention just a few examples. In the Java HotSpot VM, dynamic code generation is also used to simplify the build process and improve code quality [Griesemer 99]. More recently, with CPUs being fast enough, dynamic compilers have enabled the emulation of entire architectures. Commercial products such as Connectix' Virtual PC [Connectix] for the Apple Macintosh platform and Transmeta's Crusoe architecture [Klaiber 00] emulate the complete Intel x86 platform.

APL and Smalltalk programming environments were among the first enjoying the benefits of dynamic compilation directly. The work pioneered in [Deutsch 84] for Smalltalk was significantly extended in [Chambers 92] and [Hölzle 94] for the programming language Self [Ungar 87]. Many of these ideas found their way into a commercial product prototype [Animorphic 96] for Strongtalk [Bracha 93], a typed form of Smalltalk. The Java HotSpot VM is based on some of that work.

In the context of Java virtual machines, dynamic compilers are often referred to as Just-In-Time Compilers, or JITs, since they originally compiled a method into machine code just before its first use. Borland's JIT by Crelier [Crelier 96] was one of the first such commercial products.

8 Conclusions

We have presented an overview of the client compiler for the Java HotSpot Virtual Machine. The compiler combines state-of-the-art virtual machine technology adapted for the Java™ programming language with established code generation techniques. The resulting compiler is simple, fast, and produces excellent code. The client VM comes close to the performance of the high-end server VM, yet it requires only half the amount of memory space for compiled code and it compiles faster by an order of magnitude. We conclude that this success is due to the following reasons:

- Niklaus Wirth-style code generation is a good fit for the requirements of on-the-fly compilation: it is fast, flexible, and produces excellent code.
- Implementations of the Java programming language profit from object-oriented optimizations such as inline caches at call sites [Deutsch 84], slow-fast path splits, etc. The client compiler has been designed to support these optimizations.
- The consequent application of the 80/20 principle lead to a clean design with optimizations – and thus complications – only where necessary, i.e., where they paid off.

Acknowledgments

The authors would like to express their gratitude to the HotSpot team at Sun Microsystems, without which this work would not have been possible. Peter Kessler set up the performance measurements. Gilad Bracha, Steffen Grarup, Hanspeter Mössenböck, Hayyah Muller, Ivan Posva, Todd Turnidge, Kenneth Russel, and the referees provided valuable feedback on earlier versions of this paper. All remaining errors are of course ours.

References

[Animorphic 96] Animorphic Systems. *Strongtalk and Java™ VM Implementation.* Product prototypes exhibited at OOPSLA '96, San Jose, CA, 1996.

[Bell 73] J. R. Bell. Threaded Code. In *Communications of the ACM* 16:370-372, 1973.

[Bracha 93] Gilad Bracha and David Griswold. Strongtalk: Typechecking Smalltalk in a Production Environment. In *Proceedings of the ACM Conference on Object-Oriented Programming, Systems, Languages and Applications*, OOPSLA '93, September 1993. See also: http://java.sun.com/people/gbracha/nwst.html

[Chambers 92] Craig Chambers. *The Design and Implementation of the SELF Compiler, an Optimizing Compiler for Object-Oriented Programming Languages.* Ph.D. thesis, Computer Science Department, Stanford University. Stanford CSD Technical Report STAN-CS-TR-92-1420.

[Connectix] Connectix Corporation. *Virtual PC.* Commercial product. http://www.connectix.com

[Crelier 96] Régis Crelier. Private communication.

[Deutsch 84] L. Peter Deutsch and Alan Schiffman. Efficient Implementation of the Smalltalk-80 System. In *Proceedings of the 11th Symposium on the Principles of Programming Languages*, Salt Lake City, UT, 1984.

[Franz 94] Michael Franz. Technological steps toward a software component industry. In *International Conference on Programming Languages and System Architecture*, Springer Verlag Lecture Notes in Computer Science 782, March 1994.

[Gamma 95] Erich Gamma, Richard Helm, Ralph Johnson, and John Vlissides. *Design Patterns – Elements of Reusable Object-Oriented Software.* Addison-Wesley, 1995.

[Griesemer 99] Robert Griesemer. Generation of Virtual Machine Code at Startup. Position paper presented at the *OOPSLA'99 Workshop on Simplicity, Performance and Portability in Virtual Machine Design*, Denver, 1999.

[Hölzle 92] Urs Hölzle. Debugging Optimized Code with Dynamic Deoptimization. In *Proceedings of the ACM SIGPLAN '92 Conference on Programming Language Design and Implementation*, pp. 32-43, San Francisco, June 1992.

[Hölzle 94] Urs Hölzle. *Adaptive Optimization for SELF: Reconciling High Performance with Exploratory Programming.* Ph.D. thesis, Computer Science Department, Stanford University. Stanford CSD Technical Report STAN-CS-TR-94-1520 and Sun Microsystems Laboratories TR 95-35.

[Johnston 80] Ronald L. Johnston. The Dynamic Incremental Compiler of APL\3000. In *Proceedings of the APL '70 Conference.* Published as *APL Quote Quad* 9(4), p. 82-87.

[Kessler 90] Peter Kessler. Fast Breakpoints: Design and Implementation. In *Proceedings of the SIGPLAN '90 Conference on Programming Language Design and Implementation,* p. 78-84, White Plains, NY, June 1990. Published as *SIGPLAN Notices* 25(6), June 1990.

[Klaiber 00] Alexander Klaiber. *The Technology behind Crusoe™ Processors – Low Power x86-Compatible Processors Implemented with Code Morphing™ Software.* White paper, Transmeta Corporation, January 2000.

[Knuth 68 Donald E. Knuth. Semantics of Context Free Languages. *Mathematical Systems Theory* 2, 1986.

[Koch 98] Richard Koch. *The 80/20 Principle – The Secret to Success by Achieving More with Less.* Currency Doubleday, 1998.

[Lindholm 99] Tim Lindholm, Frank Yellin. *The Java™ Virtual Machine Specification – Second Edition.* Addison-Wesley 1999.

[Miranda] Eliot Miranda. Web posting. Search for "Ordinary Object Pointer" via www.google.com.

[Mitchel 70] J. G. Mitchell. *Design and Construction of Flexible and Efficient Interactive Programming Systems.* PhD Thesis, Carnegie-Mellon University, 1970.

[Muchnik 97] Steven S. Muchnik. *Advanced Compiler Design and Implementation.* Addison-Wesley, 1997.

[Pike 85] Rob Pike, Bart N. Locanthi, and John F. Reiser. Hardware/Software Trade-Offs for Bitmap Graphics on the Blit. In *Software – Practice and Experience* 15(2), p. 131-151, February 1985.

[Spec] Standard Performance Evaluation Corporation. SPEC JVM98. http://www.spec.org/

[Sun 99] Sun Microsystems, Inc.: *Java™ HotSpot Technology.*
http://java.sun.com/products/hotspot/

[Templ 90] Josef Templ. *SPARC-Oberon – User's Guide and Implementation.* Technical Report No. 133, Institut für Informatik, ETH Zürich, Switzerland, June 1990.

[Templ 91] Josef Templ. Design and Implementation of SPARC-Oberon. In *Software Practice and Experience*, December 1991, Vol. 15, No. 12, p. 197-205.

[Ungar 87] David Ungar and Randall B. Smith. Self: The Power of Simplicity. *In OOPSlA '87 Conference Proceedings*, pp. 227-241, Orlando, FL, October 1987.

[Wirth 85] Niklaus Wirth. *A Fast and Compact Compiler for Modula-2*. Technical Report No. 64, Institut für Informatik, ETH Zürich, Switzerland, July 1985.

[Wirth 92] Niklaus Wirth and Jürg Gutknecht. *Project Oberon – The Design of an Operating System and Compiler.* Addison-Wesley, 1992.

[Wirth 96] Niklaus Wirth. *Compiler Construction*, Addison-Wesley 1996.

Designing a Cluster Network

Hans Eberle
Sun Microsystems Laboratories

Abstract

This paper describes Clint, a network for clustered systems. Clint has a segregated architecture that separates the network into two channels, a bulk channel optimized for high-bandwidth traffic and a quick channel optimized for low-latency traffic. Each channel is limited to only one switch. The switches contain no buffer memory and forwarding delays are fixed. The bulk channel uses a scheduler that allocates transmission paths before nodes send packets. This way collisions are avoided and aggregate throughput is optimized. In contrast, a best-effort approach is taken on the quick channel. Packets are sent whenever they are available. If they collide in the switch, one packet wins and the other packets lose. The network interface supports user-level communication based on Active Messages and the Virtual Network abstraction.

This paper is also an attempt at identifying the design principles that guided me through the design process.

1 Prologue

I have had the fortune to interact with Niklaus Wirth on many occasions. I first met Niklaus in 1979. I had just begun my studies in Electrical Engineering at ETH Zurich and Niklaus was teaching my first computer science class "Einsatz von Rechenanlagen". For this class I wrote my programming assignments in Pascal-S and ran the resulting programs on a clustered system consisting of a CDC 6400 computer and a CDC 6500 computer. I still appreciate the simplicity and elegance of Pascal and occasionally use it for my everyday work. For example, referring to the work described here, I developed a behavioral simulator of the Clint network in Borland's Turbo Pascal. Also, the patent disclosure describing the least choice first arbiter explained in section 6.3 contains a Pascal program that specifies the arbitration algorithm.

In 1983 Niklaus supervised my master's project which was about a monitor board for debugging Lilith workstations. When Niklaus offered me an assistant position in his group, I accepted enthusiastically. Under his guidance I developed the Ceres workstation which was based on the first commercially available 32-bit microprocessor, the National Semiconductor NS32032. Ceres was well received. A first series of 30 machines was deployed in 1986. Further versions of Ceres were developed and by 1990 a total of 180 Ceres workstations were in use throughout ETH. It was used as the platform of many research projects such as the Oberon system and for teaching classes.

From 1993 until 1998 I held the position of an assistant professor at ETH. Now it was the time to learn to teach and I gladly accepted Niklaus' guidance. For several years Niklaus taught a class on digital design and I taught a follow-on class on computer architecture. Niklaus never read someone else's textbook to the students. He developed the course material including experimentation boards for student projects from scratch and eventually published it as a book [15]. This class also inspired Niklaus to develop a simple yet powerful hardware description language called Lola. Niklaus has always built the systems he is either researching or teaching himself since he knows that this is the only way to keep an engineer honest and credible.

My contribution to this book is a report on the cluster network Clint which I am currently working on. I believe that my work is the best testimony of how I was influenced by my teacher Niklaus Wirth.

2 Introduction

A cluster is a group of servers or workstations that work collectively as one logical system. The purpose of clustering is *high availability* and *high performance*. Since clusters capitalize on the economies of scale they are inexpensive alternatives to other fault-tolerant hardware-based approaches as well as to other parallel systems. The latter group includes systems such as SMPs (symmetric multiprocessors), MPPs (massively parallel processors) or NUMA (non-uniform memory access) machines.

Clusters have been used for decades. Early commercial systems were IBM's Job Entry System (JES) introduced in 1970 [3] and DEC's VAXCluster introduced in 1984 [6]. Lately, there has been an increasing demand for high-availability clusters in the commercial market due to the ever increasing number of businesses with an Internet presence that requires continuous operation. Products such as the Sun [TM] Cluster technology [14] and Microsoft Cluster Service [4] are targeted at these applications. These products are primarily used for failover clusters that consist of a paired server with an active node and a stand-by node. The task of the cluster management software is to detect the failure of the active node and to restart the affected applications on the stand-by node. Failover clusters typically use standard networking technology such as 10BaseT or 100BaseT Ethernet. As systems scale in size and customers raise their performance expectations, more ambitious communication solutions can be anticipated.

Clusters also provide a cost-effective platform for high performance computing. The prime example of a commercial application are distributed databases such as Oracle Parallel Server. Such systems are specialized in that they often bypass operating systems and do not rely on a general-purpose software infrastructure for cluster applications. In order for this type of cluster to gain more wide-spread acceptance, system management software has to become easier to use and more applications have to be parallelized. Thanks to their cost advantage over full-custom parallel systems we can expect the necessary investment to be made.

In this paper I describe an interconnection network for high-performance clusters. We call this network Clint. Clint differs from a LAN in the following ways. It provides lower latency in that it uses separate networks for high-bandwidth traffic and low-latency traffic. This way, the two traffic classes do not interfere with each other and low latency can be guaranteed on one network even if the other network is highly loaded. Low latency is important since the nodes of a cluster operate on shared data and, therefore, require tight coupling. In addition, given the current emphasis on clusters with a relatively small number of nodes Clint does not have to scale as well as a LAN. In fact, Clint is limited to a single switch. As I will show, limiting the scale of a network gives ample opportunities to simplify the design of the network and, ultimately, achieve higher performance.

This paper is a report on work in progress. A prototype switch with 16 ports has been built and is currently being tested. Work on the network interface card (NIC) and the corresponding application program interface (API) is still underway.

I have structured the paper as follows. Section 3 identifies the design principles that underlie the design of Clint. Section 4 gives an overview of Clint. Section 5 explains the areas where Clint breaks new ground. Section 6 describes the components of Clint in detail. Section 7 compares Clint with related work. Section 8 evaluates Clint based on the design principles in section 3. Finally, section 9 gives the conclusions.

3 Design Principles

This paper not only describes the design of a new cluster network, it also tries to identify and illustrate the underlying design principles. In this section I will describe the main principles that guided me through the design of Clint. Later, in section 8 I will evaluate the design of Clint based on these principles:

Everything should be made as simple as possible, but not simpler

– *Albert Einstein*

Simplicity has many merits. Most importantly, it is easier to show a simpler design to be correct. There are other obvious advantages such as a shorter design cycle, simpler testing, and less maintenance. All of these factors contribute to lower overall costs.

Often we do not recognize that a simpler design can lead to higher performance. This was, for example, illustrated by the CISC vs. RISC debate. While adding a feature can speed up a certain case, we tend to overlook the impact it has on the overall performance.

Identify and optimize the critical performance path

As I just outlined, it is important to identify and optimize the common case in a design since it is most critical to the overall performance. Often we try to handle every case as efficiently as possible and lose sight of the common case.

Design iteratively

Schools often like to teach us top-down design methodologies. In reality, it is of little help to create a top-level design that cannot be implemented with available technologies. Real design work is an iterative process where we revisit lower-level design abstractions on our way from top to bottom to make sure that we end up with a top-level design that can be implemented.

Codesign hardware and software

It has become popular to talk about hardware/software codesign. This effort is often mistaken for an optimization problem that consists in determining the interface between the hardware and software components based on cost functions. A more practical approach to mastering a design problem is based on stepwise refinement and design reuse. The key to this approach are clear and concise interfaces. When designing interfaces, a good understanding of the components that plug into them is essential. This is particularly true for the boundary between software and hardware.

Question flexibility

Flexibility usually comes with a price, for example in the form of higher design complexity or reduced performance. Thus, we only want to provide flexibility if its cost can be justified. To illustrate this, scalability is a form of flexibility which is often emphasized without questioning the associated cost.

4 Overview

Since a network cannot provide high throughput and low forwarding latency at the same time, we decided to provide two separate channels which we call the *bulk channel* and the *quick channel*. This is shown in Figure 1. The bulk channel is optimized for high-bandwidth traffic made up of large *bulk packets* and the quick channel is optimized for low-latency traffic made up of small *quick packets*. The

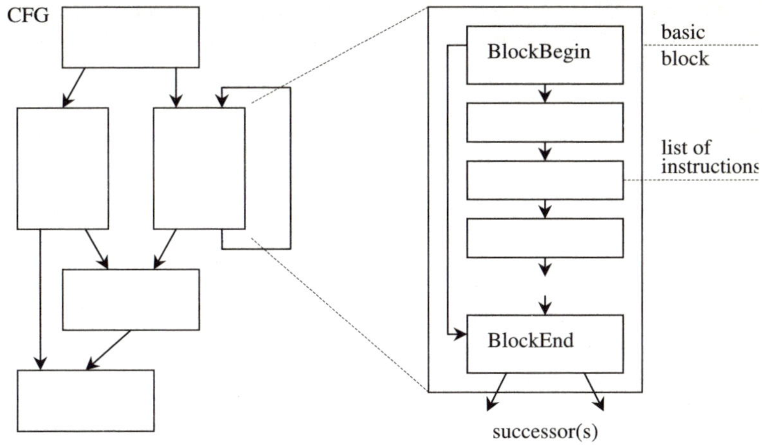

Figure 1: The Segregated Architecture of the Clint Network.

two channels use physically separate networks, that is, each channel uses its own switch as well as its own links.

Given the different optimization criteria, the two channels use different scheduling strategies when transmitting packets. Both switches are free of buffer memory and forward packets with fixed delays. They differ in how they deal with contention for output ports. The bulk channel applies an elaborate and time-consuming procedure that avoids conflicts in the switch and optimizes the aggregate throughput of the switch. This task is handled by a scheduler that calculates a conflict-free schedule before the packets leave the nodes. In contrast, the quick channel uses a best-effort approach where nodes send off packets without any coordination. As a result, packets can collide in the switch. When this happens, one packet wins and the other packets lose. The winning packet is forwarded and the losing packets are dropped.

The two switches are organized differently. The bulk channel uses a flow-through crossbar switch. This merely consists of combinational logic in the form of multiplexers. Ports as well as internal data paths are serial. The quick channel is realized as a pipelined crossbar switch. While its ports are serial, the internal data paths are parallel.

The prototype implementation of Clint has the following characteristics. Each switch has 16 ports. Links are copper cables with a length of up to 10 m. The link cable of the bulk channel has a full-duplex bandwidth of 2.5 Gbit/s and the link cable of the quick channel has a full-duplex bandwidth of 0.66 Gbit/s. These numbers consider 8B/10B-encoded data streams, that is, the bandwidths include the encoding overhead. With it, the bulk switch has an aggregate bandwidth of 40 Gbit/s and the quick switch has an aggregate bandwidth of 8.45 Gbit/s. (The bandwidth calculated for the bulk switch includes the overhead of the 8B/10B encoding since data is forwarded in its encoded form, while the bandwidth for the quick switch is obtained by using the data rates of the decoded data since data is forwarded in its unencoded form.)

Conventions

The node that initiates a transfer is called the *initiator* while the node addressed by the initiator is called the *target*.

The packet sent from the initiator to the target is called a *request packet*; the response sent back from the target to the initiator is called an *acknowledgment packet*. Since data is always pushed from the initiator to the target, the request packet contains the operation and its operands, and the acknowledgment packet contains a transmission report.

The time taken to transmit a bulk request packet is referred to as a *slot*.

5 Innovations

In this section I highlight the areas where Clint innovates. These areas are discussed in more detail in subsequent sections.

5.1 Segregated Network Architecture

Observed network traffic typically falls into two categories: there is high-bandwidth traffic mainly consisting of large packets and there is low-latency traffic mainly consisting of small packets. While a network, and a cluster network in particular, is expected to support both types of traffic equally well, this goal is difficult to achieve. Unfortunately, the two types of traffic affect each other adversely: the presence of large packets increases the latency of the small packets and the presence of small packets makes it difficult to schedule the transmission of large packets and to fully utilize the available bandwidth.

Our solution is to segregate the network into two physically separate networks called channels: a *bulk channel* optimized for the transmission of large packets with high bandwidth and a *quick channel* optimized for the transmission of small packets with low latency. Conversely, the bulk channel is not optimized for low latency, and the quick channel is not optimized for high bandwidth and, therefore, operates at a lower data rate. By having two separate channels we can characterize the channels independently. As I will show, this is beneficial since channel characteristics are often influenced by tradeoffs between high bandwidth and low latency. Typical characterization criteria are: packet size, scheduling strategy, congestion management, buffering strategy, and error rate. The tradeoffs are as follows:

- **Packet size**: Large packets cause less overhead than small packets when looking at the ratio of header size and total packet size. In other words, less bandwidth is lost to header information for large packets than for small packets. On the other hand, when competing for shared resources large packets will cause longer-lasting blockages and thus a higher increase in latency than small packets.

- **Scheduling strategy:** To achieve high bandwidth, network traffic has to be carefully scheduled, ideally so that there is a constant flow of packets. Calculating the necessary schedule can be viewed as an optimization problem. This takes time and is best done by preallocating network resources before packets enter the network. In contrast, low latency requires quick scheduling decisions. This is best achieved by scheduling network resources "on-the-fly" as a packet travels trough the network.

- **Congestion management:** If we assume random traffic patterns, high-bandwidth traffic may lead to more congestion than low-latency traffic. Thus, managing congestion might be dealt with differently for each of the two traffic classes so that a collision avoidance scheme is applied to high-bandwidth traffic while a collision detection scheme is applied to low-latency traffic.

- **Buffering strategy:** High-bandwidth traffic consisting of large packets is best described to a network interface by message descriptors referring to memory regions of arbitrary size. On the other hand, low-latency traffic consisting of small packets is best described by message descriptors that include the data to be transferred.

- **Error rate:** Transmission errors have different effects on bandwidth and latency. Since a transmission error usually requires a whole packet to be retransmitted, more data is lost when an error affects a large packet than a small packet. On the other hand, the increase in latency due to retransmission caused by a transmission error is more critical for low-latency traffic than for high-bandwidth traffic.

It is important to recognize the differences between the segregated architecture of Clint and other architectures with multiple channels. While Clint implements its two channels with physically separate networks, that is, with separate links and switches, other approaches multiplex multiple channels onto a single shared network. Some degree of decoupling can be achieved by using separate buffer queues. This technique is quite efficiently used to prevent head-of-line (HOL) blocking in input-buffered switches [2,5]. Still, the channels are competing for shared resources such as links or switching fabrics. Another important difference is the usage model for the channels. Both channels of Clint are intended for general-purpose usage. In particular, both channels are available to user programs. This is not true for networks such as HIPPI-6400 [10] that provides a control channel in addition to a regular data channel and that restricts the usage of the control channel to protocol processing.

While the outlined separation of traffic classes seems beneficial, we have yet to show how the segregated network architecture is used and, in particular, what criteria are used to select one of the two channels for transmitting a packet. Possible criteria are the size of the transfer or the type of operation performed. Yet another possibility is to have the application explicitly chose one of the channels when setting up a data transfer.

The quick channel also serves as a signaling channel for the bulk channel. Figure 1 shows how the scheduler for the bulk channel is connected to the quick channel. The scheduler's task is to collect requests from the nodes, calculate a schedule for the bulk switch, and send the corresponding grants back to the nodes. Requests and grants are communicated via the quick channel. This method of organization is attractive since the quick channel operates at a much lower data rate than the bulk channel thus making it easier to implement communication between the scheduler and the nodes.

5.2 Scheduling

Both the bulk channel and the quick channel forward packets with fixed delays. This is mainly possible since there is no buffer memory in the switches that causes variable forwarding delays. As I will show, fixed forwarding delays simplify the design of the channels and, in particular, facilitate scheduling the transmission of packets via these channels. In short, if delays are fixed, the location of a packet in transit is implicitly known. Compared to a network with variable and possibly unbound delays, this makes resource management and error detection much simpler.

Given the different optimization criteria the methods for scheduling channels look quite different. The bulk switch applies an elaborate procedure to schedule the bulk channel. By preallocating slots in the switch before nodes send off packets, collisions are avoided and packets are never dropped. On the other hand, the quick channel takes a best-effort approach to keep forwarding latencies as low as possible. No coordination of the nodes takes place and, as a result, packets can collide in the switch and be dropped.

6 Components

This section discusses the components of the Clint network in detail.

6.1 Network Interface Card

Our network interface card (NIC) is based on Active Messages 2.0 [7] and the Virtual Network abstraction [8,9]. This abstraction virtualizes the access points of the network in the form of *endpoints*. A collection of endpoints forms a virtual network with a unique protection domain. Messages are exchanged between endpoints, and traffic in one virtual network is not visible to other virtual networks.

Endpoints are mapped to the address space of a process and can be directly accessed by the corresponding user-level program or kernel program. Thus, user-level communication does not involve the operating system.

Figure 2 shows the structure of the NIC. It holds a small number of active endpoints EP - inactive endpoints are stored in the main memory. The endpoint information stored in the NIC consists of pointers to queues in the main memory. There are separate queues for the quick channel and the bulk channel. To prevent fetch deadlock of the request-response protocol described in [9], queues come in pairs, that is, there are separate queues for requests and responses. There is one pair of queues each for sending and receiving messages over the quick channel. For the bulk channel, there is one pair of send queues for each target and one pair of receive queues. In addition, there is an error queue for reporting transmission errors.

Two types of messages are supported. Quick messages containing a 64-byte payload and bulk messages containing a 2-kByte payload. Figure 2 shows the queues holding the corresponding message descriptors. The formats of the message descriptors are shown in table 1. While the quick message descriptor contains an immediate payload, the bulk message descriptor contains a payload specified by memory addresses pointing to the source and destination of the transfer. The buffers shown in Figure 2 hold this payload on its way to and from the main memory. Note that a bulk message descriptor can describe a transfer that may consist of many bulk packets.

Since endpoints are accessed directly by user-level programs, memory addresses specified by the bulk message descriptor are virtual addresses. This requires address translations when message payloads are read from memory by the initiator and

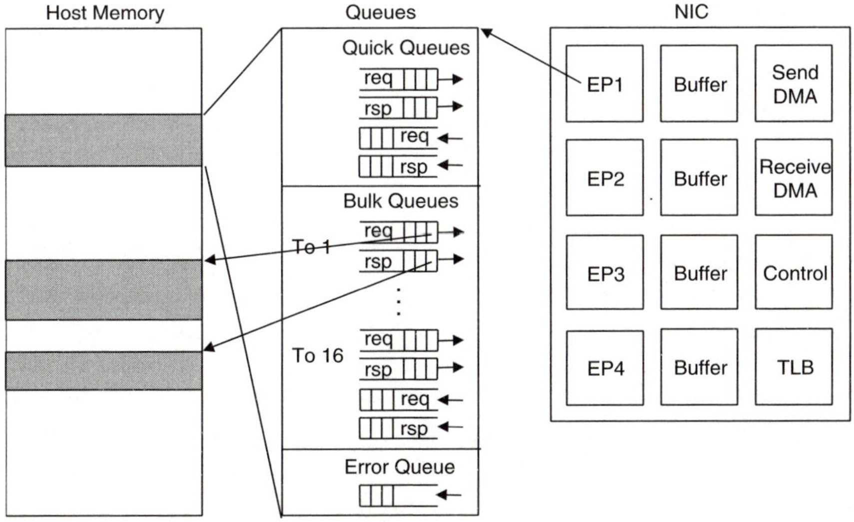

Figure 2: Organization of the NIC.

written to memory by the target. For this purpose, the NIC contains a local TLB. TLB hits are handled in hardware, while TLB misses are handled in software.

Bulk message descriptor		**Quick message descriptor**	
message type	**3 bits**	message type	**3 bits**
source node id	**4 bits**	source node id	**4 bits**
source endpoint id	**2 bits**	source endpoint id	**2 bits**
source endpoint key	**32 bits**	source endpoint key	**32 bits**
destination node id	**4 bits**	destination node id	**4 bits**
destination endpoint id	**2 bits**	destination endpoint id	**2 bits**
destination endpoint key	**32 bits**	destination endpoint key	**32 bits**
source address	**64 bits**		
destination address	**64 bits**		
transfer length	**32 bits**		
		immediate payload	**64 bytes**

Table 1: Bulk and Quick Message Descriptor Formats.

6.2 Bulk Channel

The bulk channel is optimized for high throughput rather than for low latency. A *global schedule* determines the settings of the bulk switch and the times when nodes may send packets. The schedule is conflict-free and thus bulk packets are never dropped due to resource conflicts. This is important since the loss of a bulk packet can result in the retransmission of a considerable amount of data, in particular, if we consider that a packet may be part of a larger transfer.

Scheduling the bulk channel is simplified because forwarding delays are fixed. This is possible since the bulk switch contains no buffer memory. Conflicting requests for the output ports of the switch are simply resolved by keeping packets in the buffers of the NICs until the necessary connections in the switch have been allocated. That is, a path through the switch is reserved for when an NIC sends off a packet.

The only buffer memory found in the bulk channel is located in the NICs. Logically, the bulk switch together with the buffer memories of the NICs resembles an input-buffered switch. To avoid HOL blocking caused by a single input buffer queue, the NIC contains several send buffers that can be randomly accessed and that can hold packets destined for different nodes.

A simple request-acknowledge protocol is used to detect errors on the bulk channel. For every request packet received the target returns an acknowledgment packet. The initiator detects a transmission error if it receives a negative acknowledgment or the acknowledgment is missing. A negative acknowledgment is returned if a request with a bad CRC is received, the receive queue overflows or an invalid address is received. The loss of a packet is detected if the initiator does not receive an acknowledgment within a fixed time period. If an error occurs, an error message is written into an error queue of the NIC. Fixed forwarding delays on the bulk channel simplify error detection in that the number of outstanding requests is fixed and there is a fixed timing relationship between the request and acknowledgment that does not require any timeout mechanism relying on worst-case expected delivery times.

Thanks to fixed timing and global scheduling, the bulk channel can be efficiently operated as a pipelined network. This is shown in Figure 3. Packet transmission is split up into four stages:

- **arb**: During the *arbitration stage* a slot is allocated in the bulk switch for forwarding the request packet from an input port to an output port.
- **trf**: During the *transfer stage* a request packet is transferred from a buffer on the initiator NIC to a buffer on the target NIC.
- **ack**: During the *acknowledgment stage* the target checks the integrity of the request packet and returns an acknowledgment packet to the initiator.
- **chk**: During the *check stage* the initiator examines the acknowledgment packet and, if an error has occurred, reinserts the corresponding packet into the pipeline.

Since each pair of initiator and target forms a pipeline, and the pipelines share the bulk switch in the transfer stage, the pipelines have to be synchronized. Synchronization is achieved with the help of the signaling packets described in section 6.4.

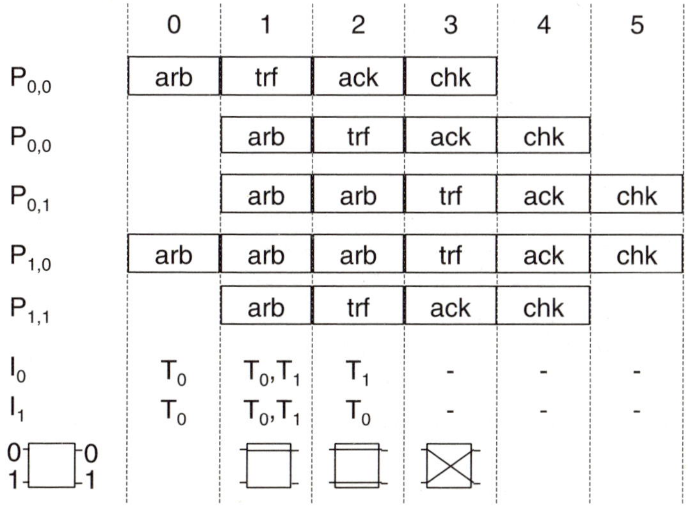

Figure 3: Pipelined Transmission of Bulk Packets.

These packets are sent simultaneously and at a fixed time relative to the bulk slot boundaries.

Only the transfer stage uses the bulk channel. Both the arbitration stage and the acknowledgment stage use the quick channel. Possible conflicts during the transfer stage are resolved in the arbitration stage. Figure 3 illustrates the operation of the bulk channel pipeline. In this example a 2x2 switch connects initiators I_0 and I_1 with targets T_0 and T_1. The transmission of five packets $P_{i,t}$ is depicted, where i stands for the initiator and t for the target. In addition to the transmitted packets, the figure shows the targets requested by the initiators and the settings of the switch. Note that the initiator generates a request for every full buffer and that, as a result, the initiator can request more than one target in a given arbitration cycle.

In slot 0, both I_0 and I_1 request connections with T_0. The request of I_0 is granted and the request packet $P_{0,0}$ is transferred in slot 1. In slot 1, both I_0 and I_1 request connections with T_0 and T_1. I_0 is granted the connection with T_0, and I_1 is granted the connection with T_1. The corresponding transfers of packets $P_{0,0}$ and $P_{1,1}$ take place in slot 2. The remaining two requests are granted in slot 2 and the corresponding packets $P_{0,1}$ and $P_{1,0}$ are transferred in slot 3.

A simple flow-through switch functions as the bulk switch. Its input and output ports as well as its internal data paths are all bit-serial. There is no sequential logic in the form of buffer memory or registers. The only logic elements used are multiplexers connecting output ports with input ports. In particular, the bulk switch contains no logic or data paths to process packets. Packets do not even have to be examined to determine their route since the scheduler exchanges the necessary information with the NICs via the quick channel.

6.3 Bulk Scheduler

We use a central scheduler to schedule the bulk channel. Referring to Figure 3 the arbiter calculates in the arbitration stage the schedule of the bulk switch for the subsequent transfer stage. An arbitration cycle starts with each node sending a *configuration packet* to the arbiter. This packet combines information supplied by both the initiator and the target residing on a node. It contains a request vector that identifies the targets for which the initiator has data packets. Also contained in the configuration packet is a enable vector which names the initiators from which the target accepts packets. An initiator is disabled if a target runs out of resources such as receive buffers or is suspected to be malfunctioning. The arbiter can now calculate a conflict-free schedule. The schedule is communicated to the initiators by *grant packets*. Each initiator receives a grant packet that reports whether one of its requests was granted and if so, which target it can address in the following transfer stage.

We have developed an algorithm which we call *least choice first arbiter* for calculating the schedule of the bulk channel. This arbiter selects the requests to be granted by prioritizing the initiators based on the number of targets they are requesting. The priorities are calculated as the inverse of the number of targets an initiator is requesting, that is, the fewer requests an initiator has, the higher its priority is. This rule can be explained as follows. An initiator with many requests has many choices and an initiator with few requests has few choices. To optimize the total number of granted requests, we schedule the high-priority initiators with few requests before we schedule the low-priority initiators with many requests. To avoid starvation we combine this algorithm with a round-robin scheduler.

To describe the arbitration scheme in detail, I will consider a 3x3 switch. In the example shown in Figure 4 initiator I_0 is requesting target T_0, initiator I_1 is requesting targets T_1 and T_2, and initiator I_2 is requesting all three targets T_0, T_1, and T_2. Targets are scheduled sequentially. Each target is scheduled in two steps. First the round-robin position is examined. As shown the round-robin positions form a diagonal which covers positions $[I_1, T_0]$, $[I_2, T_1]$, and $[I_0, T_2]$. The diagonal advances every schedule cycle so that every position in the matrix is periodically taken into account. If the corresponding request is set, it is granted. If it is not set, the request of the initiator with the highest priority is granted. If there are several initiators with the highest priority, a round-robin scheme selects an initiator. Priorities are recalculated when a new target is scheduled so that only requests for targets that have not been scheduled are considered.

In our example, T_0 is scheduled first. The round-robin position favors I_1. However, I_1 does not have a request for T_0. Therefore, the other two initiators I_0 and I_2 are considered. I_0 has only one request and thus higher priority than I_2 which has three requests. The request for T_0 by I_0 is therefore granted. Next, T_1 is scheduled. Now, the round-robin position wins, that is, the request for T_1 by I_2 is granted. Finally, T_2 is scheduled. There is no choice and the request by I_1 is granted.

As can be illustrated with the example of Figure 4 there is a tradeoff between optimizing bandwidth utilization and fairness in that higher bandwidth utilization comes at the cost of lower fairness. If we want to optimize bandwidth utilization, we can either grant $[I_0, T_0]$, $[I_1, T_1]$, $[I_2, T_2]$ or $[I_0, T_0]$, $[I_1, T_2]$, $[I_2, T_1]$. This is unfair in that the request of I_2 for T_0 is ignored. It is ignored since only two requests rather than three requests could be granted.

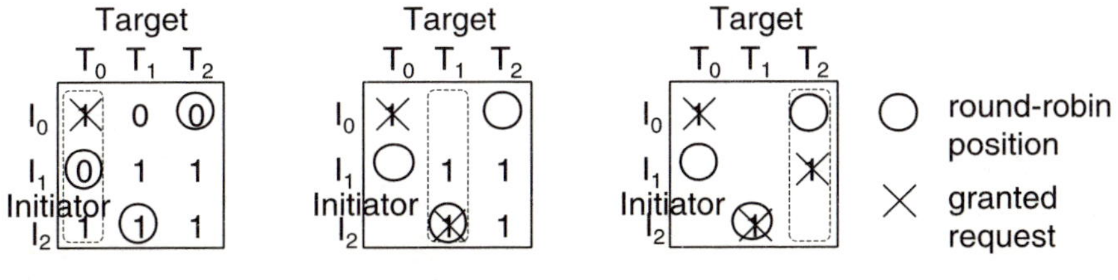

Figure 4: Least Choice First Arbitration.

6.4 Quick Channel

The quick channel is optimized for low latency rather than high throughput. In contrast to the bulk channel, nodes do not schedule the transmission of quick packets and do not allocate a path through the quick switch before they send off packets. Instead, a best-effort approach is taken in which packets are sent as soon as they are available. This approach may leadto collisions in the quick switch in which case packets are dropped. Note the difference with collisions on a shared medium such as a bus. While in our case progress is made in that one packet is forwarded, this is not the case for a shared medium that requires all packets involved in a collision to be retransmitted. Collisions in the quick switch happen infrequently since the quick channel is only lightly loaded due to excess bandwidth. While we expect typical applications to only generate light loads for the quick channel, we will probably have to add a throttling mechanism to the NIC to limit usage of quick channel bandwidth.

Similar to the bulk channel the quick channel contains no buffer memory and forwards packets with fixed delays. However, compared to the bulk channel, the quick channel is not pipelined since round-trip times are relatively short. Thus, every initiator can only have one outstanding request packet at a time.

The quick switch uses a minimal arbiter that applies a first-come, first-served policy. When a packet arrives at an input port, a request is sent to the output port specified by the routing information contained in the packet header. The corresponding header field is called *destination node id* in table 1. When quick packets collide in the switch, the packet that arrives first will win and be forwarded and packets that arrive later will lose and be dropped. If colliding packets arrive simultaneously, a round-robin scheme is used to pick the winner and discard the losers. This way starvation is avoided. Further, this scheduler is able to make quick routing decisions so that forwarding latency on the quick channel is kept low.

Unlike the bulk switch, the quick switch can process and generate packets. To allow for sufficient processing time, internal data paths are parallel and packets are latched at the switch boundaries, that is, near the input ports as well as the output ports.

Transmission errors are again recognized by a request-acknowledge protocol. A target returns an acknowledgment in response to every request. If an initiator does not receive an acknowledgment within a fixed period of time after the request was sent, either the request or the acknowledgment packet was lost and the request packet is resent.

Similar to the bulk switch the ports of the quick switch can be enabled and disabled with the help of an enable vector provided as part of the configuration packet mentioned in section 6.3.

The quick channel also serves as a signaling channel for the bulk channel. More specifically, it transports the configuration and the grant packets needed to schedule the bulk channel and it transports the bulk acknowledgment packets. These packets are transmitted at fixed times, that is, at fixed offsets within a bulk slot. This simplifies the scheduler as well as the request-acknowledge protocol. Furthermore, we make use of this property to synchronize the nodes. Since the timing of the signaling packets is implicitly known to the nodes and the switch, the grant packets are used to synchronize nodes. In addition, the grant packets are used to assign a unique identifier to each node. The node identifier corresponds to the number of the output port from where the packet was sent.

Since any loss of bulk channel bandwidth is undesirable, the signaling packets are treated differently from regular quick packets so that signaling packets cannot be dropped due to collisions. If a signaling packet collides with a regular packet, the signaling packet is given priority and the regular packet is dropped. Still, there is a possibility that signaling packets may collide with each other. While it is obvious that the configuration packets and the grant packets will not cause any collisions among themselves, the transmission of the bulk acknowledgment packets needs explaining. If we look at the switch connections needed to forward the bulk acknowledgment packets via the quick channel, we note that the connections correspond to those of the schedule calculated for forwarding the corresponding bulk request packets via the bulk channel. The difference is in the directions, which are reversed. Thus, since the schedule calculated for transmitting the bulk request packets is conflict-free, the transmission of the bulk acknowledgment packets is also conflict-free.

6.5 Link

A Clint link connecting a node with the switch consists of two physically separate cables that implement the bulk channel and the quick channel. Data directions are separated in that each full-duplex channel is realized using two pairs of wires. We use coaxial cables with a length up to 10 m. Wire pairs have a controlled differential impedance of 150 Ohms.

We use standard FibreChannel/Gigabit Ethernet transceivers to drive the cables of both the quick and the bulk channel. The transceivers of the quick channel run at 660 Mbit/s and those of the bulk channel run at 2.5 Gbit/s.

7 Related Work

Myrinet is a switched network widely used for cluster applications [1]. Switches have up to 16 ports and each port has a full-duplex bandwidth of 1.28 Gbit/s. Arbitrary topologies are possible by cascading switches. Crossbar switches are used with cut-through forwarding. Switches contain a minimal amount of receive buffers to implement stop-and-go link-level flow control. Low latency can only be guaranteed as long as the network is lightly loaded. Furthermore, Myrinet will only perform well under high load if conflicts in the switches are infrequent. However, this is only the case with certain types of regular traffic patterns; other irregular traffic patterns will degrade performance due to HOL blocking. Since the Myrinet switches together with the send queues in the network nodes logically resembles an input-buffered switch, HOL blocking occurs in the NICs. To illustrate this, if a packet is blocked in a switch, the node that sent the packet is blocked so that no other packet can be sent, even a packet that could use an available network path . While the quick channel has the same property, the bulk channel avoids HOL blocking in that it provides multiple send queues.

The global communication network of the T3E [12,13] has properties similar to those of the quick channel. Messages are transmitted by writing them into E-registers from where they are delivered to message queues mapped to user or system memory space. Status flags associated with the E-registers indicate whether the message was accepted. The sending processor checks the flags and retransmits messages if necessary. However, unlike the quick channel, the T3E network is flow-controlled. More specifically, credit-based flow control prevents the buffers of the routers from overflowing.

The use of separate mechanisms to transport short and long messages has been proposed by the Illinois Fast Messages (FM) protocol [11] and the Scheduled Transfer Protocol (ST) [10] for HIPPI-6400. The FM protocol provides two send routines: FM_send to send a long message and FM_send_4 to send a short four-word message. FM_send uses send queues in main memory, FM_send_4 uses registers on the NIC. Thus, these routines are similar to sending a bulk packet and a quick packet, respectively. Unlike our approach, both routines use the same channel. ST uses two separate channels: a high-bandwidth data channel and a low-latency control channel. The control channel is used by upper-layer protocols and is not available for the exchange of low-latency user-level messages.

8 Evaluation

Now that I have described the design of Clint, I want to illustrate the design principles outlined in section 3. Many of these principles are reflected in the following design decisions.

Limited Scalability

As I previously mentioned, current cluster installations are mainly targeted at high availability and typically consist of two nodes, that is, an active node and a standby node[1]. For example, Microsoft Cluster Server which is part of the Windows NT Server 4.0 Enterprise Edition currently supports two nodes and the Sun™ Cluster

1. There exist a few large clusters, sometimes referred to as farms, mainly used for executing scientific applications. Here, I'm interested in commercial applications.

technology 2.2 supports up to four nodes. Given the state of the art, I felt that the next evolutionary step, which addresses high performance in addition to high availability, can be well addressed by clusters of modest size. While we are often interested in scalable solutions, I viewed it as an opportunity to explore the implications of limiting the scale of a network.

Limiting the scale of Clint, and, in particular, limiting its diameter to one switch, lead to many design simplifications. Most importantly, it allowed me to build a switch without buffer memory and to enforce fixed delays for forwarding packets from one node to another node. Thanks to fixed delays the location of a packet in transit is implicitly known. This simplifies scheduling of network traffic and transport protocols. A global schedule determines when the nodes may insert packets into the bulk channel pipeline, when the packets traverse the bulk switch and which switch connections are needed for the traversal. The transport protocol uses a request-acknowledge protocol which is simplified in that there is a fixed number of outstanding packets and in that it takes a fixed amount of time to receive an acknowledgment packet after the corresponding request packet was sent. Flow control is reduced to a simple stop-and-go protocol that only takes the nodes and not the switches into account since there are no shared network resources such as buffers that could overflow.

Separation of Concerns

The performance of a network is characterized by throughput and forwarding latency. Since the two characteristics cannot be optimized with a single network, we decided to take a radical approach and separate the two concerns by providing two networks, one of them optimized for high throughput and, the other one optimized for low latency. This is an example that illustrates that a systems perspective is needed when features are optimized. For example, it is not possible to optimize a data path for high throughput without negatively affecting forwarding latency. Note that the same is true when we evaluate a system. Measuring an isolated feature can be quite misleading. Typical examples are measurements of the forwarding latency for an unloaded network or the point-to-point throughput obtained for an otherwise unloaded network.

The dual-channel architecture of Clint also demonstrates an iterative design process. When we looked into the implementation of the bulk switch we realized that building a switch with 16 ports and an aggregate bandwidth of 40 Gbit/s was challenging. We finally found integrated crossbar switches with a flow-through organization that were well-suited for our application. However, this solution made it practically impossible for the switch to process any packet received on the bulk switch. Therefore, we changed the overall organization so that any information required to operate the bulk channel was transmitted on the quick channel. This change was easily accommodated since the quick switch already had the capa-

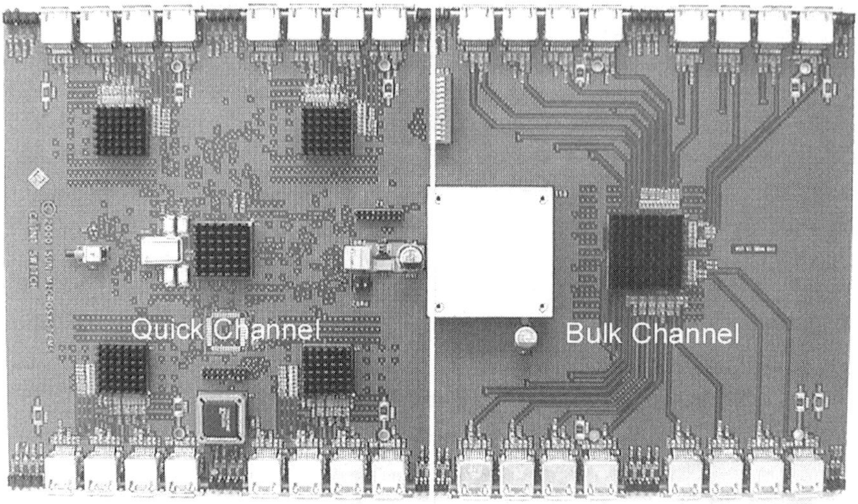

Figure 5: The Prototype Board of the Clint Switch.

bility to interpret packets to determine their route. In retrospect, considering the actual implementation early on in the design process lead us to a superior architecture that will scale well to higher-speed links.

Figure 5 shows the prototype board of the Clint switch. The bulk channel and quick channel can be easily identified.

9 Conclusions

I have described the design of the cluster network Clint and shown how segregating a network helps to optimize network bandwidth and forwarding latency. By separating these two concerns, a network architecture was obtained that contains two network channels with rather different characteristics: a bulk channel for the scheduled transfer of large packets at high bandwidth and a quick channel for best-effort delivery of small packets with low forwarding latency.

The segregated architecture also has the potential to scale well to higher-link speeds. By relieving the bulk channel of protocol processing and more specifically by using the quick channel to transport the information needed to schedule the bulk channel, a simple flow-through switch operating at high speeds can implement the bulk channel.

Limiting the scale of Clint made it possible to impose a rigid timing regime and coordinate transmission via the bulk channel with the help of a schedule that reserves switch connections and determines when nodes can send packets. This makes it possible to globally schedule all network traffic and globally optimize usage of network resources. Finally, this approach simplified network control in that the network is operated as a pipeline with fixed delays.

Acknowledgments

Neil Wilhelm helped with the initial design of Clint. Nils Gura designed and implemented an FPGA that realizes the quick switch and the scheduler for the bulk channel. Alan Mainwaring specified the NIC.

References

1. N. Bode, D. Cohen, R. Felderman, A. Kulawik, C. Seitz, J. Seizovic, W. Su: Myrinet: A Gigabit-per-second Local-area Network. IEEE Micro,vol.15, no.1, February 1995, pp.29-36.
2. W. Dally: *Virtual-Channel Flow Control*, Proc. of the 17th Int. Symposium on Computer Architecture, ACM SIGARCH, vol. 18, no. 2, May 1990, pp. 60-68.
3. IBM: *OS/390 V2R4.0 JES2 Introduction.* Document Number GC28-1794-02.
4. D. Libertone: *Windows NT Cluster Server.* Prentice Hall, 1998.
5. M. Karol, M. Hluchyi, S. Morgan: *Input versus Output Queuing on a Space-Division Packet Switch.* IEEE Transactions on Communications, C-35(12):1347-1356, December 1987.
6. N. Kronenberg, H. Levy, W. Strecker: *VAXclusters: A Closely Coupled Distributed System.* ACM Transactions on Computer Systems, vol. 4, no. 2, May 1986.
7. A. Mainwaring: *Active Message Application Programming Interface and Communication Subsystem Organization.* University of California at Berkeley, Computer Science Department, Technical Report UCB CSD-96-918, October 1996.
8. A. Mainwaring and D. Culler: *Design Challenges of Virtual Networks: Fast, General-Purpose Communication.* ACM SIGPLAN Symposium on Principles and Practice of Parallel Programming (PPOPP), Atlanta, Georgia, May 4-6, 1999.
9. B. Chun, A. Mainwaring, D. Culler: *Virtual Network Transport Protocols for Myrinet.* IEEE Micro, vol. 18, no. 1, January/February 1998, pp. 53-63.
10. National Committee for Information Technology Standardization: *Scheduled Transfer Protocol (ST).* Task Group T11.1, rev. 3.6, January 31, 2000, www.hippi.org.
11. S. Pakin, V. Karamcheti, A. Chien: *Fast Messages (FM): Efficient, Portable Communication for Workstation Clusters and Massively-Parallel Processor,* IEEE Concurrency, vol. 5, no. 2, 1997, pp. 60-73.
12. S. Scott: *Synchronization and Communication in the T3E Multiprocessor.* ASPLOS VII, Cambridge, October 2-4, 1996.
13. S. Scott, G. Thorsen: *The Cray T3E Network: Adaptive Routing in a High Performance 3D Torus.* HOT Interconnects IV, Stanford, August 15-16, 1996.
14. Sun Microsystems: *The Sun Enterprise Cluster Architecture.* Technical White Paper, October 1997.
15. N. Wirth: *Digital Circuit Design for Computer Science Students.*

Programming with Functional Nets

Martin Odersky
École Polytechnique Fédérale de Lausanne

1 Introduction

What is a good foundation of programming? Such a foundation should be simple enough to be understood without too much effort, formal and precise, so that formal reasoning about programs is supported, and universal, so that a large range of programs can be mapped into the foundation directly, without too much encoding.

Niklaus Wirth has put forward with Pascal [31, 19] such a foundation, which has turned out to be immensely beneficial for the development of computing. The programming language Pascal could be understood by its axiomatic semantics [16]. Together with the language and its semantics came the methodology of stepwise refinement [30]. Wirth's seminal work has evolved further with the introduction of the Modula-2 [32] and Oberon [33] languages. It remains very influential today.

Parallel to this, there have also been some new developments that challenge Pascal's and its successor's mold of procedures implementing predicate transformers over a global state. The global state-change view is not well suited to model objects with reference passing, or concurrent distributed systems built on message passing. While programming languages (including Wirth's own) have readily adopted these concepts, their formal foundations have tended to be left behind.

Over the last 20 years, an alternative view of program execution based on rewriting has become more widespread. In this view, a program is seen as a term in some calculus, and program execution is modeled by a stepwise rewriting of the term according to the rules of the calculus. The operational semantics still has to be complemented with a logic for program verification and a collection of laws of programming. This view is exemplified in functional programming [4, 18], in modern theories of objects [1], as well as in concurrent systems based on message passing such as CSP [15], CCS [21] or π-calculus [22].

Ideally, the terms of a programming notation should closely match the terms of the underlying calculus, so that insights gained from the calculus can immediately be applied to the language. This aim guided the design of modern functional languages such as Scheme [2], ML [24], or Haskell [6], based on λ-calculus, as well as concurrent languages such as Occam [20], based on CSP, or Pict [25] and Piccola [3], which are based on π-calculus.

This chapter gives an introduction to *functional nets* which support functional, object-oriented, and concurrent programming in a simple calculus based on rewriting. Functional nets arise from a combination of key ideas of functional programming and Petri nets [28]. As in functional programming, the basic computation step in a functional net rewrites function applications to function bodies. As in Petri-Nets, a rewrite step can require the combined presence of several inputs (where, in this case, inputs are function applications). This fusion of ideas from two different areas results in a style of programming which is at the same time very simple and very expressive.

Functional nets are introduced here by means of a sequence of examples taken from a broad range of programming areas and styles. The paper shows how functional nets can directly model sequential functional programming, imperative programming, and their object-oriented variants. It also shows how functional nets can concisely capture common schemes of concurrency control. Thus, functional nets can be taken as the foundation of a new breed of wide spectrum languages which allow flexible combinations of techniques from functional, imperative and object-oriented programming together with concurrency. Unlike some existing approaches to such languages [27, 13, 29], functional nets are based on a single concept, not an amalgamation of features coming from different domains.

Functional nets have a theoretical foundation in *join calculus* [10]. A companion paper [23] explores the relation between the two in more detail. This paper concentrates on the programming aspects of functional nets, without going too deeply into their semantics. The notation for writing examples of functional nets is derived from Funnel, a new language developed by the programming methods group at EPFL. Funnel has been designed as a small language that supports flexible combinations of functional and object-oriented programming styles with functional nets as a common basis[1]. The notation will be explained as we go along, but it is by itself not the primary focus of this paper. The principles and utility of functional nets would be equally valid using a different notation. There are also other languages which are based on join calculus, and which express the constructs of functional nets in a different way, e.g. Join [11] or JoCaml [9].

The notation used here is statically typed, using a standard type system with recursive records, structural subtyping and polymorphism. A type theoretic foundation of the notation can be developed along the lines of system $F2$ with subtyping [7]. *Local type inference* [26] is used to reduce the amount of type annotations which need to be given explicitly. Again, details are omitted here.

The work presented here follows in some respects a different approach than the one pursued by Niklaus Wirth, but he has inspired and influenced me in many

1. An earlier version of Funnel, described in [23], was named Silk. The name change was prompted by the possible confusion with the concurrent C dialect Cilk, which is pronounced the same way.

ways. There are two points in particular which I'd like to mention. First, Wirth has taught me the that when designing an artefact it is necessary to develop clear concepts at all abstraction levels, to be able to keep different abstraction levels separate yet optimize with each one of them in mind. This holds whether one designs a computer, a program, or a programming formalism. Second, I learned from him the value of simplicity and economy of resources. Niklaus Wirth is a radical when it comes to improving languages by removing rather than adding features. Even though most of us would agree to the virtue of simplicity in principle, the pragmatic incentives always go the other way. Wirth has shown us that it is possible to simplify and improve usability at the same time. I was fortunate that I had the opportunity to learn from him.

The rest of this contribution is structured as follows. Section 2 introduces a purely functional subset of functional nets. Section 3 presents the full formalism which supports concurrent execution. Section 4 shows how functional nets model imperative programming. Section 5 presents a collection of process synchronization techniques implemented as functional nets and Section 6 concludes.

2 Functions and Objects

In functional programming, the fundamental execution step rewrites a function application to a function body, replacing formal parameters with actual arguments. For example, consider the usual definition of a `min` function

```
def min (x: Int, y: Int) = if (x < y) x else y
```

and the program `min(4, 3)`. Three rewrite steps are needed to reduce the program to its answer "3":

```
   min (4, 3)
→  if 4 < 3 then 4 else 3
→  if false then 4 else 3
→  3
```

The first of these steps rewrites a function application, and the other two steps rewrite the built-in operator < and the built-in conditional expression. In principle, the built-ins can themselves be represented as functions, so that *only* the rewrite rule for function applications is sufficient. In practice, appropriate reduction rules for built-ins are assumed. In the following, we let $\rightarrow$ denote single-step reduction by application of a single rewrite rule. $\twoheadrightarrow$ denotes multi-step reduction by application of 0 or more rules.

When one has nested function applications, one has a choice as to which application to evaluate first. We will follow a *strict* evaluation strategy which evaluates all function arguments before rewriting the application. E.g. `min (4, min (3, 5))` rewrites as follows.

```
min (4, min (3, 5)) ↠ min (4, 3) ↠ 3
```

Some functional languages, such as Haskell, follow a *lazy* strategy instead, where arguments are passed unevaluated.

Aggregation

Functions in Funnel can be aggregated to form records. Here is an example of a record type (with several more functions left out for brevity):

```
type Complex = {
  def re: Float
  def im: Float
  def plus (c: Complex): Complex
}
```

This defines a record with three functions, `re`, `im`, and `plus`. Functions `re` and `im` are parameter-less, whereas `plus` takes a single parameter of type `Complex`. A complex number can be constructed using a function like `makeComplex`:

```
def makeComplex (r: Float, i: Float): Complex = {
  def re = r
  def im = i
  def plus (c: Complex) = makeComplex (re + c.re, im + c.im)
}
```

Values of type complex can then be formed by calling the constructor function:

```
val one = makeComplex (1.0, 0)
val i   = makeComplex (0, 1.0)
```

Value definitions like these evaluate the right-hand sides, binding it to the name given on the left-hand side. Contrast this with a parameterless function definition like

```
def oneExp = makeComplex (1.0, 0)
```

This definition does not entail any evaluation itself, but each time `oneExp` is used, the right-hand side is evaluated anew.

As usual, fields of record values are selected by an infix period. E.g. the expression `one.plus(i)` evaluates to the complex number $1+i$.

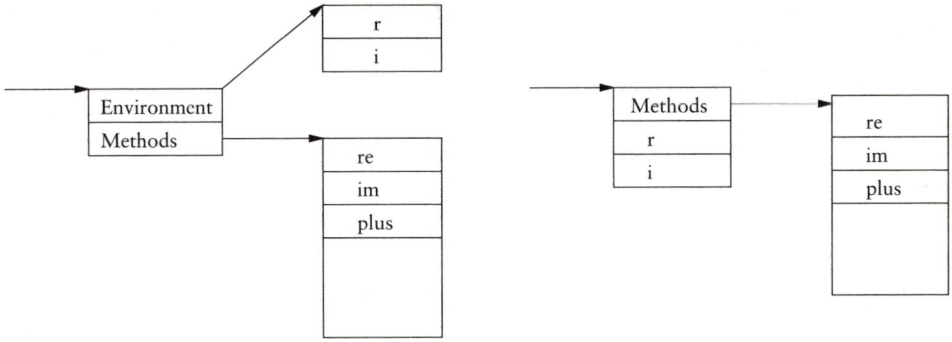

Figure 1: Object Representations

Objects

So far, our notation was explained in terms of functions and records. Equally well, one could have used object-oriented terminology. Records are then called objects, and their fields (which are always functions in our case) are called methods. Unlike in many object-oriented programming languages, there is no need for a special syntactic form for object construction such as **new**. Instead, an object is simply defined by constructing its record of methods. The construction can be wrapped in a function itself, as was demonstrated by the case of `makeComplex`. Furthermore, the record methods may refer to variables bound in their environment. For instance, the methods in the record created by `makeComplex` refer to the parameters of `makeComplex`.

Looking at the situation from an implementation viewpoint, this has two consequences. First, since the created record survives the execution of the enclosing creator function, it will have to be stored in the heap rather than on the stack. Second, together with the record, the values of `makeComplex`'s actual parameters need to be stored since these values can be accessed during evaluation of the record's methods. A good place to store these *environment variables* is as instance variables of the created heap object itself. The methods, on the other hand, need not be allocated once per call to `makeComplex`. Since their code is the same each time `makeComplex` is called, their implementation among all calls to `makeComplex` can be shared. A record can thus be represented by a *method table* and an *environment*, as depicted on the left side of Figure 1. When calling a method, the environment is passed as an additional parameter. This is very similar to the *closure* representation used in functional programming for first-class functions. The only difference is that a closure consists of an environment and a single function code pointer, whereas our record representation shares a single environment between all methods of a record.

One can also eliminate the indirection to the environment by making the method pointer itself the first entry of the environment. A record is then identified by just a pointer to its environment. This situation is depicted on the right of Figure 1. It corresponds exactly to the standard object layout used in many object-oriented languages. Two differences remain, however. First, fields of an environment are local to the object itself, so that they can be accessed only through a method of the record. In object-oriented terms, one would say that all instance variables are *private*[2]. Second, fields in an environment are always immutable, reflecting the purely functional nature of the language presented so far. The next sections will introduce a richer language which lets us express mutable variables. But for now we stay in the purely functional subset.

Record type definitions can be recursive, as is shown in the following definition of a type for lists.

```
type SimpleList [t] = {
  def isEmpty: Bool
  def head: t
  def tail: SimpleList [t]
}
```

This says that a `SimpleList` is a record consisting of three functions. Function `isEmpty` returns `true` if the list is empty, function `head` returns the first element of a (nonempty) list and function `tail` returns the list consisting of all elements but the first one. The definition has a type parameter 't' which represents the element type of the list. To distinguish type parameters from value parameters, we always enclose the former in square brackets `[...]`. Both types and functions can have type parameters.

Given a definition of lists as above, how can values of this type be defined? As in the case of `makeComplex`, we create constructor functions for lists. Two constructor functions are needed, depending on whether the constructed list is empty or not. The following code defines the two list constructors `Nil` and `Cons`.

```
val SimpleList = {
  def Nil [t]: SimpleList [t] = {
    def isEmpty = true
    def head = error ("Nil.head")
    def tail = error ("Nil.tail")
  }
```

2. Actually, the term private does not have a standard meaning in OOP. In Simula or Smalltalk a private field can only be accessed from within methods of the same object, whereas in Java or C++ it can be accessed from any object which is a direct instance of the class which defined the field. Our scheme implements the Simula/Smalltalk meaning of the term.

```
def Cons [t] (x: t, xs: SimpleList [t]): SimpleList [t] = {
  def isEmpty = false
  def head = x
  def tail = xs
}}
```

The Nil function creates an empty list. Taking the head or tail of such a list results in an error, which is expressed here by calling the predefined error function. The Cons function creates a list consisting of a given head x and a given tail xs. Both Nil and Cons take a type parameter t. We also say they are *polymorphic* in the element type of the constructed list. The constructors Nil and Cons are themselves methods of a record value called SimpleList. This record plays the role of a module in Modula-2 or Oberon. Note that SimpleList is used as a name for both a record type and a record value. This is possible since Funnel has different name spaces for types and values.

As examples of clients of the SimpleList abstraction, consider the following definitions of a length function and a non-destructive append function.

```
def length [t] (xs: SimpleList [t]) =
  if (xs.isEmpty) 0
  else 1 + length (xs.tail)

def append [t] (xs: SimpleList [t], ys: SimpleList [t]) =
  if (xs.isEmpty) ys
  else SimpleList.Cons (xs.head, append (xs.tail, ys))
```

Actually, one could equally well define length and append as *methods* of SimpleList objects. The following code defines a List type which is itself defined in terms of SimpleList and adds a set of methods to it.

```
type List [t] = {
  with SimpleList [t]

  def tail: List [t]
  def length: Int
  def append (ys: List [t]): List [t]
  def forall (p: t → Bool): Bool
  def filter (p: t → Bool): List [t]
  def map [r] (f: t → r): List [r]
}
```

The **with** SimpleList[t] clause at the beginning of the List record simply inserts the definitions for those methods of SimpleList which are not defined later in the List record. In our case, because tail is redefined later, the cause would be equivalent to the two definitions:

```
def isEmpty: Bool
def head: a
```

The effect of **with** is analogous to *inheritance* in object-oriented programming, and the redefinition of tail is analogous to *method overriding*.

Constructors for List are also defined in terms of the constructors for SimpleList. Each constructor in List simply wraps the corresponding constructor in SimpleList in an application of function fromSimple. This function constructs a record which inherits the given SimpleList parameter, redefines function tail and adds the newly defined methods.

```
val List = {
  def fromSimple [t] (xs: SimpleList [t]): List [t] = {
    with xs
    def tail = fromSimple (xs.tail)
    def length = if (isEmpty) 0 else 1 + tail.length
    def append (ys) =
      if (isEmpty) ys else List.Cons (head, tail.append (ys))

    def forall (p) =
      p (head) && tail.forall (p)
    def filter (p) =
      if (isEmpty) List.Nil
      else if (p (x)) List.Cons (head, tail.filter (p))
      else tail.filter (p)
    def map (f) =
      if (isEmpty) List.Nil else List.Cons (f (head), tail.map (f))
  }
  def Nil [t]: List [t] =
    fromSimple (SimpleList.Nil)
  def Cons [t] (x: t, xs: List [t]): List [t] =
    fromSimple (SimpleList.Cons (x, xs))
}
```

The final type for lists is defined in terms of a basic implementation with just the operations isEmpty, head, and tail. Actually, it is possible to define lists with even fewer basic methods. It would be sufficient to have a single method match which takes a *visitor* [12] record as an argument. Depending on whether the list was empty or not, one of two methods of the visitor would be invoked. This structure essentially models the *algebraic data types* found in many functional languages, with the visitor taking over the role of a pattern matching case expression. Details are found in [23].

Higher-Order Functions

To keep the presentation short, we have restricted ourselves in the definition of the List data structure to a representative sample of methods. Besides length and append there are three other methods which all take functions as parameters:

- The method `forall` takes a predicate and returns `true` if all elements of the list satisfy the predicate. The predicate is a function from the element type of the list `t` to `Bool`. Function types are expressed with an infix arrow, e.g. the given predicate has type `t` $\rightarrow$ `Bool`.

- The method `filter` also takes a predicate and returns a list of all those elements which satisfy the predicate.

- The method `map` takes a function `f` from list elements to some arbitrary result type `r` and returns the list resulting from applying `f` to each element.

The standard definition of `List` in Funnel defines these methods and several others as well. Functions such as `forall`, `filter`, and `map`, which take functions as arguments or return them as results are called *higher-order* functions. To streamline the application of such functions, a lightweight form of functional abstraction is introduced which lets us define anonymous functions: the expression (x_1, ..., x_n | E) denotes a function which maps its formal argument x_1, ..., x_n to the value computed by the expression E (which may refer to x_1, ..., x_n). For instance, the following expression would yield a list consisting of the squares of elements of a given list:

```
xs.map (x | x * x)
```

To demonstrate the expressive power and convenience of higher-order functions we conclude this section with a presentation of an algorithm for topologically sorting a graph. For a given `Node` type, we define the type `Edge` as a pair of two nodes, and the type `Graph` as a record of nodes and edges:

```
type Node = ...
type Edge = (Node, Node)
type Graph = {
  def nodes: List [Node]
  def edges: List [Edge]
}
```

A topological sort function maps a given graph to a list of all nodes in the graph, so that the predecessor of every edge appears in the list before its successor. This is possible only if the graph has no cycles; for cyclic graphs an error should be reported. An implementation of `topSort` is as follows.

```
def topSort (g: Graph): List [Node] = {
  def isSource (n: Node) = g.edges.forall (x, y | n != y)
  val sources = g.nodes.filter (isSource)
  if (nodes.isEmpty) nodes
  else if (sources.isEmpty) error ("topSort of cyclic graph")
  else
     sources.append (topSort {
        def nodes = g.nodes.filter (x | ! isSource (x))
        def edges = g.edges.filter (x, y | ! isSource (x))
     })
}
```

The implementation of this function is very close to the following high-level constructive definition of topological sorting: "To sort a graph, form a list consisting of all sources of the graph, followed by a sort of the remaining graph which results from removing all original sources and all edges emanating from them. A node is a source of a graph if it is not the successor of any edge in the graph." The functional definition is concise and elegant, even though it is not optimally efficient. Nevertheless, the present formulation is very attractive as either a prototype implementation or a high-level design which is to be improved in its efficiency by program transformations.

3 Forks and Joins

The subset of the Funnel language we have seen so far was purely functional. There was no way to express a side effect or a concurrent computation of several threads. We now extend Funnel to make it into a general purpose programming language in which these concepts can be expressed. Surprisingly little new mechanism is needed for these extensions. We will concentrate in this section on basic concurrency constructs. In the next section, we will show how the same constructs also express imperative programming.

Any concurrent language needs an operator to initiate parallel computation. We introduce for this purpose the *fork* operator `&`. The term `A & B` executes its operands `A` and `B` in parallel.

A concurrent language also needs mechanisms for synchronizing threads running parallel and for communications between them. A large number of different methods for doing this have been proposed. We use here the following simple scheme which fits very well with the functional approach we have followed so far. We admit the `&` operator not only in function bodies on the right-hand side of a rewrite rule, but also in function headers on the left-hand side of a rewrite rule. For instance, the definition

```
def a (x) & b (y)  =  c (x + y) & d ()
```

would be interpreted as follows: "If there are two concurrent calls to functions a(x) and b(y), then these calls are to be replaced by two concurrent evaluations of c(x + y) and d(). As long as there is only one call to a or b, this call will block until its partner in the rule is also called." An occurrence of & on the left-hand side of a definition is called a *join*, since its effect is the joining of two previously independent threads of computation. Consequently, a left-hand side containing & symbols is also called a *join pattern*.

Asynchronous Channels

As a first example of join synchronization, consider an implementation of an asynchronous channel which connects a set of producers with a set of consumers. Producers call a function put to send data to the channel while consumers call a function get to retrieve data. An implementation of a channel is realized by the following simple functional net.

```
def get: T & put (x: T) = x
```

This definition jointly defines the two functions get and put. Only put takes a parameter, and only get returns a result. We call result-returning functions like get *synchronous*, whereas functions like put are called *asynchronous*. The definition rewrites two concurrent calls to put(x) and get to the value x, which is returned to the caller of the get operation. Generally, only the first function in a join pattern can return a result, all other functions are asynchronous. Likewise, only the first operand of a fork can return a result, all other operands are asynchronous or their result is discarded.

Here is an example of a program that uses the channel abstraction.

```
def get: Int & put (x: Int) = x
def P = ( val x = get ; P & put (x + 1) )
P & put (1)
```

The program repeatedly reads out a number which was sent to a channel and sends back the number incremented by one. Initially, the number 1 is sent to the channel. A reduction of this program starts with the following steps (where we abbreviate the above definitions of get, put and P to **def** D).

```
    def D; P & put (1)
→   (by rewriting P to its definition)
    def D; { val x = get ; P & put (x + 1) } & put (1)
→   (by joining put (1) and get)
    def D; val x = 1 ; P & put (x + 1)
→   (by expanding the val)
```

```
    def D; P & put (1 + 1)
```

→ (by numeric simplification)

```
    def D; P & put (2)
```

→ (by rewriting P to its definition)

```
    def D; { val x = get ; P & put (x + 1) } & put (2)
```

→ ...

This program is still deterministic, in the sense that at each point only one reduction is possible. But we can change this by adding another process Q:

```
def get: Int & put (x: Int) = x
def P = { val x = get ; P & put (x + 1) }
def Q = { val x = get ; P & put (x – 1) }
P & Q & put (1)
```

There are now many possible reduction sequences of this program, since either *P* or *Q*, but not both, can react via their get operation with a previous put operation. The sequence in which the two processes execute is arbitrary, controlled only by the channel's rewrite rules. Generally, we do not assume *fairness*, so that it would be possible for P to execute infinitely often without any intervening execution of Q (or *vice versa*).

Channels can be turned into reusable abstractions by packing their operations in a record with a type parameterized with the type of messages:

```
type Channel [t] = {
  def get: t
  def put (x: t): nil
}
def newChannel [t]: Channel [t] = {
  def get & put (x) = x
}
```

The type of put is a function from t to **nil**, which represents the empty type.

A note on precedence. We assume the following order of precedence, from strong to weak:

```
( )  (&)  (=)  (,)  (;)
```

That is, function application binds strongest, followed by parallel composition, followed by the equal sign, followed by comma, and finally followed by semicolon. Other standard operators such as +, *, == fall between function application and & in their usual order of precedence. When precedence risks being unclear, we'll use parentheses to disambiguate.

A Note on Indentation. As a syntactic convenience, we allow indentation instead of `;-separators` inside blocks delimited with braces { and }. Except for the significance of indentation, braces are equivalent to parentheses. The precise rules are: (1) In a block delimited with braces a semicolon is inserted in front of any non-empty line which starts at the same indentation level as the first symbol following the opening brace, provided the symbol before the insertion point is not already a semicolon. The only modification to this rule is: (2) If inserted semicolons would separate two **def** blocks, yielding **def** D_1 ; **def** D_2 say, then the two **def** blocks are instead merged into a single block, i.e. **def** D_1, D_2. (3) The top level program is treated like a block delimited with braces, i.e. indentation is significant.

Qualified Definitions

The asynchronous channel suffers from a potentially unbounded pile-up of undelivered messages if messages are produced at a higher rate than they are consumed. This problem is avoided in bounded buffers which limit the number of unconsumed messages to some given number. For instance, the following functional net implements a one-place buffer in which the number of `put` operations cannot exceed the number of `get` operations by more than one:

```
def get: T & full (x: T)    =  x  & empty,
    put (x: T): () & empty =  ()  &  full (x)
```

There are two definitions which define four functions. Functions `put` and `get` are meant to be called from the producer and consumer clients of the buffer. The other two functions, `full` and `empty`, reflect the buffer's internal state, and should be called only from within the buffer.

In contrast to the situation with asynchronous channels, both `get` and `put` are now synchronous functions. The `put` operation returns the empty tuple `()` as its result. Its result type, also written `()`, consists of just this single value. Functions that return `()` are called *procedures*. The explicit `()` result is important since it tells us that the call to procedure `put` has terminated. If nothing was ever returned, `put` would be an asynchronous function, the termination of which cannot be observed. The "side effecting" part of the expression is `full(x)`. Like `empty`, `full` is an asynchronous function. Its sole purpose is to enable calls to `get` and to pass the stored element `x` along.

When faced with the task of turning one-place buffers into a reusable abstraction, we encounter some problems. First, not all functions of a one-place buffer should be turned into methods of a record – `empty` and `full` should remain hidden. Furthermore, before using a buffer abstraction we also need to initialize it by invoking the `empty` method. But `empty` is supposed to be internal, hence it cannot be initialized from outside! One possible solution would be to have a local definition of the four functions making up a buffer and then constructing a record with the get and put methods, which forward to the corresponding local method. But the code for this, presented below, is rather cumbersome.

```
def Buffer [t] = {
  def get: t
  def put (x: t): ()
}
def newBuffer [t]: Buffer [t] = {
  def get': t & full (x: t)       =  x  & empty,
      put' (x: t): () & empty     =  ()  &  full (x)
  { def get = get',
       put (x) = put' (x) } & empty
}
```

A more streamlined presentation can be obtained using *qualified definitions*. Qualified definitions mirror the qualified names used for accessing record elements. As an example, consider a re-formulation of the newBuffer function.

```
def newBuffer [t]: Buffer [t] = {
  def this.get & full x         =  x  & empty,
      this.put (x) & empty      =  () & full x
  this & empty
}
```

The left-hand side of a definition can now contain not just simple identifiers but qualified names like this.get and this.put. In the above example, the local definition thus introduces the three names this, full, and empty. this represents a record with two fields, get and put, while empty and full represent functions. Note that the naming of this is arbitrary, any other name would work equally well. Note also that empty and full are not methods of the record returned from newBuffer, so that they can only be accessed internally.

The identifiers which occur before a period in a join pattern always define new record names, which are defined only in the enclosing definition. It is not possible to use this form of qualified definition to add new fields to a record defined elsewhere.

We can now explain the anonymous form of record definition as an implicit qualified definition, where every defined method is prefixed with the name of the record being defined. I.e. the newChannel function given above would be regarded as syntactic sugar of the following expanded version:

```
def newChannel [t]: Channel [t] = {
  def this.get & this.put (x) = x
  this
}
```

The new interpretation gives up structured record values as a primitive language feature, replacing it by simple names. This view fits well with the join calculus theory underlying functional nets, since that calculus also represents every intermediate result with a name. Details are found in [23].

A simple usage of the one-place buffer abstraction is illustrated in the following example.

```
def newBuffer [t]: Buffer [t] = {
  def this.get & full x        =  x  & empty,
      this.put (x) & empty     =  () & full x
  this & empty
}
val b: Buffer [Int] = newBuffer
b.put (1) & ( val y = b.get ; b.put (y + y) )
```

There are two client processes composed in parallel. One process `puts` the number 1 into the buffer. The other process tries to `get` the buffer's contents and once it succeeds, puts a modified value back into the buffer. We will now trace the rewrite steps of this program. As a first step, the `newBuffer` call is replaced by its definition, yielding

```
def newBuffer [t] = ...
val b: Buffer [Int] = {
  def this.get & full x         =  x  & empty,
      this.put (x) & empty      =  () & full x
  this & empty
}
b.put (1) & ( val y = b.get ; b.put (y + y) )
```

The complex right-hand side of the **val** definition can be simplified by "pulling out" all elements which do not form part of the result (Precise rules for such permissible rearrangements of terms can be found in [23]). This yields:

```
def newBuffer [t] = ...
def this.get & full x       =  x  & empty,
    this.put (x) & empty    =  () & full x
val b: Buffer [Int] = this
b.put (1) & ( val y = b.get ; b.put (y + y) )  & empty
```

A simple-minded rearrangement of definitions from a local to a global scope may possibly create name clashes or shadow names that were visible before. We avoid these pitfalls by systematicly renaming the locally defined names where necessary. In our example, renaming is not necessary, but let's do it anyway to demonstrate the principle. The following program is identical to the previous one, except that `this` has been renamed `B`.

```
def newBuffer [t] = ...
def B.get & full x          =  x  & empty,
    B.put (x) & empty       =  () & full x
val b: Buffer [Int] = B
b.put (1) & ( val y = b.get ; b.put (y + y) )  & empty
```

The next rewrite step expands out the value definition, yielding:

```
def newBuffer [t] = ...
def B.get & full x          =  x  & empty,
    B.put (x) & empty       =  () & full x
B.put (1) & ( val y = B.get ; B.put (y + y) )  & empty
```

Abbreviating the two initial **def** blocks to **def** D, we finish with the following rewrite sequence:

```
    def D ; B.put (1) & ( val y = B.get ; B.put (y + y) ) & empty
→  (by joining B.put (1) and empty)
    def D ; () & B.full (1) & ( val y = B.get ; B.put (y + y) )
→  (by joining B.full (1) and B.get)
    def D ; () & B.empty & ( val y = 1 ; B.put (y + y) )
→  (by expanding the val definition)
    def D ; () & B.empty & B.put (2)
→  (by joining B.empty and B.put (2))
    def D ; () & () & B.full (2)
→  (by discarding the second () result)
    def D ; () & B.full (2)
```

4 Mutable State

The mechanisms introduced so far are also sufficient to explain imperative programming, where programs manipulate a state of mutable variables. After all, a mutable variable can be easily modeled as a functional net with the following two defining equations.

```
def value: T & state (x: T)             =  x  & state x,
    update (y: T) & state (x: T)        =  () & state y
```

The structure of these equations is similar to the one-place buffer in Section 3. The two synchronous functions `value` and `update` access and update the variable's current value, which is carried along as a parameter to the asynchronous function `state`.

The function state in the above definition appears on the left-hand sides of both equations. There is nothing strange about this. Remember that equations are rewrite rules. It is certainly possible for a function symbol to appear on the left-hand side of more than one rewrite rule, as long as all such rules form part of the same **def** block. On the other hand, it is not allowed that the same function appears several times in a single join pattern, i.e. **def** state (x) & state (y) = ... would be illegal.

Building on these definitions, we can create an abstraction for first-class mutable variables (also called a *reference cells*). The abstraction defines a type Ref [t] for reference cells and a function newRef for creating them. Here are the details.

```
type Ref [t] = {
  def value: t
  def update (y: t): ()
}
def newRef [t] (initial: t) = {
  def this.value & state (x: t) = x & state (x),
      this.update (y: t) & state (x: t) = () & state (y)
  this & state (initial)
}
```

As a simple usage example, consider the following program which creates a reference and defines and applies an increment function for it:

```
val r: Ref [Int] = newRef (0)
def increment  =  r.update (r.value + 1)
increment
```

Variables

The last program shows that while it is possible to use references, it is certainly not very pleasant. To obtain a more conventional and streamlined notation we introduce the following syntactic abbreviations:

– The definition **var** x := E expands to the three definitions

```
val _x = newRef (E)
def x = _x.value
def x! = _x.update
```

The first of these creates a reference cell while the second and third definitions introduce an *accessor* function x and an *update* function x!. Only the last two names are visible whereas the name of the reference cell _x is meant to be inaccessible for user programs.

- Analogously, a signature **var** x: T in a record type expands to a pair of signatures for the accessor and update function.

```
def x: T, x!: T→()
```

- Simple assignment expressions x := E expand to simple calls of the update function, e.g. x!(E).

- Qualified assignment expressions Q.x := E expand to qualified calls of the update function, e.g. Q.x!(E).

With these expansions, programs can be written using a customary syntax for variable definition and access. For instance, the previous increment program can now be written more concisely as follows.

```
var count := 0
def increment  =  count := count + 1
increment
```

Loops

The second important aspect of imperative programming are its loop control structures. In principle, such structures can be written as higher-order functions, thus implementing their standard definitions directly. For instance, here is an implementation of a function for while loops:

```
def whileLoop (cond: ()→Bool) (body: ()→()) =
  if (cond ()) { body () ; whileLoop (cond) (body) } else ()
```

And here is a usage example which employs two anonymous functions for the condition and the body of the loop.

```
def exp (x: Int, y: Int) =  {
  var m := 1
  var n := y
  whileLoop (| n > 0) (| m := m * x ; n := n – 1 )
  m
}
```

The example of Smalltalk blocks [14] has shown that it is quite possible to base all control structures on higher-order functions. But in the interest of readability we will retain the usual forms of control structures, with their meaning established by expansions like the one above.

Implementation Aspects

Our presentation so far has shown that imperative programs can be seen as a special class of functional nets, and that, at least in principle, no new constructs are necessary to support them. So far, we have not yet touched on the issue of efficiency. Clearly, a literal implementation of mutable variables in terms of joins and forks would be much less efficient than a direct implementation in terms of memory cells. But nobody forces us to actually use the literal implementation. We could equally well choose an implementation of the abstract Ref type in terms of primitive memory cells. Such an implementation could no longer be represented as a functional net, but its high-level interface, as well as the programs using it, could.

Another source of inefficiency lies in the indirection entailed by reference cell objects. In many cases, it is possible to avoid the indirection by "inlining" variables at the point where they are defined. This is particularly attractive for our high-level **var** syntax since this syntax does not permit access to the variable as a first class reference, only read and write operations are permitted. Nevertheless, care must be taken because functions accessing variables can escape the environment where the variable is defined. Example:

```
def newCounter = {
  var count := 0
  def this.reset  =  count := 0,
      this.increment  =  count := count + 1,
      this.value =  count
  this
}
```

In this example, the count variable may not be stored in newCounter's stack activation record, since the record returned from newCounter still accesses count. The standard object representation of reference cells avoids the problem since we assume that objects are always stored on the heap. Good techniques exist for *escape analysis* which tell whether a variable can be stored on the stack or whether it must be stored on the heap.

Functions and State

We now present an example which demonstrates how imperative and functional code can be combined with and substituted for each other. An often-used function for lists is reduce, which uses a given binary operator ⊕ and a zero value z to reduce all elements of a list to a single value:

$$\text{reduce}\ (\oplus,\ z,\ (x_1,\ \ldots,\ x_n))\ =\ (\ \ldots\ (z \oplus x_1) \oplus \ldots\ ) \oplus x_n\ .$$

Here's a purely functional implementation of reduce:

```
def reduce [s,t] (f: (s,t)→s, z: s, xs: List [t]): s  =
  if (xs.isEmpty) z
  else reduce (f, f (z, xs.head), xs.tail)
```

An equivalent imperative implementation is:

```
def reduce [s,t] (f: (s,t)→s, z: s, xs: List [t]): s  =  {
  var acc := z
  var rest := xs
  while (! rest.isEmpty) {
    acc := f (acc, rest.head)
    rest := rest.tail
  }
  acc
}
```

Once defined, reduce can be used in a large number of programming tasks. Examples:

- To sum up a list of operands:
```
def plus (x, y)  =  x + y;
def sum xs  =  reduce (plus, 0, xs)
```
- To compute the product of a list of factors:
```
def times (x, y)  =  x * y;
def product xs  =  reduce (times, 1, xs)
```
- To reverse a list:
```
def snoc (xs, x)  =  List.Cons (x, xs);
def reverse xs  =  reduce (snoc, List.Nil, xs)
```
- To form the scalar product of two vectors represented as lists:
```
def scalprod (xs, ys)  =  reduce (plus, 0, map (times, zip (xs, ys)))
```

Here, zip is a function which takes two lists and forms a list of pairs which combine corresponding elements of the two lists. This function can be defined as follows.

```
def zip [s, t] (xs: List [s], ys: List [t]): List [(s, t)] =
  if (xs.isEmpty || ys.isEmpty) List.Nil
  else List.Cons ((xs.head, ys.head), (xs.tail, ys.tail))
```

Stateful Objects

Objects with state arise naturally out of a combination of functional objects and variables. The newCounter function which was presented earlier provides an example. On the other hand, we can also implement stateful objects in a more direct way, by extending the implementation scheme for reference cells. An object with methods $m_1, \ldots, m_k$, and instance variables $x_1, \ldots, x_l$ with initial values $i_1, \ldots, i_l$ can be coded as follows.

```
def this.m_1 & state (x_1, ..., x_l)  =  ... ; state (x_1^1, ..., x_l^1),

    this.m_k & state (x_1, ..., x_l)  =  ... ; state (x_1^k, ..., x_l^k);
this & state (i_1, ..., i_l)
```

Here, the dots after the equal signs stand for elided method bodies. The object's instance variables are represented as arguments of a `state` function, which is initially applied to $i_1, \ldots, i_l$. Each method m_j consumes the current state vector of all instance variables and terminates by installing a new state in which instance variables have new values $x_1^j, \ldots, x_1^j$. Here is a re-formulation of counter objects using the new scheme.

```
def newCounter = {
  def this.reset & state (count: Int)  =  state (0),
      this.increment & state (count: Int)  =  state (count + 1),
      this.value  =  count & state (count)
  this
}
```

This representation technique achieves a common notion of information hiding, in that an object's instance variables cannot be accessed from outside the object. It further achieves mutual exclusion in that only one method of a given object can execute at any one time. After all, each method starts by consuming the state vector which is not re-established before the end of the method's execution. Thus, after one method commences, all other method calls to the same object are blocked until the first method has terminated. In other words, objects implemented in this way are *monitors*.

5 Concurrency

We now show how common constructs for concurrency control can be expressed as functional nets. The main problem in handling concurrency has to do with *process synchronization*. How can one process wait until some condition is established by some other process(es)? How can we ensure that certain operations are *atomic*, that is that they are performed from start to finish by one process at any one time, without other processes starting execution of the same action? In the following, we'll present several well-known schemes to handle this task and show how they can each be expressed as functional nets. For reasons of bounded space, we can only present a selection of common constructs. We refer the reader to [23] for a description of further constructs.

Semaphores

A common mechanism for process synchronization is a *lock* (or: *semaphore*). A lock offers two atomic actions: `getLock` and `releaseLock`. The lock starts its life in released state. A call to `getLock` succeeds and returns `()` if the lock is in released state. At the same time, the lock is put into locked state, in which other calls to `getLock` block until the lock is put back into released state by an operation of `releaseLock`. Here's the implementation of a semaphore as a functional net:

```
type Lock = {
  def getLock: ()
  def releaseLock: nil
}

def newLock = {
  def this.getLock & this.releaseLock  =  ()
  this & this.releaseLock
}
```

A typical usage of a semaphore would be:

```
val s = newLock ;
...
s.getLock ; "< critical region >" ; s.releaseLock
```

It is interesting to note the similarities in the definitions of semaphores and asynchronous channels.

Critical Regions

One problem with the previous usage pattern of semaphores is that it is easy to forget the `releaseLock` call, thus locking the semaphore forever. A safer solution is to pass the critical region into a higher-order function which does both the `getLock` and `releaseLock`:

```
type Proc = () → ()
type Mutex = Proc → ()
def newMutex: Mutex = {
  val s = newLock
  ( region: Proc | s.getLock ; region () ; s.releaseLock )
}
```

A typical usage pattern for this would be:

```
val mutex = newMutex
...
mutex (| "< critical region >")
```

Monitors

Modula-2 has popularized *monitors* [17] as a synchronization method. A monitor exports a set of functions f_1, ..., f_k while ensuring that only one of these functions can be active at any one time. At the end of Section 4, we have already seen a scheme to implement monitors by joining methods with a state vector containing all instance variables. Alternatively, we can represent instance variables as normal variables in a record's environment and use a `turn` "token" to achieve mutual exclusion. Here is an implementation of counters using this scheme.

```
def newSyncCounter = {
  var count := 0
  def this.reset & turn = { count := 0 ; () & turn },
      this.increment & turn = { count := count + 1 ; () & turn },
      this.value & turn  =  { val x = count ; x & turn }
  this & turn
}
```

Many monitors are more involved than this example in that a process executing in a monitor also needs to wait for conditions to be established by other processes. We can use join patterns to implement this form of waiting as well as mutual exclusion. As an example, consider the following implementation of bounded buffers.

```
def newBoundedBuffer [t] (N: Int): Buffer [t] = {
  val elems: Array [t] = newArray [t] (N)
  var in := 0; var out := 0

  def this.put (elem: t) & available & turn  =  {
    elems (in) := elem ; in := (in + 1) % N
    () & filled & turn
  }
  def this.get & filled & turn =  {
    val elem = elems (out) ; out := (out + 1) % N
    elem & available & turn
  }
  var i := 0
  while (i < N) { () & available ; i := i + 1 }
  this & turn
}
```

The basic implementation of the buffer is as in [32]. Buffer elements are stored in an array `elems` with two variables `in` and `out` keeping track of the first free and occupied position in the array. These variables are incremented modulo `N`, the size of the buffer. What's new here is how processes wait for their preconditions. A producer process has to wait for the buffer to become nonfull, while a consumer process has to wait for the buffer to become nonempty. Our implementation mirrors each filled slot in the buffer with a `filled` token. Each unfilled slot in the buffer is mirrored with an `available` token. Thus, the total number of `filled` and `available` tokens always equals `N`, the number of elements in the buffer. Initially, all slots are free, so we create `N` avaliable tokens. Each subsequent `put` operation removes an `available` token and creates a `filled` token, while each `get` operation does the opposite; it removes a `filled` token and creates an `available` token. Mutual exclusion of the `get` and `put` operations is ensured by the standard `turn` token technique.

Signals

Instead of join patterns, Modula-2 uses *signals* to let processes executing in monitor wait for preconditions. The implementation of such signals as functional nets is a bit subtle. On the surface, a signal is quite similar to a semaphore. Like a semaphore, a signal also offers two operations, which are now called `send` and `wait`. The `wait` operation of a signal corresponds to the `getLock` operation of a semaphore in that it waits until there is a call to `send` and then returns. A `send` operation of a signal on the other hand will unblock a pre-existing `wait` but does nothing at all if no call to `wait` exists. Unlike the `releaseLock` operation of a semaphore, a `send` will not interact with a `wait` that is issued later. Hence, in the execution sequence `releaseLock ; getLock`, the `getLock` operation will always succeed, whereas in the sequence `send ; wait`, the `wait` will always block since the previous `send` got lost. A first attempt to implement signals as functional nets could be:

```
type Signal = {
  def wait: ()
  def send: nil
}
def newSignal: Signal = {
  def this.wait & this.send = (),
      this.send             = nil
  this
}
```

The idea is that if there are calls to both `send` and `wait`, the `wait` operation will return with `()`, whereas a `send` alone will reduce to process **`nil`**, which does nothing at all.

This implementation of signals would work if join patterns were always tried in sequence, with earlier join patterns taking precedence over later ones. Unfortunately, there's nothing that stops an implementation of functional nets from always immediately reducing a `send` operation to **`nil`**, so that a `wait` might block even after subsequent `send`'s. Hence, our first attempt to implement signals fails.

It is still possible to formulate signals as functional nets. Here's one way to do it:

```
def newSignal: Signal = {
  def this.send & inactive = inactive,
      this.wait & inactive = wait1,
      wait1 & this.send    = () & inactive
  this & inactive
}
```

The solution makes use of a token, `inactive`, which signals that there are no active `waits`. A `send` in inactive state simply leaves the state inactive. A wait in inactive state suppresses inactive state and continues with the blocking operation `wait1`. Finally, a `wait1` and a `send` return `()` to the `wait1` and re-establish inactive state.

The second implementation of signals "feels" more deterministic than the first one, but its correctness is not easy to establish. Indeed, if we compare actual reduction sequences we find that every reduction sequence of `send`'s and `wait`'s possible in the first implementation is also possible in the second and vice versa. The problem is that even with the second formulation of signals a processor might never reduce an incoming `wait` to a `wait1`. For instance, it might be busy doing other things indefinitely. Therefore, `send`'s might still overtake `wait`'s and get lost. So have we gained nothing by refining the implementation of signals? Not quite. The second formulation still has the following property, which is generally good enough for reactive systems: Say some process in a reactive system issues a `wait` on some signal and eventually all processes of that system block. If at some later time, some process is triggered by an external event and, once resumed, issues a `send` on the same signal, then the `wait` (or some other wait on the same signal) is guaranteed to be able to proceed.

We now reformulate the bounded buffer example to closely match the implementation in the Modula-2 book, making use of our signal abstraction. This implementation provides an explanation of the interaction between monitors and signals, which is also quite subtle. Here is the code:

```
def newBoundedBuffer [t] (N: Int): Buffer [t] = {
  val elems: Array [t] = newArray [t] (N)
  var in := 0; var out := 0; var n := 0

  val nonFull: Signal = newSignal
  val nonEmpty: Signal = newSignal

  def this.put (elem: t) & turn  =  {
    n := n + 1
    while (n > N) { waitUntil (nonFull) }
    elems (in) := elem ; in := (in + 1) % N
    if (n ≤ 0) nonEmpty.send
    () & turn
  }
```

```
    def this.get & turn  =  {
      n := n – 1
      while (n < 0) { waitUntil (nonEmpty) }
      val elem = elems (out) ; out := (out + 1) % N
      if (n ≥ N) nonFull.send
      elem & turn
    }

    def waitUntil s = ( s.wait & turn ; reEnter )
    def reEnter & turn = ()
    this & turn
  }
```

The correct interaction of signals with monitors, hidden in Modula-2 by the underlying implementation, requires some effort to model explicitly. When waiting for a signal, a process has to re-issue the `turn` token, to let other processes enter the monitor. On the other hand, once a process wakes up, it has to re-consume the `turn` token to make sure that it executes under mutual exclusion. The re-issue and re-consumption of the `turn` token is done in functions `waitUntil` and `reEnter`. Because a process might block waiting for its `turn` after being woken up by a `send`, it is not guaranteed that the awaited condition will still be established when the process finally resumes. Hence, the awaited condition needs to be tested repeatedly in a **`while`** loop. This style of monitors has been discussed together with other alternatives by Hoare [17].

The second implementation of bounded buffers is more complicated than the first. But one might still prefer it because of efficiency considerations. After all, the implementation in terms of signals uses fewer tokens than the first implementation, because it sends a signal only when a process is waiting for it. This does not invalidate our initial implementation, however, which remains attractive as a concise and executable design.

6 Conclusion

Functional nets are an attempt to distill a large number of programming concepts into a uniform and very simple kernel. We have presented here a tour through functional, object-oriented, imperative and concurrent programming concepts, which were all mapped into our kernel language Funnel. A companion paper [23] takes this approach further, by translating Funnel itself to object-based join calculus, a simple operational semantics which can be described comfortably on a single page. The reduction of a large number of phenomena to a common foundation is inherent to a large part of science. Like in other areas, it is also useful in programming since it helps to clarify the meaning of derived constructs and the interactions between them.

An analogous approach is well established in the field of functional programming, where elaborate functional programming languages are reduced to λ-calculus as a kernel language. Classical λ-calculus [8, 5] is ideally suited as a basis for functional programs, but less well suited for imperative and reactive programs. Extensions of λ-calculus for modeling these aspects have been devised, but these extension quickly become too complex to seem completely natural. Join calculus, on the other hand, supports all these aspects in the kernel language itself. Consequently, it is possible to express a much wider variety of programming constructs than with λ-calculus alone.

The introduction given here remains necessarily sketchy. Issues which have not been addressed include a formal language specification of Funnel including its type system, a program logic, programming methodology and laws of programming, implementation and optimization techniques, and the modeling of more involved programming concepts such as classes and inheritance. These issues are topics of current research.

Acknowledgements

Matthias Zenger and Christoph Zenger designed several of the examples and suggested numerous improvements to the presentation.

References

[1] Martin Abadi and Luca Cardelli. *A Theory of Objects Monographs in Computer Science*. Springer Verlag,1996.

[2] Harold Abelson, Gerald Jay Sussman, and Julie Sussman. *The Structure and Interpretation of Computer Programs*. MIT Press, Cambridge, Massachusetts, 1984.

[3] Franz Achermann and Oscar Nierstrasz. Applications = comonents + scripts – a tour of Piccola. In *Software Architectures and Component Technology*. Kluwer, 2000.

[4] John W. Backus. Can rogramming be liberated from the von neumann style? *Communications of the ACM*, 21:613–641, 1978.

[5] Hendrik P. Barendregt. *The Lambda Calculus: its Syntax and Semantics*, volume 103 of Studies in Logic and the Foundations of Mathematics. North-Holland, Amsterdam, revised edition, 1984.

[6] Richard Bird. *Introduction to Functional Programming using Haskell*. Prentice Hall, 1998. 2nd edition.

[7] Luca Cardelli, Simone Martini, John C. Mitchell, and Andre Scedrov. An extension of system F with subtyping. *Information and Computation*, 109(1–2):4 –56, 1994.

[8] Alonzo Church. *The Calculi of Lambda-Conversion*, volume 6 of *Annals of Mathematics Studies*. Princeton University Press, second edition, 1951.

[9] Fabrice Le Fessant. *The JoCaml reference manual*. INRIA Rocquencourt, 1998. Available from `http://join.inria.fr`

[10] Cédric Fournet and Georges Gonthier. The reflexive chemical abstract machine and the join-calculus. *In Proc. 23rd ACM Symposium on Principles of Programming Languages*, pages 372–385, January 1996.

[11] Cédric Fournet and Luc Maranget. *The Join-Calculus Language.* INRIA Rocquencourt, 1997. Available from `http://join.inria.fr`

[12] Erich Gamma, Richard Helm, Ralph Johnson, and John Vlissides. *Design Patterns: Elements of Reusable Object-Oriented Software.* Addison-Wesley, 1994.

[13] Alessandro Giacalone, Prateek Mishra, and Sanjiva Prasad. Facile: A symmetric integration of concurrent and functional rogramming. *International Journal of Parallel Programming*, 18(2):121–160, April 1989.

[14] Adele Goldberg and David Robson. *Smalltalk-80; The Language and Its Implementation.* Addison-Wesley, 1983.

[15] C. A. R. Hoare. *Communicating Sequential Processes.* Prentice-Hall, Englewood Cliffs, New Jersey, 1985.

[16] C. A. R. Hoare and Niklaus Wirth. An axiomatic definition of the programming language Pascal. *Acta Informatica*, 2:335–355, 1973.

[17] C. A. R. Hoare. Monitors: An operating system structuring concept. *Communications of the ACM*, 12(10), October 1974.

[18] Paul Hudak. Conception, evolution, and application of functional programming languages. *ACM Computing Surveys*, 21(3):359–411, 1989.

[19] Kathleen Jensen and Niklaus Wirth. *PASCAL: User Manual and Report*, volume 18 of *Lecture Notes in Computer Science.* Springer-Verlag, 1974.

[20] Jon Kerridge. *Occam programming: a practical approach.* Blackwell Scientific, 1987.

[21] Robin Milner. *A Calculus of Communicating Systems*, volume 92 of *Lecture Notes in Computer Science.* Springer-Verlag, New York, 1980.

[22] Robin Milner, Joachim Parrow, and David Walker. A calculus of mobile processes. *Information and Computation*, 100:1–77, 1992.

[23] Martin Odersky. Functional nets. In *Proc. European Symposium on Programming*, number 1782 in LNCS, pages 1–25. Springer-Verlag, March 2000.

[24] L. C. Paulson. *ML for the Working Programmer.* Cambridge University Press, 1991. ISBN 0-521-39022-2.

[25] Benjamin C. Pierce and David N. Turner. Pict: A rogramming language based on the pi-calculus. Technical Report CSCI 476, Computer Science Department, Indiana University, 1997.

[26] Benjamin C. Pierce and David N. Turner. Local type inference. In *Proc. 25th ACM Symposium on Principles of Programming Languages*, 1998.

[27] The Munich Project. *CIP, Volume 1: The Wide Spectrum Language CIP/L*, volume 183 of *Lecture Notes in Computer Science.* Springer-Verlag, 1985.

[28] W. Reisig. *Petri Nets*, volume 4 of *EATCS Monographs on Theoretical Computer Science.* Springer-Verlag, 1985.

[29] John H. Reppy. CML: A higher-order concurrent language. In *Proc. ACM SIGPLAN Conf. on Programming Language Design and Implementation*, pages 293–305, June 1991.

[30] Niklaus Wirth. Program development by stepwise refinement. *Communications of the ACM*, 14(4):221–227, 1971.

[31] Niklaus Wirth. The rogramming language Pascal. *Acta Informatica*, 1:35–63, 1971.

[32] Niklaus Wirth. *Programming in Modula-2.* Springer-Verlag, 2nd edition, 1983.

[33] Niklaus Wirth. The programming language Oberon. *Software Practice and Experience*, 18(7):671–690,1988.

Part V
Mastering Simplicity – in the Industry

Lilith Meets the World of Business

Bernhard Wagner

Abstract

Lilith was an advanced prototype computer that had many new features, which only became commonplace five to ten years later. However the obvious idea, to make a commercial product out of Lilith, failed several times. Three attempts to bring Lilith to the marketplace are described, namely the offer to a large company, the efforts of a startup company, and the attempt to market Lilith as a special purpose tool. By means of selected computer developments in the early eighties of the last century, namely the commercially successful personal computer from IBM and the workstation from SUN Microsystems, and by reviewing the Macintosh and the Lisa computer from Apple, the reasons for Lilith's failure are discussed. Finally it is shown that in the field of commerce, Lilith has faced similar problems to those faced by the Alto computer from Xerox PARC some time earlier, and a possible scenario for commercial success is presented.

1 The Lilith Computer

If it is quite natural today to have a personal computer in one's office, or at home, equipped with a user interface based on mouse clicks and window technology, this is the result of a research effort conducted in the seventies and early eighties of the last century. Around then the first workstations and desktop computers were built; the Star by Xerox, the Apple II and the Macintosh by Apple, workstations by SUN Microsystems and Apollo, and the IBM personal computer (PC), to name just a few very popular machines. Throughout this paper we call these new types of computers *office/home computer*, in order to avoid the term *personal computer* which is associated with the PC from IBM and its clones.

At the Federal Institute of Technology (ETH) in Zurich Niklaus Wirth's group, too, worked in this field and as the result of their research the Lilith computer [Wir81] was presented in 1980. Lilith was new, in comparison to mainframe computers, in several aspects.

- Lilith was an office/home computer, small enough to fit under a desk. Interesting enough to the user it seemed to have about the same performance as a mainframe computer. This impression was induced by Lilith's architecture, a kind of virtual machine implemented in microcode, which was well-suited for the generation of compact and fast code.

- Lilith's user interface was not the then wide-spread character-oriented 80 × 24 screen on which arcane system commands had to be typed in, but on Lilith's portrait-shaped screen individually accessible pixels were displayed. That allowed characters in arbitrary fonts to be displayed. The screen could be separated into several windows, each of them having different content, and a mouse as an additional input device could replace most of the typing by cut/copy/paste operations.
- In order to support such a user interface, Lilith had special hardware instructions for screen manipulation, which were implemented as micro-programs for the AMD 2901 bit-slice processor.
- All of Lilith's software including operating system, device drivers, etc was written in the – as we call it today – 3rd generation language Modula-2; there was no assembly language. This was new in the respect that Modula-2, other than C in which Unix was written, provided strong type checking and supported separate compilation. The clean interfaces to the operating system, together with a Modula-2 specific linking loader and debugger made Lilith to an ideal tool for software engineering [Pom85].
- With clever software, Lilith was able to control a Canon laser printer, which for example, allowed users to print fonts not only on the screen but also on paper.

In summary, Lilith was a first class prototype computer, which showed that all these new concepts could be implemented together on a single machine. For such a highly innovative computer it seemed obvious to most people that Lilith would also be a self running product on the computer market, particularly because many concepts like the raster screen, windows, mouse, which are commonplace today, were already implemented in Lilith. All attempts however to establish Lilith on the market and sell it in larger quantities failed. In retrospect, with the experience of 20 years personal computing, Lilith's failure on the market is no surprise, although (or because) it was far ahead of its time.

The remainder of this article is organized as follows. We describe three attempts to transform Lilith into a commercial product and discuss by means of similar developments why each attempt failed. Section 2 describes why Lilith wasn't accepted by the large company Siemens, and we compare it with the PC from another large company, i.e. IBM, which was launched some time after Lilith was rejected by Siemens. In Section 3 the efforts of a startup company, which was founded as a spin-off from Wirth's group, are set in relation to the workstations built by SUN Microsystems and Apollo Computers. Section 3.3 compares Lilith with Lisa and Macintosh, the products of Apple Computer Inc. The reasons for the failure of another startup company, which sold Lilith as a special development tool, are examined in section 4. When concluding in section 5 that an excellent prototype does not imply a commercially successful product and vice versa, we also answer the questions "Could one have known better?" and "Could it have been done better?"

2 Large Established Companies

2.1 Siemens AG

In 1981 the Munich based Siemens AG was Germany's largest manufacturer of hard- and software. Within its department of basic software development, a group headed by Manfred Sommer had just made the programming language *Pascal* to an official Siemens product. The status of an official product implied some investments by the company: guaranteed support by trained staff, professionally made manuals, training courses open to customers, presentation at computer fairs and road shows, etc.

Because of these investments, there are high requirements for obtaining the status as an official product. In the case of Pascal for example, it was not sufficient to implement just another code generator, therefore the compiler was embedded in a programming environment which facilitated the edit-compile-run cycle. On the other hand, a new product has also to fit into the range of Siemens products and to support existing applications. That implied that Pascal had to be extended in order to support, for example, index-sequential files and atomic transactions (see [Wag82]).

When Niklaus Wirth and Manfred Sommer met one day, the idea of presenting Lilith at Siemens was born. The realization of this idea in spring 1981 however, initially faced a serious obstacle. Nowadays nobody cares if you cross the border with a notebook computer on the backseat of your car, which is at least 100 times more powerful than a Lilith computer. But 20 years ago it was quite unusual to carry around computers, especially those that have no serial number. Hence customs required a lot of paperwork which could be done only by the Siemens office in Zurich – the advantage of a large company.

The presentation of the Lilith computer at Siemens had two goals:

1. to convince the upper management that personal computing is a promising field in which Siemens should be engaged by constructing a workstation of its own.
2. to use Lilith as this workstation and to transform it into an official Siemens product.

The first goal was in part achieved by presentations, which deeply impressed basically all visitors, and by a well attended talk about Lilith, given by Jirka Hoppe. For the sake of fairness one has to admit however, that Lilith does not deserve all the credit. The products of Xerox, Three Rivers, and Apollo also showed that it was possible to build workstations.

The second goal was not fulfilled, mainly because Lilith was too far advanced compared to the computing paradigms of that time. In 1981 Siemens and its main competitor IBM manufactured mostly large mainframe computers which were accessed by simple character-oriented 80 × 24 terminals. Although nowadays features like mouse and windows are commonplace, twenty years ago each of Lilith's new concepts alone already meant a step in a new direction, away from the mainstream. Hence Lilith required too many steps at once; large companies with many different customers whose investments have to be protected aren't flexible enough to march in new directions at this pace.

Another reason is that in large companies there are usually too many managers who have to be convinced about the usefulness and low risks of such a highly innovative project. The latter is hardly possible, since the more innovative a product is, the higher the investments required to fit it into the range of the company's products and to support existing applications. As it will be shown in sections 3.2 and 3.3, in order to market it, Lilith would have required an enormous amount of both hardware and software development and engineering.

- The end of the "will-be" Siemens – Lilith liaison is quickly told. Eventually Siemens established co-operation with Apollo Computers and even if Lilith couldn't convince Siemens as a whole, it did at least convince me. After having presented Lilith so often, I left Siemens and followed her to Zurich where I joined Jirka Hoppe's group.

2.2 The IBM PC

About the same time as Lilith's presentation at Siemens, IBM developed the personal computer (PC) which was then released in the following year. The PC may serve as another example that large and well-established companies seldom bring really new and innovative products to the market, products, which may revolve the paradigms of computing. Compared to IBM's mainframe computers, the PC was new in one aspect only: it was a small desktop computer. Most of the features of the list above, which Lilith already had, e.g. mouse, windows, etc. were added to the PC only during the following six to seven years. To the user, the PC with its 80 x 24 monitor looked like a mainframe, except that it was slower and always short on memory.

Despite the user interface, in their basic design Lilith and PC were completely different in the processor, but had a common design principle for their operating systems. Both of their operating systems, *Medos* for the Lilith (see [Knu00]) and *DOS* for the PC were designed for stand-alone office/home computers. This allowed the operating systems to be kept small and simple – DOS, a rebuild of CP/M, was so simple that it bore more resemblance to an interrupt handler than to an operating system.

The drawback of such a design was that both operating systems were brand-new, which implied that originally no application software existed for them. For DOS that was no problem. Because of the well established brand name *IBM*, many companies saw an opportunity to make money by selling DOS applications to a large number of customers and therefore, shortly after the launch of the PC, a lot of third party software was available for it. On the other hand, the lack of application software may explain why Lilith had no commercial success.

Although Medos had some features which supported remote procedure calls and transparent remote file access (see [Knu00]), it is important to note that, because of their design for the use in stand-alone single-user computers, neither Medos nor DOS were originally suitable for use in local area networks (see section 3.2). Hence at the latest by the mid eighties, when the paradigm changed from personal computing to client/server computing, both operating systems became obsolete.

As already mentioned, Lilith and PC differed in the type of processor. Lilith used the AMD 2901 bit-slice processor which was the technology of 1978 and which became more or less obsolete when the one-chip microprocessors were available around 1980. IBM's design principle was to assemble the PC only from existing components, which could be bought elsewhere. So the 8088 microprocessor from Intel was used, which was much less capable than the Lilith (it did not efficiently support pixel operations for example), but this design had the advantage of minimizing the time and costs of development.

Another difference between Lilith and PC was the programming language. Apart from a few third party compilers, the PC supported only Basic, a very simple language. Maybe too simple, since DOS itself was written in assembly language. On Lilith, as already mentioned, only Modula-2 was available, in which also all of Lilith's software was written.

The PC was incredible successful on the commercial market, its monthly sales figures were higher than those of any other office/home computer, despite the fact that Lilith was not only by far the better computer, but also faster and less expensive computers were also available at this time. The commercial success of the PC, which seems to contradict all market laws, is based on two key factors: the price and the tag IBM on the box. Both factors contribute jointly to its success, they cannot be regarded independently from each other.

The success of the PC in the industry has its roots, at least in part, in the way large companies are managed. Its middle managers usually have a budget, which allows them to make smaller investments under their own responsibility. Because the price mostly fit the frame of this budget, a PC could be bought without approval from IT's computer professionals. Although most managers didn't understand e.g. the implications of the obsolete operating system DOS, they were convinced that the PC is a useful tool since they had bought the same brand of computers which the computing center was full of. This way of establishing PCs in a company without approval of the IT department is a sad example for misplaced empowerment.

The widespread use of the PC in smaller businesses and private homes is due to an impact of the design, which IBM probably didn't anticipate. Since IBM bought nearly all components for the PC from third party manufacturers, it had no copyright on them, except for the BIOS. So when the company *Chips & Technologies* implemented all functions of the PC's motherboard in five chips and another company called *AMI* reprogrammed the BIOS without violating IBM's copyright, the production of PCs became very cheap and clones, which were assembled in countries with low wages, could be offered for half IBM's price. It came to the paradox situation that IBM lost market shares to companies like Dell and Compaq, although the sales figures for the PC went up.

The fact that PCs with the more than inappropriate operating system DOS could still be sold ten years later is another story, stemming from the establishment of a quasi monopoly position by aggressive marketing methods and from its misuse (see State of New York, et al. vs. Microsoft Corporation, conclusions of law, civil action no. 98-1233 (TPJ), 2000 D.C.Cir.). But that story is beyond the scope of this paper.

3 Small Startup Companies

The two examples of Siemens and IBM show that bringing new and innovative products to the market remains an opportunity for small flexible (startup-)companies. Therefore it is no wonder that the follow-up attempts to market Lilith were undertaken by such companies.

3.1 Diser AG

When Heinz Waldburger, an IT-manager at Nestlé SA, saw the Lilith for the first time, he was convinced that he had finally found the tool he needed in order to realize his vision. That was to build what we would today call a multimedia information server connected to personal computers as clients by a company-wide intranet. Thus he gave up his job to found Diser AG; the name is an acronym for Data Image Sound Emitter Receiver.

Heinz Waldburger wrote a business plan, organized about three million USD venture capital, hired some of Wirth's coworkers and students, leased office space in a building close to ETH's computing center and Wirth's office, and established Diser AG in spring 1983.

The business plan was basically as follows. Diser AG would need two years to deliver DISER-Tool (the client), DISER-Central (the information server), and DISER-Net (the network), as they were called. To generate revenues during this time, the Lilith should be reengineered and brought to the marketplace as a workstation for software engineering or as an advanced typesetting machine. It is pointless to speculate if the first goal of the plan, namely the DISER-project could have been achieved in time, or for example if Lilith was the appropriate machine for a DISER-Central, because Diser AG already failed to reach the second goal.

The reengineering of the Lilith, performed by Diser, was marginal and mostly cosmetic: a controller for Winchester disks, a new box, another keyboard, to name a few changes. Lilith's inherent weaknesses however, weren't tackled. Lilith was incompatible to everything else in the world of commercial data processing. It was a first class prototype computer, which showed how software engineering could be done, but to earn money an IBM mainframe was needed on which database applications in Cobol could be written.

To position Lilith as a typesetting machine, a lot more engineering would have been needed, as well as specialists for marketing and finance, who Diser didn't have. Apart from the incompatibility problem mentioned above, as a typesetting machine Lilith was useless without a laser printer. The price for a Lilith was about CHF 47,000 (USD 18,000) plus CHF 19,000 for the printer, which was very expensive for small shops like lawyers. In addition, professionally organized offices require a backup and an archive function, which Lilith didn't have at all. Also users of typesetting machines are not necessarily computer literate, which requires that Lilith is immune to errors that a computer specialist would never think of. I will explain this using an example.

Wirth's secretary used Lilith's word processing software in her daily work. Whenever she had written a letter, she stored it as a file under the recipient's name. That worked well until a letter should be sent to Mr. Müller. The word processing tool stored it without any warning message, but the command interpreter didn't accept Umlauts, so the secretary could neither access the letter any more, nor print it. This is particularly cumbersome for example for a lawyer who has an urgent letter to print and who doesn't have computer specialist in the office next door to fix the problem, unlike Wirth's secretary.

Even though Diser had sales offices in France and also in several US cities, in retrospect it is no surprise, because of the above mentioned weaknesses of Lilith, that the sales figures remained far behind expectations. With its price Diser positioned Lilith in the upper segment of the workstation market. In order to compete there with Sun, Apollo and others (see section 3.2), Lilith's weaknesses would have to have been eliminated by a complete reengineering of the original machine. Thus it is doubtful if, as stated in [Fur93], more venture capital alone, without rethinking the strategy, would have created better results.

Finally in spring 1984, in a meeting in the Zunfthaus zur Meisen in Zurich, the shareholders decided with overwhelming majority to stop Diser's businesses and to liquidate all its assets. For some of the shareholders this decision meant the definitive loss of a very large amount of money; in their cases Lilith's seduction was stronger than economic prudence.

3.2 Workstations

Intuitively workstations are different from personal computers although there is no precise definition for them. Adele Goldberg in [Gol88] gives the only definition we found: *A workstation is a relatively large and expensive personal computer, which is used by professionals for their work.* We'll leave it up to the reader to decide if Lilith was a workstation in conformance with this definition, but since Lilith had to compete with workstations on the market for office/home computers, we have to consider them in this article too.

The history of Sun Microsystems has some parallels with Diser AG, so it is interesting to see which differences may have lead to Sun's overwhelming success. In the early eighties at Stanford University work was in progress on an internal network consisting of workstations based on the 68000 chip from Motorola. When Andreas von Bechtolsheim, a PhD student and principal designer of the workstation, realized that there was some demand for it, he offered the workstation to several companies, but none of them were interested in marketing it. So in 1982, Andreas together with three former students from Stanford and Berkeley founded Sun Microsystems (the name is an acronym for Stanford University-Network).

Sun did not build its workstation from scratch, but used existing components with standardized interfaces whenever possible. The processors were taken from the Motorola 68000 family, originally 16-bit microprocessors which were upgraded to 32-bit later on, and the operating system named SunOS was a rebuild of Berkeley Unix. In this way, Sun wasn't forced to write a lot of application software for its machines. To establish local area networks Sun workstations used the Ethernet and had already implemented TCP/IP, later to become the protocol of the Internet. A SCSI bus could be used to add disks and other peripheral devices. Sun used the term *open system* for its design principle.

It is of interest to note that Sun was not the first company that built Unix-based workstations. Apollo Computers for example, founded in 1980 by Bill Poduska who formerly worked on the Multics project at MIT, combined the 32-bit single-chip microprocessor from Motorola with Berkeley Unix, but used its own network protocol *Apollo Domain*.

At first glance, the use of powerful 32-bit processors and of the multi-user operating system Unix in office/home computers seemed over the top. But it turned out later that this design contained the concepts for the future and it was thus one of the key factors for Sun's commercial success. Workstations became more and more integrated in local area networks. In 1984 Sun released the source code of its network file system (NFS), which made the physical location of a file (nearly) transparent to the user, and rightly claimed: *the network is the computer.* It's obvious that a network is a multi-user computer and that the local operating systems had to reflect this fact.

When the computing paradigm shifted to client/server computing, Unix was the appropriate operating system for servers. Since homogeneous networks are easier to administrate and to maintain than heterogeneous ones, Unix was used in the client computers too, although some of its features were needed in servers only. But with a 32-bit address size and the decreasing costs of hardware, memory size was no longer an issue.

Finally it is important to note that for computers used by professionals, security is an issue. Without going into detail, it is commonly known that multi-user systems are less susceptible to viruses than single-user systems like DOS. Not to forget that Unix was almost entirely written in the 3rd generation language C, which made this language the lingua franca for system development.

In summary, with their operating system the workstations were ready for the upcoming developments, whereas Lilith, with its simple single-user system Medos was stuck in a dead end. The graphical user interface, the only advantage that Lilith initially had compared to workstations, was quickly overtaken, at the very latest by XWindows from MIT. Transforming Lilith in a commercially successful workstation-like computer would therefore have required a complete redesign of its hardware and operating system – but would the result still have been a Lilith computer?

3.3 Apple's Lisa and Macintosh

The discussion about the reasons for Lilith's commercial failures would be incomplete without mentioning Apple's products *Lisa* and *Macintosh*. Both computers have some similarities with the Lilith and with each other, but contrary to the Macintosh, Lisa was a commercial flop. In the following we will examine this astonishing result more closely.

In our classification of large vs. startup companies, Apple Computer Inc is a hybrid. Founded in 1976 by Steven Wozniak and Steve Jobs, five years later Apple had a strong experience in designing and building hard- and software for office/home computers. With the Apple II, they also had a nearly self-selling product. With several thousand employees one could consider Apple as a large company, well established on the market for office/home computers.

On the other hand Apple's chairman was not a business man but the cofounder and technical visionary Steve Jobs. He had less interest in the sales figures of the next quarter or the upcoming year, but more in thinking about what computers will look like in ten years. So Apple took higher risks in developing very advanced computers, which usually characterizes startup companies.

Lisa

In 1979 Jobs had seen the Alto computer at Xerox PARC (see also section 5.1), which convinced him that the upcoming computer generation would have a user interface consisting of a raster screen, windows, icons and mouse. Jobs managed to hire one of Xerox's key designers and Apple established a team to develop a successor for the Apple II. The result was the Lisa computer, which was brought on the market in 1983.

Apart from the processor – Lisa used the 68000 chip from Motorola –, Lilith and Lisa were pretty similar. After Xerox's Star (see section 5.1), Lisa was the first commercially available computer with a graphical user interface (GUI), including mouse, bitmap screen, windows, and icons. A new operating system was also developed for Lisa. Because of the GUI and the new operating system, Apple had to write all the software for the Lisa, which made the development particularly expensive (the rumor is more than USD 100 million development costs). It is hard to estimate if the costs and the duration of reengineering Lilith would have been in a similar order of magnitude?

Three reasons why Lisa's sales figures remained behind the expectations were identified: this computer was too slow and too expensive and it came at the wrong point in time.

Too slow: Although Lisa had a 68000 chip initially, this chip only ran with a 4 to 5 MHz clock rate. Additionally it had no supporting chips, as for example the Amiga from Commodore and the Atari ST had at that time. To allow the user to fully enjoy the GUI however, more power would have been necessary.

Too expensive and at the wrong point in time: Lisa was officially unveiled exactly at that time when the potential customers were eager to see IBM's first PC. Though Lisa was one of the most innovative computers at this time, two circumstances may have spoken against the purchase of a Lisa. It cost about four times more than an IBM PC and at the official presentation of Lisa, Steve Jobs told the audience about the soon to be released Macintosh computer. The new machine would have basically the same capabilities as the Lisa, would be cost only a fraction of it and would be incompatible to it.

Eventually Lisa was renamed Macintosh XL and it could emulate MacOS programs, but its sales figures remained minimal.

Macintosh

The Macintosh computer was developed mostly parallel to the Lisa. Initially Steve Jobs was the head of the Lisa development team. In 1980, when Apple Computers underwent a major reorganization, he lost this position but a couple of months later, he headed the (smaller) Macintosh development team. Jobs directed the team to his ideas which hadn't much changed since he had left the Lisa group. So the Macintosh was also equipped with a Motorola 68000 processor running at 8 MHz clock rate, and had a GUI with raster screen and mouse like the Lisa. Its multitasking operating system *MacOS* was also developed from scratch (and incompatible to Lisa's *Work*). Obviously MacOS also required some new software called MacWrite, MacPaint, MacTerminal, etc.

Finally Jobs demanded that everything except the keyboard fit into a small box, so that the Macintosh became the first portable computer. Developed faster and with less people and less money, the Macintosh was unveiled only a year after the Lisa at a quarter of its price, announced by only one advertisement during Super Bowl 1984.

Even so, initially the Macintosh didn't sell as expected. The fact that it had not enough memory was fixed within a few months, but that didn't improve the situation. The breakthrough came only with the twin introductions of the LaserWriter, the first affordable PostScript laser printer for the Macintosh, and the PageMaker software. Together they made the Macintosh an inexpensive tool for desktop publishing.

The examples discussed so far, show that the good design of a computer does not necessarily guarantee commercial success. In many cases only an application tailored to the machine is the impetus for a customer to buy it. Consequently, the last attempt to market Lilith was to sell an application program with it.

4 Lilith as CAD Tool

As one of Niklaus Wirth's coworkers during the design and implementation of the Lilith, Richard Ohran's never ending intention was to market Lilith. So he was involved in Diser AG as one of its first employees, hoping that Lilith's obsolete hardware would soon be replaced as promised. But Diser's management changed its mind after a month or so and Richard quit the job in order to establish his own company.

In 1984 Modula Corp. was founded by Richard and his brother in their hometown Provo, UT, where wages are lower than in Switzerland or in silicon valley. The latter should not be disregarded since Modula Corp. had approximately only one sixth of Diser's funding; not to mention Apple's budgets for Lisa and Macintosh (see section 3.3). It was the year when the Macintosh was unveiled and hence Lilith was no longer a prototype computer with the most advanced GUI. Therefore fundraising for Lilith became more and more difficult.

Richard had recognized that Lilith's fundamental hardware technology was already obsolete in 1984, but its software architecture was a promising platform for development. Because a complete redesign of the hardware wasn't affordable for Modula Corp., not even a change of the CPU to 32 bit or to put it on a single chip, the company didn't try to market Lilith directly, but to profit from its inherent ideas.

To start, Modula Corp. had a few orders from universities and research departments within the industry, for example from ETH. So some minor improvements to the original Lilith were carried out. The removable 10 MB disk was replaced by a 50 MB fix disk in Winchester technology, a floppy disk drive was added, and the whole machine was put in a wooden box half the original size. Finally the Kermit protocol [DaC84] was implemented in order to allow data exchange with other computers via the serial interface.

Modula's main emphasis however, was on the development of CAD software for circuit board layout using the Modula-2 programming language and Lilith as development tool. With this suite of software Modula Corp. could sell about 250 Lilith machines as CAD workstations, for example to customers like Signetics (see [BOB00]). The goal however remained to migrate the CAD software as quickly as possible to a viable commercial platform, which, it was recognized, Lilith would never be.

The software was eventually migrated to the IBM PC, but even then it failed to succeed. It is beyond the scope of this paper to examine all reasons for the failure of this CAD program to compete in the CAD marketplace. One was certainly the miniscule amount of support that Modula Corp. could afford. Neither on Lilith nor on PC did the software generate enough revenue, so the company was caught in a circulus vitiosus. Because it had no credit at the bank, it had to cut back on people, which reduced the support and therefore the revenue further, until there was nothing left. So the last attempt to market Lilith ended 1988 by simply running out of money.

5 Conclusion

Nowadays the development lines of PC and workstation have converged and for most users there are no more differences in terms of performance and/or comfort between, for example a Pentium with Linux or Windows NT and a PA-RISC with HP-UX. In the early eighties however, workstations and PCs were completely different in nearly all aspects such as operating system, performance, user interface, and price. Lilith fell into the gap between workstation and PC. That's the main reason why it wasn't successful on the commercial market. Being neither fish nor meat, Lilith implemented too far advanced concepts for the PC, but its processor and operating system were inappropriate for a workstation.

Another computer in this gap, similar to the Lilith, was the Macintosh from Apple. The amount of time and money Apple needed to make it commercially successful, was so high that no startup company could afford it and no larger company took the risk to do the same for Lilith. So less than one thousand Liliths were built in total, the last one in 1987.

5.1 Could one have known better?

I think "probably yes", looking at the fate of Xerox's computers Alto and Star. The research lab PARC of the Xerox Corp. had the vision of personal distributed computing and this vision materialized in the first prototype of the Alto computer in 1973 ([TML79]). At PARC, there were visions of the office of the future, in which computers play a dominant role and the Alto had all the features to become such an office computer.

The Alto had strongly influenced Lilith's design; it already had many features that Lilith had too: a bitmapped screen, a WYSIWYG word processor, a mouse, laser printer, Smalltalk language, Ethernet, and software for combining text and graphics in the same document. Initially the Alto was very expensive, but with some improvements to the hardware in 1976 its price came down to the order of magnitude of twice the price of Xerox's most expensive copy machine.

But the Alto still wasn't offered on the market for the same reason, as Siemens didn't accept Lilith: it was too far ahead of its time. In the mid-seventies Xerox made money by renting copy machines. That was the kind of business with which the top management was familiar, which they could calculate and correctly predict, but they had no experience in the computer business. So, for example, they didn't believe in flexible programmable word processing, but did favor type writers in which text processing was locked in hardware.

These are certainly not the only reasons why Xerox didn't market the Alto computer; for a more detailed description see [SmA99].

Times were changing, the appearance of the Apple II in 1978 implied that computers were no longer banned to back offices and Xerox's upper management changed its mind too. About 1500 Altos were built and many were given to universities, used for marketing trials and instructing sales people in the usage of the complex technology.

Finally, Xerox transformed the Alto into a product, which was brought to the market as the Star computer in 1981. The Star however was a commercial disaster. It was incompatible to all existing computers and therefore no software existed for it. Xerox did not publish its API and programming language, so that no application programs could be written by third parties. They were exclusively implemented by engineers within Xerox, but without the help of the marketing and finance departments. One result was that the Star didn't have a spreadsheet program, whereas VisiCalc was the reason why many people bought an Apple II computer.

The second obstacle to the commercial success was the price. Not only that the price of more than USD 15,000 was about ten to twelve times higher than that for an Apple II, a single Star computer wasn't useful. One had to install a couple of Stars and a laser printer, all connected by an Ethernet. Since in the early eighties the intended customers for the Star did not have much experience in personal computing, such a high investment in a Star network seemed too risky to many IT-managers, in particular because the low risk alternative Apple II existed.

The stories of Alto and Lilith sound pretty similar don't they?

5.2 Could it have been done better?

In retrospect, I think one has to affirm this question. As innovative as Lilith was, the methods for marketing Niklaus Wirth's ideas could have been just as revolutionary. Namely giving away the source code of all of Lilith's system software, i.e. operating system, Modula-2 compiler, linking loader, debugger, command interpreter, etc. for free. Giving away source code is nothing particular today, well known under the term *open source* (see [OSD97]), although admittedly today it's easier to organize than it was in the pre-Internet times. In the case of Lilith, the distribution of software had to be accompanied by founding a company like Modula Corp., which carried out only minimal improvements to Lilith's hardware and produced it inexpensively. We will now examine this scenario further for the time around 1980.

Apart from the much larger and less well structured Unix, Lilith's software would have been the first publicly available operating system for office/home computers. The clean interfaces of its modules would have made it an ideal candidate for use in operating system classes at universities. Lilith computers certainly would also have been used in most of these classes, because the understanding of the principles of a system does not necessarily require the most modern hardware.

On the other hand, if someone wanted to adapt the software to a different hardware and/or processor, he or she would have needed a Lilith computer as a development system and for cross compilation. This would have been true in particular for Apple computers. Why should they spend money on developing their own operating systems for Lisa and Macintosh, if there is one around which supports all functions of the planned GUI. And why should Bill Gates have bought the CP/M derivative for USD 50,000 if he could get another operating system for free?

In summary, by the proposed approach Lilith certainly could have been sold in the order of a few thousand machines. This doesn't mean that it would have piled up as much money as possible, which by the way, never was the goal of professor Wirth's research. But Lilith would most likely have saved mankind from MS-DOS, which would have outweighed any commercial success by far.

6 Acknowledgements

I have to thank Jirka Hoppe, Richard Ohran, David Peet, Peter Salus, Manfred Sommer, Chuck Thacker, and Heinz Waldburger for providing me with valuable information about the beginning of personal computing and for commenting on earlier drafts of this paper. Thanks are also deserved by my wife Petra and the Zivi Andreas Witzel, who supported me in getting and reading the necessary literature. Without the help of all of these people it would have been impossible for me to write this article.

7 References

[BOB00] R. Burton et al.: The chip company that made $100M with Modula-2, in L. Böszörményi et al. (eds.), The School of Niklaus Wirth, Heidelberg, 2000

[DaC84] F. Da Cruz, B. Catchings: Kermit: A File-Transfer Protocol for Universities, Part 1 and 2, BYTE, June/July 1984

[Fur93] F. Furger: Informatik-Innovationen aus der Schweiz? Verlagsgemeinschaft Technopark Zürich, 1993

[Gol88] A. Goldberg: History of Personal Workstations, Addison-Wesley, New York 1988

[Knu00] S. E. Knudsen: Medos in Retrospect, in L. Böszörményi et al. (eds.), The School of Niklaus Wirth, Heidelberg, 2000

[OSD97] The Open Source Definition, Version 1.7, http://www.opensource.org/osd.html

[Pom85] G. Pomberger et al.: Lilith und Modula-2, Werkzeuge der Softwaretechnik, Carl Hanser Verlag, München 1985

[SmA99] D. Smith, R. Alexander: Fumbling the Future, toExcel, New York, 1999

[TML79] C. Thacker et al.: Alto: A personal computer, XEROX Corp. Palo Alto Research Center, 1979, technical report CSL-79-11

[Wag82] B. Wagner: Das Dateikonzept der Siemens Pascal Programmiersysteme, in H. Langmaack et al. (eds.), Implementierung Pascal-artiger Programmiersprachen, Teubner, Stuttgart, 1982

[Wir81] N. Wirth: The Personal Computer Lilith, ETH Zurich, Institut für Informatik, 1981, technical report n. 40

The Chip Company that Made $100M with MODULA-2

Robert Burton, Farrell Ostler, Philips Semiconductors
Thom Boyer, Novell Corporation
Fon Brown, Evans and Sutherland
Matt Morrise, Intel Corporation

Abstract

In 1981 the Philips/Signetics design group in Orem, Utah learned about Modula-2 and the Lilith computer.

Within two years, 25 chip designers each had a Lilith computer to do schematic capture, device modeling, and circuit simulation. All the programming had been done by two student programmers. The programs were ecstatically reviewed by a team of outside consultants hired by Philips to review all the available CAD software.

The Orem operation became extremely profitable, and every type of CAD and system software was written in Modula-2 by a small and changing group of student programmers.

1 The Lilith Revolution

Niklaus Wirth is justly famous for his computer languages. He and Richard Ohran also took the engineering workstation out of hiding at Xerox [10] and made it available to anybody with $10K. The Lilith [14, 9, 11] was half a Vax 780 when 780's cost $200K. Coupled with Modula-2 [15], an elegant modular programming language, and an economical but complete software environment [3, 4, 6, 7], Lilith was ripe fruit, ready to be plucked and put to work on real-world problems. At the Philips/Signetics integrated circuit design center in Orem, Utah there was no shortage of such problems [2].

1.1 Designer (and Programmer) Heaven

In 1983 Philips Semiconductors hired Productivity Products, Inc. to review their CAD software and hardware worldwide. In their final report, PPI devoted 7 pages to Orem, far more than to any other location. Their Orem review begins with the following paragraph:

"Working on the hairy edge of corporate regulations, Dr. Burton acquired a powerful workstation and a programmer for the design group in Orem. In two years, the most capable CAD environment in Philips had been developed from scratch. This Utah 'skunk-works' resides in a house trailer without a toilet and uses software components supplied by a very small and unknown workstation vendor. The CAD environment contains less than 12,000 lines of Modula software which provides the only integrated CAD environment in the company."

PPI reports widespread dissatisfaction among CAD users and developers, but notes that "In Orem, designers and developers were saying such things as, 'Gee it's really fun to work here' and 'The reason Orem is profitable is that people have the tools to actually work here.'"

1.2 What Happened?

PPI comments "This dramatic software development story may have occurred because of the confluence of two rare elements – an excellent programming environment and a super-star programmer." The environment was the Modula editor, compiler, and debugger supplied by ETH along with the Lilith computer. The programmer was Matt Morrise.

The harvest really came in 1984. The Orem design group was supposed to be second sourcing a family of chips specified by another company, but they were able to become the leading supplier. Throughout 1984 net profits ran about $5M per month, even though every imaginable expense in the company was being charged to the Orem operation. The circuit design mangers, Jim Dunkley quickly followed by Dick Morrell, had made a gamble that was going to pay off handsomely for a decade.

2 The Love Affair with Modula

The Lilith had a long life for a computer, and was replaced by another, much faster Modula computer called the Eve, which is described in a later section. Virtually all the CAD programs used in Orem were written and used on these machines. In roughly chronological order, they included the following:

Program or Hardware	Authors
Transistor circuit simulator [8]	Matt Morrise, Bob Burton
Schematic editor	Matt Morrise
Device model generator	Tom Fletcher, Jim Dunkley
Long Real compiler	Thom Boyer, Matt Morrise
Color graphics board for Lilith	David Brewer
Layout editor	Bob Schillmoeller, Brian Jarvis
Structured Modeling Language	Fon Brown
Layout design rule checks	Thom Boyer, Fon Brown
Device parameter extraction	Ed Weagel
Leadframe LRC program	Bob Burton

Program or Hardware	Authors
68020/68881 Modula-2 system	David Brewer, Thom Boyer
Netlist extraction from layout [5]	Brian Jarvis
Layout versus schematic check	Fon Brown, Thom Boyer
Logic simulator and HDL	Matt Morrise
Eve computer	Farrell Ostler
Eve microcode	Fon Brown
Eve multi-tasking operating system	Fon Brown
Eve compiler, debugger	Thom Boyer, Matt Morrise
Hardware support and Eve "production"	Steve Reilly
Semi-automatic layout program	Matt Morrise
Automated chip characterization	Tim Frodsham
Networking	Fon Brown, Thom Boyer
Automatic routing, Edit port	Doug Lee

The Lilith provided open source code for the operating system and a simple architecture. These two points were important because they removed the barriers which often make software production so difficult, namely the virtually infinite complexity of the programming environment and impossibility of finding out what is really going on inside there. The Lilith was a tool to be used, not a barrier to be overcome.

These two traditions continued with the Eve. Imagine having the hardware designer, and authors of the operating system and compiler all available to those writing applications. In most computing environments you can't buy access like that for any price.

In 1991, Philips Semiconductors had recently lost a lot of money. Although Orem was still profitable, the plant was old and its closure was announced in January 1992. The design group would be transferred to Albuquerque, the Eves and the CAD software would go with them, but the programmers would be left behind. The programmers formed a company called Orem Programming Partners, and Philips gave OPP non-exclusive rights to the software, and an Eve for each programmer.

OPP secured a contract from the US Air Force to port the logic and circuit simulators to the IBM PC and make improvements:

Project	Principal Author
Port to TopSpeed Modula on PC	David Owens
Good CAD program documentation	Keith Howick
Concurrent logic simulation with VHDL	Matt Morrise
Additions to circuit simulation	Fon Brown
Cross compilers to C and ADA	Thom Boyer

Bob Burton went to Albuquerque with Philips. He wrote a circuit optimization program on the Eve. It was ported to the HP workstations that replaced the Eves, using Thom Boyer's cross compiler to C and an X-Windows interface by David Owens. It is being extensively used and has made a real contribution.

In a just completed final report on a minor project, Burton wrote "Listings of programs written exclusively for this project are given in Appendix B. [25 pages] The programming language is Modula-2, which is as readable as pseudo code. All of these programs have been cross-compiled into C, and are running on the HP workstations."

3 Eve You Would Love to Spend Your Life With

By 1987, the Lilith computer and Modula-2 CAD software were established and reliable performers. The decision to base a production environment for chip design on Professor Wirth's ETH work had proven to be a wise one.

The group was willing to tackle enhancements to the underlying hardware and software where this was needed to support our targeted applications. This was evidence of a "can do" attitude but also a necessity; there was no outside maintenance or support available. In any case, our efforts to maintain and evolve the system were blessed by being based on a system of clarity, limited complexity and, therefore, considerable accessibility.

At this point in time, the Lilith technology was about ten years old, which is pretty old in "computer years". Applications were starting to bump into some of Lilith's inherent limitations of a 16-bit data word, limited address space, and speed, particularly the speed of the floating-point operations needed for circuit simulation.

A project was undertaken to transform Lilith into her own successor, Eve. In a happy coincidence, the fastest floating-point chipset available at the time was also the only one that also supported integer, shift and logic operations. A new microprogrammed CPU was designed around this chipset. When converting a Lilith into an Eve, the three printed circuit boards that held the former CPU were replaced by two boards, one being the new CPU and the other a new memory. The rest of the Lilith was retained. The reuse of peripherals helped to save dollars and manpower.

The Eve was an evolution of the Lilith and retained Wirth's fundamental concepts in the hardware, instruction set and system software. There were, however, some distinguishing features. We mention now, in brief, some of the characteristics of the Eve system, including new features that Wirth, given his high threshold for including a feature in a design, might well have challenged.

3.1 Writeable Microcode

As the Eve chipset was being designed, it was determined that the microcode would be executed from RAM rather than ROM, since no ROM was available that was fast enough for the purpose. The writeable control store, in conjunction with compiler and operating system support allowed for the introduction of microcode modules, discussed below.

3.2 Putting Parity to Work

Modula-2 programmers, unless they are very careful, will be familiar with the pesky and hard to diagnose errors caused by uninitialized variables. While the parity circuit of the Eve memory board was being designed, it was realized that, if we were willing to combine parity errors and uninitialized variable errors into a single class, a writable parity bit could enable runtime detection.

With an instruction for invalidating the parity on a range of memory, it was simple to add an option to invalidate all allocated or freed memory, and to have the compiler invalidate all local and global variables. Thus, any access to uninitialized memory would cause a run-time exception, allowing the Signetics programmers to virtually eliminate that class of errors, which, it was discovered, existed even in long-used production programs.

3.3 Instruction Set

The Eve instruction set [1] continued in the spirit of its predecessor; that is, it was both compact and efficient. Given equivalent clock speeds, Eve code ran slightly faster than the 680X0 and 80X86 but took half the space.

The instruction set was extensible; microcode modules could be loaded at run-time. This made it possible to use highly optimized application specific instructions. An example of this was the circuit simulator, whose inner-loop LU-factorization routine was re-implemented as a microcoded procedure, resulting in significant speedup.

3.4 Operating System

The operating system of the Eve (called Eden) was patterned after that of the Lilith (MEDOS) with a few notable exceptions: 1) it had a hierarchical file structure, 2) it was fully multi-tasking, and 3) it managed both regular and microcode modules. The user interface was simple and intuitive, and it provided a seamless network interface to other Eve computers.

3.5 Dynamic Arrays

Besides the ability to create separately compiled modules, probably the most important advance in Modula relative to Pascal was the addition of open array (`ARRAY OF` *`type`*) parameter types. This made it possible to create library routines of much more general applicability.

However, a frequent nuisance in writing real world applications is the fact that many times array sizes are not known at compile-time. The typical solution is to declare a pointer to a huge array, but to initialize it at run-time with a memory allocation that is only as large as necessary. This does work, but the resulting program looses the protection of effective bounds checking.

The underlying concept of open array parameters inspired Thom Boyer to add dynamic arrays (`DYNAMIC ARRAY OF` *`type`*). Both types are implemented as a pointer and an integer, which indicate the address and size of the array. Dynamic arrays differ from open arrays in two ways. First, open arrays are always parameters, but dynamic arrays can be variables as well. Second, the pointer of an open array is managed completely by the compiler, whereas a dynamic array is always heap-allocated and must be managed by the programmer via explicit calls to NEW, DELETE, and RESIZE. Dynamic arrays maintain the actual size of the array at runtime, so array bounds checks, when enabled, actually check the right thing.

Although dynamic arrays were created primarily to allow for more general implementations of types like vectors and matrices, their greatest benefit on a daily basis was probably that `DYNAMIC ARRAY OF` *`CHAR`* made strings much easier to deal with.

4 Why Didn't Modula Take Over The World?

We believe this is an important question. The Orem environment was essentially a university environment. Bob Burton was a Brigham Young University professor, and all the programmers started as students.

After the favorable outside review, Orem was invited to bring some Liliths to the company headquarters in California and demonstrate. The designers were very impressed and the atmosphere was "how many of these machines can we get?" There was a large meeting at the end of the demo, and the Diser salesman was asked, "How will you maintain these computers in Sunnyvale?" He replied, we will give you complete schematics and documentation so you can maintain them yourselves.

This was a very sensible answer. The technicians in Orem were less expensive and far more competent than those supplied by outside vendors. But the USA branch of Philips managed its computer hardware by the same dictums as most other US corporations:

(A) No one ever got fired for buying from IBM.
(B) If you are very daring, you might buy from DEC.

If a power cord fell out of the socket, they called IBM or DEC to plug it in again. Now days, we call EDS.

On the software side, the history of Modula would have been completely different if Microsoft had adopted it. But if Modula didn't take over the world, it appears that Lilith or at least a Lilith-like architecture might. The similarities between the Lilith architecture and the Java Virtual Machine are obvious: a stack machine operating on short instructions compiled from a language co-designed with the architecture. The inventors of Java credit Modula as a predecessor of Java. Would they consider Lilith a predecessor of the Java VM?

4 Acknowledgments

Our co-workers and managers, many of whom have been mentioned in the text and its tables, are gratefully acknowledged (with apologies for inevitable oversights). We hope that our colleagues, as do we, remember fondly the Orem period as an exciting and rewarding one in their professional lives.

The evangelism of Richard Ohran resulted in Robert Burton becoming aware of the Lilith computer.

One might ask what role Niklaus Wirth played in establishing, encouraging and supporting the work at Signetics, Orem. The answer, perhaps surprisingly when we note that academicians are often motivated to actively pursue industrial liaisons, is that he played no significant direct role at all. We consider it a testament to the soundness of his ideas and the quality of his (group's) work that an industrial enterprise, with virtually no hardware or software support, was able to build a significant production CAD environment on the Lilith/Eve platform. Every day we were beneficiaries of his insistence on uncluttered, transparent design in computer systems.

For that silent but thunderous contribution to our commercial success we give our most heartfelt thanks.

References

1. Brown, F: *The Design of an Instruction Set for the Eve Engineering Workstation*, MS Thesis, Computer Science Dept., Brigham Young U., Provo, Utah, 1989.
2. Burton, R., Brewer, D., Penman, R., Schilmoeller, R: 'A Cost-Effective CAD System', *Proc. of the IEEE 1985 Custom Integrated Circuits Conf.*, pp. 356-362.
3. Geissmann, L, *et al*: *Lilith Handbook*, Institut für Informatik, Eidgenossiche Technische Hochschule, Zurich, 1982.
4. Gutknecht J: *System Programming in Modula-2: Mouse and Bitmap Display*, Eidgenossiche Technische Hochschule, Zurich, Berichte des Institutes fur Informatik, Nr 56, 1983.
5. Jarvis, B: *Determination of the Electrical Network from a Hierarchical Graphics Database*, MS Thesis, Computer Science Dept., Brigham Young U., Provo, Utah, 1990.
6. Knudsen, S: *Medos-2: A Modula-2 Oriented Operating System for the Personal Computer Lilith*, Dissertation 7346, Eidgenossiche Technische Hochschule, Zurich, 1983.

7. Knudsen, S: Medos in Retrospect, in this book, 2000.
8. Morrise, M: *Mathematical Modeling of Integrated Circuits*, MS Thesis, Mathematics Dept., Brigham Young U., Provo, Utah, 1984.
9. Ohran, R: *Lilith: A Workstation Computer for Modula-2*, Dissertation 7646, Eidgenossiche Technische Hochschule, Zurich, 1984.
10. Thacker, C., *et al*: *Alto: A personal computer*, XEROX Corp. Palo Alto Research Center, 1979, technical report CSL-79-11.
11. Wagner, B: Lilith Meets the World of Business, in this book, 2000.
12. Wirth, N: *The Personal Computer Lilith*, Eidgenossiche Technische Hochschule, Zurich, Berichte des Institutes fur Informatik, Nr 40, 1981.
13. Wirth N: The Personal Computer Lilith. *Proc. 5th Intl. Conf. on Software Engineering* 1981, 2-16.
14. Wirth, N: The Personal Computer Lilith, A Wassermann Ed., *Software Development Environments*, IEEE Computer Society Press, 1981.
15. Wirth, N: *Programming in Modula-2*, Third Corrected Edition, Springer-Verlag, 1985.
16. Wirth, N: From Programming Language Design to Computer Construction (Turing Award Lecture). *Comm. ACM* 28(2): 159-164, 1985.

FFF97 – Oberon in the Real World

Dr. Josef Templ
Software Templ OEG

Abstract

The Oberon programming language and system, subsequently called the Oberon technology, are well known in the software research community. Few applications, however, exist outside academic institutions. This paper describes one of them (FFF97), which constitutes a database front end application that has been in mission critical use by more than 25 concurrent users since 1998. FFF97 makes full use of Oberon's innovations including dynamic loading, commands, garbage collection, type extension, integrated text and form system, component technologies, model/view separation, low resource consumption, etc. It is claimed that choosing the Oberon technology and a particular approach to software construction, known under the term 'Prototyping', was of vital importance for this project, which, as one of the rare examples of custom software development projects, was completed within the scheduled time and budget without compromising quality or functionality.

1 Introduction

The successful application of research results to real world problems can be considered the ultimate justification for spending money on pure research and as a proof of the correctness and relevance of the research results. In the field of software engineering, one controversial research project was the Oberon project [1], carried out by N. Wirth and J. Gutknecht at ETH Zurich starting in the late 80s. Many computer professionals still doubt the advantages and relevance of this technology because it started from scratch and ignored industry standards, and because it appears to be too simple to compare favorably against industry standard technologies. This paper describes the story of FFF97, a database front end application based on the Oberon technology, that has been in mission-critical use by more than 25 persons since 1998. FFF97 embodies a perfect example of applying the results of the Oberon project to the real world, not because it shows that the problem could equally well be solved in Oberon, but because it shows that the problem could *better* be solved in Oberon. In fact, we are not aware of any other system that would have been suited better to this particular task.

In the following chapters we will describe the application domain, the chosen approach to software development, the rationale for choosing the Oberon technology, architectural and implementational aspects of the developed system. We will also present a summary of vital points and some general remarks.

2 The Application Domain

FFF97 is a tool to manage funding for applied research projects by an Austrian governmental organisation (FFF, Forschungsförderungsfonds der gewerblichen Wirtschaft). Activities include registration of all sorts of received postal matter (most notably applications for funding), grading applications with respect to technical, economic and other properties, requesting additional or missing information, maintaining groups of applicants for joint applications, association of FFF staff with individual applications and subtasks, maintenance of funding proposals and funding decisions, maintenance of a calendar of monthly presidential decision sessions, communication with applicants, answering ad-hoc queries for applicants, automatic or semi-automatic production of printed letters to applicants, automatic reminders for various purposes, full text search in text documents, printer management, checking access rights based on user roles, keeping track of travels to applicants and other travels, generating address lists for a large volume of letters, maintaining variables for current interest rates for various purposes, maintenance of third party funds and communication funding proposals and decisions with third parties, grading the project outcome and monitoring how money is spent, carrying out payments, maintaining liabilities, automatic statistics for the yearly funds report and for accounting purposes as well as for the distribution of workloads among the FFF staff, automatic account creation and booking in an electronic accounting system, automatic payments in both directions, etc.

The above list is by no means complete and is continually extended with new services and refinements to existing services. However, it should be sufficient to show that it is a real world problem and it is non-trivial by the sheer amount of different activities. At first glance it appears to be a typical database application where one of the many existing 4GL tools would provide the perfect development environment. However, complications arise when the target platform and environment is taken into account and the need for text integration is investigated further.

3 The Target Platform

FFF97 was supposed to run in an existing Windows PC network, featuring Intel i486 CPUs at 33 or 40 MHz with 16 MB of main memory. The operating system being used was Windows 3.1 with a Novell file server. In 1996 this was no longer on the cutting edge , but quite common in offices that cannot afford to upgrade all their PCs every two years. Upgrading the CPUs was not possible for technical reasons, because the low-cost motherboards were simply not compatible with any CPU upgrade available then. Given the tough hardware limitations, 4GL tools were ruled out completely, because they tend to create bulky and slow solutions as can be seen by the project history.

4 The Project History

FFF had been using a Philips P4000 database system with dumb terminals for applications management and accounting parallel to a Windows PC network for other typical office activities. It decided to move to a unified PC solution in order to

- upgrade to state of the art client-server technology,
- get rid of the dependency on no longer supported P4000 systems,
- increase the speed of database operations,
- eliminate the duality of two completely incompatible systems (P4000 and the Windows PC network) on every desktop,
- provide for more flexibility in respect to new services,
- improve client interaction, and to
- improve integration of text documents.

A first attempt by a subsidiary of an Austrian bank corporation to create a solution based on Oracle Forms4 failed due to unbearable response times and other user acceptance problems. The system used Microsoft Word as a text component and was able to create texts with database information included, which was quite reasonable in principle. For unknown reasons, however, it took several minutes and thousands of database requests until a simple data input form opened on a user's desktop PC. This behavior, among other problems, could not be repaired, so the solution was abandoned and the project was started again from scratch.

5 Restarting From Scratch

Given the tough hardware limitations and previous experience with Oracle's 4GL tool reported to us, we decided to rule out 4GL tools altogether and focus on an efficient and innovative general purpose programming system available then under the brand Oberon/F from the ETH spin-off company Oberon microsystems [2]. Oberon/F (later called BlackBox Component Builder) incorporated all the innovative ideas of the Oberon project in a form that was well suited for Windows PC users. In particular it used standard Windows look and feel (overlapping windows, menus and other GUI elements), supported Windows file systems and provided a database interface. Dynamic loading, command activation, garbage collection, an efficient compiler for a slightly extended version of the Oberon language and, most notably, text integration were preserved. Given these prerequisites, we estimated the initial development work as two man-years and the development time as one calendar year.

6 Prototyping

In order to avoid repeating the mistakes of the failed predecessor project it was decided to base the new project on prototyping. This means that there is no written detailed specification of the functions to be implemented. Instead, the developer creates a prototype of a functional unit based on a vague specification of the tasks to be performed. The working prototype is presented to the users and leads to more detailed requirements based on user feed-back. This takes into account that it is virtually impossible to specify the requirements of a complex system in detail and has the advantage that the user sees what (s)he will get long before the project is finished, thereby avoiding unpleasant surprises. An unbiased judge is installed that both parties (developers and users) agree to call if there is no agreement in the termination of the feed-back loop. The decision for one particular offer from among several companies was also made based on prototyping a subset of the required functionality in order to demonstrate the availability of adequate development tools and skills. For more details on prototyping see [3].

A few years later, refined variants of this approach to software development became known under the term *Extreme Programming* [8], which is based on four guiding principles in order to embrace change: Communication, Simplicity, Feedback, and Courage. Since we used the term prototyping throughout the project we shall stay with this term in the following.

7 Integrated Development and Execution Environment

A rapid application development system (RAD) is the technical foundation of any prototyping approach. Obviously, slow compilers and linkers as well as bulky executables are contradictory to prototyping. Even state of the art integrated development environments (IDEs) such as Visual Studio or Delphi are not sufficient. They provide a graphical user interface and sophisticated wizards for various common tasks, but under the hood they are little more than point-and-click interfaces for traditional command line tools and do not exceed the traditional application development model. They still need to link an application even if linking can make use of dynamic link libraries (DLLs). In order to run a modified version of a program, the program has to be rebuilt and started from the main entry point. Any internal program state between multiple executions is lost. Oberon's idea of an integrated development *and* execution environment (IDEE) makes it much more efficient to perform incremental changes to a program. Only the modules that have been changed are reloaded, the rest of the program is retained and preserves its state. Furthermore, any kind of repeating activity can be automated by means of user-defined commands, which can be executed from within the IDEE.

With BlackBox's form subsystem it is even possible to make many user interface changes by simply editing the form (just like editing graphics). There is no code generator involved. The form is stored as a document in a file and can be reloaded and used from there. This idea is based on the Gadgets[4] user interface toolkit of the ETH Oberon System 3 project and turned out to be an invaluable simplification of the development process. It clearly separates user interface concerns from the functionality of a program and permits real time GUI changes interactively with users, without even restarting the application.

Another aspect of rapid application development is the production of documentation in the form of online help texts. We used BlackBox's integrated text subsystem for writing help texts (as well as program texts) which avoids the need for external tools that make it slow, inconvenient and unreliable to create online documentation, especially for a large project.

In summary, with BlackBox we essentially end up with an "IDDEE", an integrated development, documentation and execution environment, which goes beyond what standard tools support.

8 Component Interaction

The following illustration gives an overview of FFF97's interaction with other components.

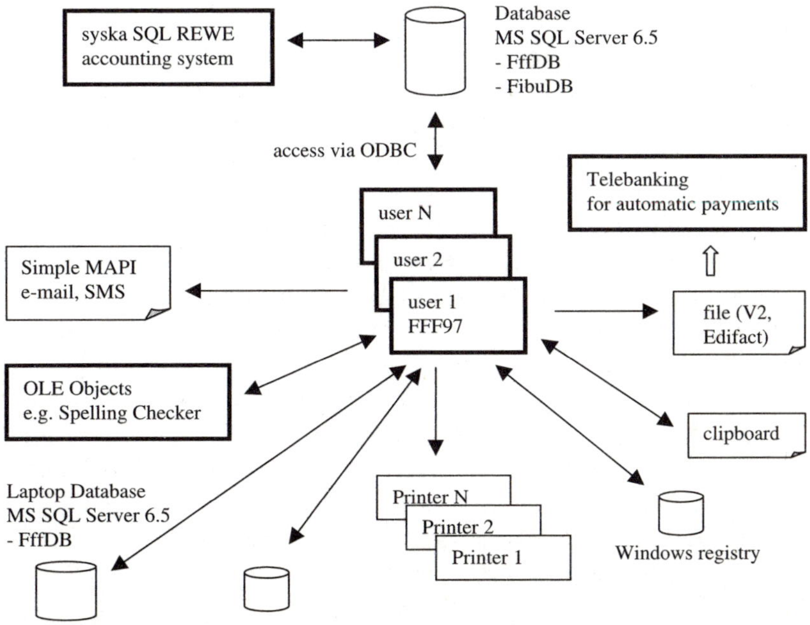

There is a common database server for both the FFF projects database and the database of the accounting system. This simplification has become possible by selecting an accounting system that is based on a client-server architecture (syska SQL REWE [5]) and supports Microsoft SQL Server [6], which we also managed to connect with FFF97. It allows us to access both databases from within FFF97 using only one database connection and even allows SQL commands that access both databases within one command. A second database connection is used for optional selective export of data to a local laptop database for users who use a laptop when travelling to applicants. So far, modified data cannot be imported from a laptop database, since this would require additional version control mechanisms (merge replication) not provided by MS SQL Server 6.5.

A standard telebanking program is used for carrying out automatic payments. The interface is simply a file that follows a particular syntax (called V2 or "Normdatenträger" and in the future will be an EDIFACT interchange consisting of PAYMUL and DIRDEB messages).

FFF97 can access any Windows file system and load and store files in various formats (ASCII formats, RTF, etc.). It can also import and export data using the Windows clipboard and can print to any Windows printer.

The Windows registry is used to store default settings per user, such as configurable window items, settings for automatic logins, printer configurations, etc. The Windows registry turned out to be a rather volatile database, especially when Windows is run in a Novell network, because with nearly every Novell upgrade or reconfiguration (carried out by a professional network administration company) all registry settings have been lost so far.

Since the FFF staff is distributed across multiple offices on multiple floors, each user has access to different printers and FFF97 allows each user to configure printers for various kinds of paper, e.g. blank paper on Printer 1, letter paper on Printer 2 and so on. Whenever a document is printed that is known to need letter paper, the preconfigured letter printer (defined by printer name, input tray and orientation) is provided as a default, which speeds up printing and avoids using the wrong kind of paper. Printer selection is not part of the standard BlackBox libraries, so we had to go through the intricacies of the Windows API for this purpose.

BlackBox supports integration of COM/OLE objects and we made use of this for connecting the Microsoft office spelling checker. This worked in principle but requires one of the Office Applications (e.g. Excel) to be loaded in order to get access to the spelling checker. The result is some waste of memory, startup delays, memory leaks (inside Excel) and slow communication with the spelling checker. The built-in BlackBox text subsystem also supports integration of OLE objects, which we used mainly for bitmap objects, but which the users also use sometimes to include Excel spreadsheets or other objects.

9 FFF97 Program Architecture

FFF97 is a 32 bit Windows application which runs under Win 3.1 (in the Win32s subsystem) and under Windows 95/98/NT. Under Win3.1 it uses 16-bit ODBC drivers that run under a 'generic thunk', under Windows 95/98/NT it uses 32 bit ODBC drivers. The syska SQL REWE accounting system also supports ODBC, but in 1996 it was a 16 bit application which needed 16 bit ODBC drivers also under Windows 95/98/NT. This caused conflicts with 32 bit drivers in various situations. Figuring out working combinations of server OS, client OS, client applications and ODBC drivers was a hard task at the beginning and took weeks of trial and error.

At the level of the development system FFF97 there is a subsystem called fff, which is represented by its own root directory at the same level as the text, forms, sql or development tools subsystem. A running application is the combination of all available subsystems. The directory fff contains subdirectories for the source code, the object code, symbol files, resource files, documentation and more. For the task of migrating legacy data, we introduced a second subsystem called P4000.

Any user of FFF97 has zero or more roles that allow access to selected parts of the program. The roles are maintained within FFF97 by a system administrator, which again is a special user role. Currently there are 28 different roles that can be freely combined. The user logs in to the database server using a generic login name and password. In addition the user types his FFF97 login name and password used to determine his role(s) in FFF97 and control his access rights. We deliberately do not rely on the much less flexible database features for access protection, thereby avoiding dependencies on the database server product.

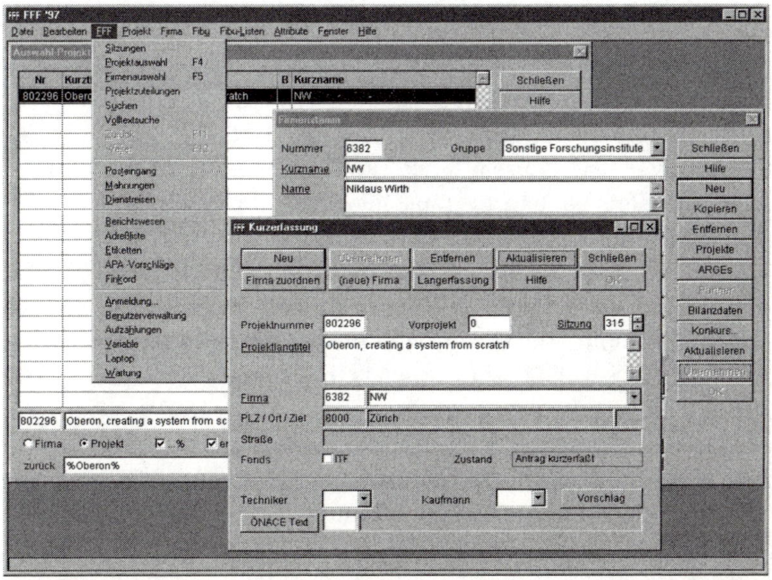

From a user's point of view, FFF97 appears as a Windows MDI (multiple document interface) application, which allows the user to open any number of (sub)windows in an application window. Of course, it is also possible to start FFF97 more than once, in which case multiple application windows are opened at the expense of starting multiple application processes. Subwindows typically are of one of two kinds: (1) input forms, and (2) text documents. Both kinds allow non-modal use of the system, i.e. it is possible to switch from one window to another or to activate menu items at any time. There are exceptions to this rule, however, which appear in the form of requests to the user to answer a yes/no question or to acknowledge a message. Such dialog message boxes are, in good old Windows tradition, modal.

An unexpected consequence of making input forms non-modal was the disabling of keyboard accelerators for command buttons. Normally, under Windows, you can define a keyboard shortcut for a button, which allows you to activate the button without leaving the keyboard. This is not possible with non-modal windows due to Microsoft's user interface conventions.

10 Data Model and Legacy Data Transfer

First of all, we had to deepen our knowledge of SQL, which obviously would become of vital importance for the implementation of the system. We also had to familiarize ourselves with the peculiarities of MS SQL Server 6.5. This includes server installation and administration and SQL language extensions and limitations. We learned most of the more subtle points on demand as we proceeded with the design and implementation of the new relational data model. We deliberately did not look at the legacy data model on the P4000 at this time, but designed from scratch and migrated the old data model to the new one using scripts with SQL-statements (so called batches) at a later stage.

Exporting the legacy data from P4000 turned out to be a rather slow process, because the only way was to use a serial 19200 baud link and it took two days to complete data transfer. We had to implement data format conversion routines in order to be able to import the exported legacy data into SQL Server tables. After that, we had access to the old data model by means of a 1:1 representation of the old tables in the SQL Server and could apply batches to convert the old data to the new data model. By doing that, it turned out that the old data was highly redundant and contradictory as well as incomplete, meaningless or incorrect. We had to prepare scripts to repair the data in many places in order to get useful data for our new data model.

We decided not to do a full transfer of accounting data to the new accounting system but to transfer the accounting plans and balances only, which is quite common when switching from one accounting system to another. We also had to split several accounts to make them compatible with the new data and accounting model. Most of the accounting data transfer was done automatically, i.e. only a few accounts had to be opened or corrected manually. Fortunately, accounting data was much more consistent and less redundant than project data, so we could transfer the accounts with a lot less development effort than the project data.

All in all, the Microsoft SQL Server 6.5 turned out to be a stable product with few surprises and was fairly easy to learn and manage even for a novice. The most unpleasant thing is probably that empty strings are stored as a string containing a single blank character (fixed in 7.0), which implies that all potentially empty strings must be trimmed not only before writing but also after reading. It was possible to normalize the new data model (with very few exceptions) without running into performance problems.

11 SCP – SQL Client Pages

One of the fundamental requirements of FFF97 was the need for text integration in the application. It should be possible to type in texts, store them in the database, generate read-only texts from database contents (reports) and generate writeable texts from database contents (e.g. templates for individual letters with the letterhead and parameterized standard texts filled in automatically). All these requirements are essentially variations on the same theme, coping with text, and this is where Oberon (and BlackBox) really shines. Based on the integrated text subsystem it was easy to provide for something that might be called SQL Client Pages (SCP) in analogy to Java Server Pages (JSP) or Active Server pages (ASP). We therefore defined a simple syntax that allows us to mix a text with SQL-Select statements, which are executed, and to substitute text variables with fields of the result set. The statement syntax is SQL, the SELECT statements are executed on the database server and the text expansions and substitutions take place on the client. The following simple template should illustrate the mechanism:

```
Clearing Code Name
<@SELECT code, name FROM Bank ORDER BY code;
<code>        <name>
>
```

This defines a report consisting of underlined column titles and an ordered list of pairs of all the banks contained in the table *Bank*. *code* is the clearing code of a bank, *name* is its name. The construct <@SELECT ... > opens a scope for field names (code, name) and a range for text expansion. The character ";" separates the SELECT statement from the text section. The text section is instantiated and appended for every row of the result set and within every text instance the values of the fields of the current row are available as <variableName> (<code> and <name> in the above example). The text may contain arbitrary formatting attributes and embedded elements, which are preserved during instantiation. It should also be noted that the mechanism may be nested recursively, i.e. within a text section there may be another <@SELECT...> phrase and it is allowed to use the variables of the enclosing SELECT within an enclosed SELECT statement and text section. There is some additional syntax for formatting numeric fields, date values and other special formats, for inclusion of files, for conditional text expansion, and, most notably, there is an extension mechanism in the form of an arbitrary command, whose output is embedded in the text.

```
<@COMMAND M.P param1 param2 ... >
```

This construct calls command M.P and replaces itself by the result produced by M.P, which writes text (including arbitrary elements floating within a text) into a text buffer. Examples include inserting bitmaps for scanned signatures, inserting hyperlinks or generation of non-static header or footer elements into the generated text.

We provide several ways of activating SCPs, including opening the resulting text as read-only text windows, as writeable database text windows, or as a view object that is not immediately opened as a window but may be further processed by the caller (e.g. as an e-mail attachment). The files containing the SCP specifications are called *templates* and are stored in a separate directory.

It might be argued that it should also be possible to use one of the many commercial report generators for the task of generating reports. While this is true in principle, it would be a tremendous waste of resources, introduce extra license costs, complicate report definition, limit the report structure to RPG-style reports, preclude an extension mechanism, complicate the inclusion into an application and serve only for read-only reports. The task of creating letter templates would still require a special solution. We have also observed that other programs switch to custom report generators after experimenting with standard tools (the syska SQL REWE is a prominent example for this).

12 Customized Visual Components

During the course of the project it became evident that the predefined visual objects, such as text editor, input controls, etc. were not sufficient for our specific needs and that customized components would become necessary.

Normal BlackBox texts, for example, are stored as a file and contain little more document information than the location and file name. For storing texts into a database there must be additional information available in the form of a database key which allows modified text to be replaced at a later stage. We therefore extended the standard text views by our own wrapper class that introduced the missing instance variables (database key, document type and paper type). This turned out to be a straightforward process, although it necessitated some delving into the details of handling visual components and working with wrappers, which are the BlackBox's preferred method of introducing subclasses. There were more visual components to be created, most notably a data grid component (based on a simple prototype provided by Oberon microsystems) which serves to display a database query result set and permits navigation and selection of entries. Other visual components include an editor for grading projects with respect to certain properties, attributed straight lines, and specialized date and currency input controls.

BlackBox provided all the prerequisites necessary to create such components and it was never necessary to switch to a different development system in order to create such classes.

13 Meta-Programming Facilities

The original Oberon system provides meta-programming using the concept of commands alone, which are exported procedures without paramters. BlackBox component builder goes beyond that and provides full access to variables and commands with parameters comparable to the one in [7]. Two important applications exist: forms with user interface components and the database interface.

The forms subsystem allows the linking of user interface components to program variables and procedures. A text input field, for example, is linked to a character array or an integer variable and displays the contents of this variable. This makes it very much like a 4GL programming system, because it allows a program to access the values contained in user interface components as normal program variables. Optionally, two procedures, a notifier and a guard may be linked as well. Both constitute commands with parameters. The notifier is called whenever a particular event, such as typing a key, occurs and may trigger related actions. The guard is called in order to inquire about the state of a component, which may be disabled, read-only, or normal. The forms subsystem and not the application program is responsible foractivating guards and notifiers, which simplifies programming significantly. Without such a mechanism it is hopelessly difficult to realize self guiding forms, i.e. forms that guide the user by disabling user interface components that are currently not applicable.

The BlackBox database interface allows the user to deal with whole records, not just with individual fields, for reading query results and composing SQL commands. When reading a row of a result set, a record variable may be used that matches the structure of the row. After reading, the record fields retains the values of the (positionally) corresponding fields in the result set row, which again would otherwise require a 4GL programming system. The Sql-subsystem is not hard coded in the BlackBox runtime system but simply uses the meta-programming facilities provided by BlackBox in order to traverse record variables and to fill in the field values in an appropriate format. When executing an Sql-command, the notation :M.V, where M denotes a module and V denotes a variable, may be used in order to expand a record to a comma separated sequence of record fields. This saves a lot of typing especially in Insert statements, as for example in "INSERT V VALUES (:M.V)".

In both examples the runtime overhead introduced by using the meta-programming facilities is marginal, the benefits for the application programs are huge.

14 Statistics

The following list contains some key matrices about FFF97.

- Source code: 86 modules with a total of 1,3 MB, 21.000 Semicolons
- Templates: 167 files with a total of 758 KB
- Resource files: 102 files with a total of 520 KB
- Documentation: 100 files with a total of 594 KB
- Object code: 86 files with a total of 1.2 MB
- Executable process size: about 6 MB
- Databases FibuDB and FffDB: 160 MB each, about 70% filled
- Number of text documents in FffDB: 19.000
- Number of database objects: 39 tables with a total of 450 fields, 1 View, 1 stored procedure.

15 Summary of Vital Points

Let us now summarize the points which we believe were vital for the success of the project.

- Prototyping turned out to be possible to circumvent the writing of detailed specifications, which nobody is able to accomplish for a complex project. It depends, however, on efficient tools and the close cooperation of all participants. The short feed-back loop avoids developments in the wrong direction, so we never had to throw away big pieces of work. Without an Oberon style IDDEE tool, we believe, it would have been impossible to achieve the required number of development cycles.

- Error avoidance is of vital importance for a prototyping approach, since long debugging times simply cannot be afforded. Oberon's approach of using an airtight type system and automatic garbage collection turned out to be an invaluable asset even in the world of commercial data processing. The procedure activation stack dump provided in case of a runtime exception and the possibility of inspecting global variables were sufficient for debugging logical errors. This is, by the way, more than one gets in traditional IDEs, since Oberon does not make a distinction between release (without debugging) and debug version.

- Efficiency of the resulting programs in terms of time and memory consumption can only be achieved with a compiled general purpose programming language and reasonably designed libraries. Both is the case with *BlackBox*, which made it possible to run the application on i486/33Mhz with 16MB main memory. It is still an advantage after switching to bigger PCs, because it allows the user to start more than one FFF97 process or other office tools in order to perform certain parallel tasks . It is also an advantage when working offline on a Laptop, which must host a database server locally. A small disk footprint is also an advantage when starting a program via a network from a central file server.
- Oberon's dynamic loading strategy turned out to be of three-fold benefit to us: (1) it avoids the extra linking step during development, (2) it allows the application to be installed on a central file server and to be loaded incrementally with almost unnoticeable loading delays even on a 10Mbit network with about 30 active users, and (3) it allows us to maintain and update the system incrementally via remote access over a single 64 Kbit ISDN line.
- Text integration pioneered by the original Oberon project and continued by BlackBox turned out to be at the very heart of our application. A simple SCP report generator needed just a few weeks of coding and allowed us to create text templates for a broad range of applications including reports and letters with little effort and great flexibility.
- Meta-programming support in BlackBox introduces many features of 4GL programming systems and allows a tight integration of the program with databases and user interface components. There is no extra coding required and there is also no code generator involved.

16 Concluding Remarks

The following contains some thoughts about lessons learned during the course of the FFF97 project. Some of the points are actually statements made by Prof. N. Wirth that proved to be more than true in practice.

- "Keep it as simple as possible, but not simpler" (Einstein, often quoted by Wirth) is especially important in a prototyping approach in order to be flexible enough to incorporate additional or deviating needs. Whenever it is unclear what the user really needs, do not invest a big effort in a preliminary solution.
- A user interface should be created using visual design tools, not by means of lengthy statement sequences. There is no need for a code generator within such a form editor, which simplifies development and the development system significantly. It also provides a clear separation of concerns, GUI design on the one hand and functionality behind the buttons on the other. Programmed user inter-

faces are only justified in exceptional cases, where highly dynamic layouts are needed.

- The lack of static typing in the database world constitutes a major problem for client applications whenever the data model needs to be changed. It is impossible to test all dependent programs systematically. With the common approach of using dynamic SQL inside a general purpose programming language, this situation cannot be expected to change in the near future.
- Modern database systems and programming interfaces exhibit a degree of complexity that is hard to digest for someone used to the simplicity of the Oberon system. Most of the complexity stems from irregularities and exceptional cases that would better be omitted from the specifications. This might free some resources for introducing higher level concepts such as type extension into a database management system, which is still a long way off.
- Wasting resources is never a good idea even if the resources appear to be unlimited, as is the case with disk space nowadays. With a highly normalized data model and compact representation of text documents we were able to fit the database into less than 160 MB, a small fraction of a modern hard disk. There are advantages, though. Backup is fast and our database fits almost entirely into the main memory of a modern server computer, where 256 MByte and more are the norm. The same argument holds for every level of the memory hierarchy.
- Compiler construction is at the very heart of computer science. Even in a commercial data processing application, one can make good use of a simple language and a recursive descent parser as can be seen by the SCP example.
- Custom software projects such as FFF97 are always at the technological limit. With improved hardware and software technology user expectations are raised, because standard software created with thousands of man-years raises the standard of comparison to new heights. Keeping up to those expectations is everything but easy considering the limited development resources for custom software.
- What a user wants is not always what a user needs. Taken literally, the wishes formulated by users range from trivial to unsolvable. They often include *how* to do it, based on a particular idea, and not only *what* to do. It is the developer's task to find the intersection of realizable and powerful concepts, which in many cases deviates significantly from what the user originally wanted.
- Sometimes the user is not able to distinguish between "always" and "often" and between "never" and "seldom". This can easily lead to oversimplifications that do not take exceptional cases into account.

– Oberon microsystems Inc. did an excellent job of hiding the complexities of the Windows API and preserving the spirit of Oberon in a Windows environment. There are some points left to be improved (e.g. advanced GUI interface elements), of course, which are mainly due to limited manpower. The complexities and irregularities of the Windows API make it difficult to integrate Windows services and components seamlessly with a reasonable effort.

– The FFF97 project would certainly not have been possible in 1996 and would still not be possible in 2000 using the much hyped Java technology. Although Java resembles Oberon in some aspects (e.g. garbage collection, strong typing), its library is far from being useful for this kind of application. It would require at least five times the memory, execution time, development effort and program startup time, let alone the unsolved problem of text integration and printing.

17 Acknowledgements

Without the contribution and support of many people FFF97 would not have been finished successfully. I wish to thank my business partner and brother Dipl.-Ing. Erwin Templ, with whom I had the pleasure to work on this project. He was always a highly motivating and inspiring discussion partner both in solving problems of detail and for developing the big picture. Prof. Gustav Pomberger supervised and coordinated the project and played the role of the unbiased judge, and who, thanks to his wise project management, we rarely had reason to call. The FFF management deserves respect for taking the risk of charging a young, small and unknown company with the development of their mission critical software. The FFF staff was a patient and constructive prototype tester and did its best to communicate its needs to us. Susanne Litschauer shouldered the burden of organizing meetings and writing reports and was always a competent and friendly contact person. For the rare cases where we needed help or bug fixes Oberon microsystems Inc. responded quickly and cut out a lot of red tape. I also want to thank Hanspeter Mössenböck and Eva Jaksch for proofreading this paper. Last but not least I want to thank Prof. N. Wirth for the technological ground work he laid together with J. Gutknecht in the Oberon project and for the privilege of working with him at ETH Zurich.

References

1. N. Wirth, J. Gutknecht, Project Oberon – The design of an Operating system and Compiler, Addison Wesley, 1992
2. Oberon microsystems Inc, http://www.oberon.ch
3. G. Pomberger, L.J. Heinrich: Prototyping-orientierte Evaluierung von Software-Angeboten., Theorie und Praxis der Wirtschaftsinformatik, Heft 197, Sept. 1997
4. A. Fischer, H. Marais, The Oberon Companion, VDF Hochschulverlag AG, Zürich 1998

5. syska SQL REWE, http://www.syska.de
6. Microsoft SQL Server, http://www.microsoft.com/sql
7. J. Templ, Meta-programming in Oberon, PhD thesis, ETH Zurich, 1994
8. Kent Beck, Extreme Programming Explained: embrace change, Addison Wesley 1999

Part VI
The World According to Wirth – Personal, Anecdotal Reviews

Serendipity

Kathleen Jensen
Reading, England

It was 1971 when I arrived in Zurich. I had just graduated from the University of California at Santa Cruz, where I was one of the first 10 students earning the brand new degree in "Information and Computer Science."

I can't recall whether the term "culture shock" was in vogue yet, but that's what I faced upon landing in Switzerland. Not only were my hippie clothes not appreciated, but the attitude to computing was also different. In California computers were beginning to capture the imagination of an infant industry. But at the more conservative Eidgenössische Technische Hochschule (ETH), my impression was the study of computer science had yet to earn acceptability as a discipline. (Never mind that ETH could boast some of the field's pioneers among its faculty.)

A result of this mistrust was a greater supply than demand of research and teaching assistantships in the "Informatik" department. And it was into this happenstance that Wirth received my letter inquiring of a position.

Although I lacked the qualifications (the prerequisite diploma being more on par with a US masters degree than my BA), I had the advantage of a recommendation from my professor, Bill McKeeman. As it turns out, McKeeman was Wirth's first PhD student at Stanford, and I was among McKeeman's "first born" at UCSC. So when Wirth met me in Zurich, he proclaimed how hiring me was like becoming a grandfather. It was this touch of sentimentality that secured my position!

In many ways such accidents of circumstance drove our industry in those days. It was a fun and fertile field for discovery and invention, a field where people focused on engineering the product rather than marketing or selling the result.

Wirth had published the original definition of Pascal in November 1970 as an internal report. During my three years at ETH, my colleagues (most notably Urs Ammann) worked on improving the compiler. Urs also developed the portable Pascal-P compiler, upon which most non-CDC implementations of the time were based. And Wirth continued to perfect the language definition – much to many students' frustration upon discovering a previously functioning program failing to compile!

Perhaps it was Wirth's instinct, or maybe just another coincidence, but Pascal also benefited from some non-technical aspects of product development. Because English was my mother tongue and because I was the most junior of the assistants,

I was asked to improve the user documentation. I don't think we've ever analyzed the impact of having more accessible documentation had on the adoption of Pascal. Yes, I know the first edition is a bit terse, but still a great improvement on what previously existed! (And Wirth felt *very* strongly that a language as well formed as Pascal should be documented in less than 100 pages – just as the well-written program needn't be cluttered with comments to be understandable.)

Perhaps even more important in promoting the use of Pascal were the introductions of the *Pascal Newsletter* (first edited by George Richmond) and Pascal *User's Group*. Yes, Pascal is a beautiful language, elegant in its simplicity, rich in function without the hint of excess – but it also profited from some tentative steps into marketing and promotion.

As the software industry has matured, the emphasis on engineering product versus marketing the result has changed immensely. Upon leaving ETH, I joined Digital. During my 24 years at Digital, I experienced technical and business cycles that would have taken many times those years to unfold in other industries. It was an exciting place to work, and I feel very fortunate for the experience. But to its commercial detriment, Digital remained an environment where its engineering skills exceeded its marketing acumen – in an industry whose pendulum had swung much the other way. Superior product development alone does not ensure commercial success. I'm now convinced that if a tree falls in the forest and nobody is there to hear it, it doesn't make the slightest sound.

I haven't mentioned I was quite terrified of Wirth during my ETH days. While clearly a genius, he was not always one to instill confidence in others. After leaving Switzerland, I met Wirth on handful of occasions, each exposing a more approachable and engaging man.

Our last and most enjoyable meeting was when I traveled to Zurich to hear his retirement farewell lecture. As a final coincidence of circumstance, his retirement coincided with my own, mine being hastened by a take-over in an industry that can afford generous redundancy terms. We had a delightful lunch overlooking the city of Zurich, and he showed me around a very much grown-up computer science department (one now beyond opening its doors to an under-qualified UCSC graduate). It was one of those "passages" you read about in pop psychology books: we were both setting off on a new life – and I hope he's enjoying his as much as I'm enjoying mine!

Daily Life with N. Wirth

Jirka Hoppe

Summary

This article describes a number of daily life situations at the "Institute for Informatics" at the Swiss Federal Institute of Technology where the author worked for nine years with N. Wirth. Daily problems, daily fights, victories and losses. These situations give an informal insight into the environment where the ideas of Wirth developed.

The author worked (besides on a large number of small tasks) in Wirth's team in the following areas: the thesis on the classification of operating systems, the development of the first Modula compiler, the development of the computer Lilith and finally the introduction of distributed computing for Lilith.

The Swiss Like to Save Money

It is well known about the Swiss (and possibly the Scottish) that they are miserly about money. The Swiss (even very wealthy people) try to save everything – not only physical money but all other resources too: they try to save water, save air, they collect empty glass bottles (so that not a single bottle is lost) and they collect aluminum yogurt lids – in order to save aluminum.

In this dimension, Wirth is very Swiss. Possibly he is even more Swiss than other Swiss citizens – he has another dimension to saving that is not available to other people: he was able to save bytes of main memory, bytes on disks, lines of code.

Saving bytes became a part of daily life: The number of program lines was a quality attribute of each program. Less lines was a sign of a good program, more lines was a clear property of a bad program.

Once we were developing the basic part of an operating system. We called it "Nucleus" – it was that component that is responsible for creating and managing processes and for communication between them. As usual, one of the goals was to keep this Nucleus as small as possible. With this goal in mind, we developed a really minimal Nucleus (actually a good property). But fully applied, this goal prevented any enhancement to the Nucleus. We felt a necessity to add a time handling to this Nucleus – it would enable e.g. handling of timed waits. This idea had to be abandoned – the main argument against such an enhancement (if not the only one) was that it would make the Nucleus a few bytes larger.

Similarly saving the execution time of a program was a well accepted goal. Each code line was measured by the execution time. This optimization sometimes overshot the target: the first version of the Modula compiler was overoptimized. When we first investigated the instruction set for the PDP-11 computer, we found that the access to global variables (at a fixed address) was really fast. For that reason the first compiler was designed to work with global variables only – accessing variables on the stack seemed to be too slow. A second check revealed that stack variables could be accessed with about the same speed as global variables – the difference was very minimal. We had to rewrite the compiler to allow stack variables and consequently to allow recursive procedures.

Universities Always Grant Very Limited Funds

Besides Wirth's natural property described above to save any and all resources, there was outside pressure to save money. No university in the world grants anybody an unlimited amount of money – each project has to live within a limited budget.

And Wirth succeeded in finding his position in this money-saving world. Most probably he even felt more comfortable in such a situation than in a situation where there was money in abundance. He enjoyed living with a limited budget and not asking for additional funding. Every Swiss Frank was checked twice as to whether we should spend it.

But there was a way around this problem. Instead of spending actual money we had a huge amount of another resource: manpower. At universities there is a huge amount of cheap manpower – all students and all assistants work nearly for free. We inverted the famous saying "buy instead of build" – at the institute everything was built instead of bought.

A famous example of such an approach was a device that writes content into read-only memories – a so called "ROM burner". This "ROM burner" was needed to program the micro-code of Lilith. Such a device may be bought in every second electrical hardware shop and it does not cost a fortune. But even for such an amount there was no money. We spent a lot of time building our own burner; building it, experimenting with precise timing, finding hardware bugs. Actually we saved some money by not buying the burner. But taking the labor costs into account, this ROM burner could have been made of gold.

Similarly, the budget for hardware to build a Lilith was also very limited. Part of the original Lilith prototype was built using second-hand material. We found a collection of second hand ROMs – they were for free, but every second one was broken. Since there was plenty of time, we burned each ROM many times till we finally found a ROM that was fault-free and could be burned.

Even the Brightest Ideas Need Practical Experience

Wirth's actual background was electrical engineering – he got his first university diploma in electrical engineering before he fully converted to computer sciences. There are rumors (unproven) that he once built his own television set by soldering single capacitors, resistors and valves together. But since then technology has changed. When starting with the design of Lilith, there was not much practical knowledge about building computers at the institute. Richard Ohran (from Brigham Young University) was the only one who knew something about state-of-the-art digital design methods. We were very enthusiastic about building such a complex thing as a computer, but we had almost no practical knowledge. This lack of experience cost us a lot.

The first Lilith prototype had a beautiful and a nearly final architecture, but a lot of small technical details hindered the work. The first prototype was not built in a metal box, but on a wooden frame. There was no motherboard with a solid ground, there was no standard shield box around it. The wiring was done with thin wires and the quality of soldering was as good as can be expected from people with no education in soldering. We had to learn that building a computer requires a lot of knowledge in the handcraft of electrical engineering: the first Lilith prototype somehow worked, but it was completely unreliable. Sometimes it worked, sometimes not.

We spent a lot of time on small improvements. Each time we experienced some unreliability we added more grounding wires, we soldered in some more capacitors. With time (and with a lot of additional capacitors) we finally arrived at a prototype that worked.

Although Wirth based his work (nearly) always on a solid theoretical background, this exceptional experimental approach showed the other side of his attitude to computer science: in addition to theoretical work he always required real experience. Theoretical research is important, but everything must always be supported by "hands on experience". Both in the hardware as well as in the software area.

Demonstrating Lilith

Every invention needs some sales support. Even the brightest idea will not be automatically accepted if the responsible people are not aware of it.

Demonstrating Lilith was a part of our daily life. Not only at the ETH, but in many places throughout Switzerland we showed Lilith to a broad audience. Some demonstrations were carried out without problems, some others needed a lot of luck and a lot of fast fix-ups in order to make the demonstration successful.

The unreliable wooden prototype was once demonstrated to the ETH management. The goal was to get more funding to continue development. The demonstration was given by a perfect team. Wirth was giving the main talk, the other part of the team was standing by as instant support for potential hardware and software crashes. Such support was needed. During such a demonstration Lilith failed again. But the emergency team did a good job. Wirth continued with his talk (talking slowly on purpose). Christian Jacobi (who wrote a code generator part of the Lilith compiler and knew the code by heart) used the switches of the hardware panel, manipulated the code in real time and restarted the demonstration. The talk went perfectly. None of the management realized this perfectly camouflaged failure.

Lilith was once presented in the main auditorium of the nuclear research center in Geneva (CERN). We transported Lilith across half of Switzerland, installed it, checked it, and prepared for the talk and demonstration. Everything was ready, but the main speaker of the event – Wirth himself – could not be found. He was invited to a nice business lunch with wine, coffee and dessert. The time of the talk came around, but there was no speaker. Again the emergency team went into action. The audience started asking questions about Lilith and the team answered them. Suddenly somebody brought a microphone, TV cameras were put in operation, the lights were on. The emergency team did a good job. They gave a perfect talk about Lilith in the main auditorium. When Wirth appeared (some time later), he was happy – he knew that he could rely on his team.

Another demonstration almost had legal consequences. Lilith was demonstrated as a part of the research division during the largest Swiss computer exhibition, Orbit in Basle. The success was overwhelming. The entire exhibition concentrated on the technology of 1980 – character-oriented displays. If anything was anything like "edge of technology" – it was a color display. And suddenly – among such technology a bitmap screen with graphics, proportional fonts, dithered pictures, and animated graphics appeared. The audience was no longer interested in character displays and wanted to see the modern technology. As a result, several companies were considering taking legal steps against Lilith – demonstrating this technology was considered as illegal competition. They were afraid that nobody would be interested in their character displays if the audience were to be "infected" by the modern bitmap technology.

Social Life

The Wirth team consisted of hard working and really motivated people. But we were not hard-working all the time. A little pleasure was always part of our life. There was a custom that each first success was celebrated with champagne. A compiler being able to compile a statement "i := 0;", the first character on a screen or a disk head starting moving were all good reasons to have champagne. Looking back it is hard to say whether we were officially allowed to drink alcohol in the University, but we did it without asking for a permission.

Once Lilith was again able to do a little bit more. It was again time for champagne. Everybody came to the Lilith, grabbed a glass and the champagne bottle was opened in a small ceremony. That time either the champagne was too warm, had been shaken too much or the person holding the bottle (yours truly) had nervous hands. The bottle was opened, the cork flew out and the champagne poured out of the bottle. Unfortunately there was an expensive device called a "logic state analyzer" just where the champagne was headed. Such a device has a huge number of small buttons to control it. The effect of the sparkling wine on these buttons was overwhelming. When the champagne dried out, it was nearly impossible to press any of these buttons – they were glued by the champagne. This was the most expensive celebration and the most expensive "small progress" of the Lilith.

Moral of the Story

These little stories from daily life with Wirth give a short informal insight into the environment in which great ideas were developed. Such stories may be not very scientific and sometimes they may show the more negative side of our work. But they demonstrate the circumstances under which Wirth's ideas evolved. They show that even fantastic scientific results have been created by human beings. They show that the way to success was not always a straight path without setbacks. Each success was the result of a lot of iterations and a lot of mistakes and errors.

But looking back, all these small mishaps and all things that went wrong had a significant positive influence on the way of thinking, on the philosophy of the author of this article. The way, Wirth taught me to work and to think is still (after many years) reflected in my daily decisions.

Looking back, I would say that the most essential things I learned from Wirth are the following:

- Keep everything simple and small. Only simple and small programs and computers will work. Usually the simplest solution is sufficient to make everybody happy. Simple solutions are not only inexpensive to develop, but moreover they are inexpensive to maintain.
- Find the real needs of your customer. Average customers usually ask for more than they really need. You may spend a fortune on implementing a functionality that a customer will never use.
- Work only in a small team. With up to 7 members, the team concentrates on the real work. Large teams spend all their time organizing themselves – they do not work – they just organize.
- Avoid committees. Committees are the most efficient way to spend money and the most inefficient way to get results.

– Have a strong leader in the team that is able to decide. Such a leader may sometimes make wrong decisions. But the fact that everything is created in one head results in a better and more consistent result.

Third Millennium Culture

Ann Dünki

I floated into the Swiss Federal Institute of Technology at Zurich, the ETH-Z, on the initial European tides of the era we today associate with the World Wide Web. In the early 1970's Arpanet was exerting its pull on the academic and research world outside of the United States. I was given the opportunity to work with a small research group representing Switzerland on a European Community project to build up and link European universities and research centers into a packet switching network.

Our team was concerned with layered architectures, virtual terminals, and the networking of widely diverse systems and facilities. We were sponsored by the Swiss government and, although based at the ETH-Z, we existed outside of the normal academic structure. We were a tiny Swiss nucleus tied into an exiting European adventure and in need of a strong intellectual home base.

Today we know about intelligent objects which traverse a network and behave smartly in varied remote locations and situations. But in the early 1970's my project seemed, even to me, far afield from compiler and language theory. But, while the post worried that we might do something radical such as use this new network to exchange mail, the Institute for Applied Mathematics opened its mind and extended its curiosity to embrace our activities. Those interactions let me – just – glimpse the contours and possibilities of self-contained intelligence in a networked world. I was pulled into the vortex of academic life at the ETH and somewhere along the line was given the opportunity to pursue a doctoral degree based upon my research work with this five year project.

Niklaus Wirth, who would chair the Institute for Informatics when it was finally created, became my doctoral advisor.

We studied Informatics at a university that offered neither graduate nor undergraduate degrees in that subject. This bothered some people but it did not bother Berkeley, Xerox Parc or any of a number of universities and corporate think tanks that exchanged people and ideas with Niklaus Wirth. Nor did it prevent the Hoare's and the Dijkstra's from addressing us in the comfort of our lecture halls.

The ETH-Z was slow in promoting Informatics to an independent discipline but somehow it did not matter all that much because we had Niklaus. Through him the digital age – with its technology, its language, its culture, and its lack of boundaries – was virtually a reality well before Informatics was ever formally recognized at the ETH-Z. Perhaps Niklaus Wirth understood something that we, on the brink of the third millennium, are only now realizing – that the digital age is something much bigger than technology.

Niklaus understood the dynamics of the global village and leveraged the world to our delight and advantage. Just one small example:

Niklaus needed his own computer – one that would do his bidding and behave according to his and Modula's rules. The ETHZ hadn't the right skills for such an enterprise but the world at large did; Niklaus enlisted Richard Ohran and half of the Mormon state to bootstrap the ETHZ into the realm of modern computer design and production. Richard came to us from the Brigham Young University in Utah. In Zurich he began the design of the Lilith. But a computer had not only to be designed, it had also to be built and the project needed more skilled hands than were available. Thus started an unusual intercontinental commute. Every three months, or just within the limits of the law, some young graduate assistants from Utah appeared at the ETHZ's doorstep and took over the building baton from their equally young predecessors who had to hightail it out of Switzerland or suffer the wrath of the Labor Department.

Someone reading this may be tempted to lift an eyebrow, but it was legal. And it was a precursor to the networked ventures that today occur without the long commute. It was natural to use the resources available in this large world. We approved. We profited from the exposure to new technology, to new people, even to a new religion.

Niklaus also understood that great ideas do not come from genius in isolation, that great advances in our digital society come from sharing one's intellectual assets – through dialogue, arguments, questions, knowledge sharing.

He had that rare talent in Switzerland – he created discussion! He had the temerity and the talent to be provocative and the sense to enjoy the discussions he provoked. He was determined that his intellectual offspring would learn more than compiler design; he wanted his students to think in a networked fashion. He was the one who led the way. He would question both the heavyweights and the lightweights, open up discussions, bring life into the lecture room. He beseeched with stamping feet, invited, and implored his students to do the same. He was intimidating but never hierarchical and so drew us into a large circle with bright light.

Niklaus made acceptable both unconventional approaches – as in "do what needs to be done but get it done"; and discussion – as in "heated and creative". In the 1970's Niklaus pioneered more than Pascal, he pioneered global work groups, knowledge sharing, networked thinking. The rest of the world is just catching up.

Authors and Editors

László Böszörményi is a full professor of computer science at the University Klagenfurt, Austria. His current main research area is distributed systems with emphasis on multimedia infrastructures. László Böszörményi was born in Budapest, Hungary and studied at the Technical University of Budapest. He became acquainted with Niklaus Wirth in 1977, when he spent an academic year at the ETH in Zürich. Since then László Böszörményi has returned as a visitor for longer stays at the ETH. He ported the ETH-Modula-2 compiler to a Motorola-based workstation designed by his research group. László Böszörményi is the author of a textbook on introductory programming with Modula-3, the high-end successor of Modula-2. He has been a disciple of Niklaus Wirth for 23 years, and plans on retaining that status far into the future.

laszlo@itec.uni-klu.ac.at

Thom Boyer received B.S. and M.S. degrees from Brigham Young University in Provo, Utah. His first job after college was with Signetics, where he was responsible for extending Lilith's Modula compiler to support extended precision reals. Later he created the Modula compiler for Eve (the 32-bit updated version of Lilith). He has worked in the Advanced Technology Group at WordPerfect, and at several small startup companies. He is currently with Novell, where he is responsible for maintaining the NetWare port of Symantec's Java just-in-time compiler.

Fon Brown received B.S. degrees in Electrical Engineering and Mathematics from Utah State University, an M.S. degree in Computer Science from Brigham Young University, and a Ph.D. in Electrical Engineering from Utah State University. He worked at Signetics from 1984–1992 developing algorithms for circuit simulation, netlist comparison and design rule checking. During that time he became involved in a project to upgrade the Lilith wherein he developed the microcode and operating system for the new Eve workstation. He is currently working at Evans & Sutherland Computer Corporation as a system architect for high performance image generators that are used for real-time visual simulation.

Robert Burton received a Ph.D. from the University of North Carolina in Chapel Hill. He then worked at Brigham Young University in Provo, Utah where he became a professor of mathematics and computer science. He was a pioneer in moving large-scale rocket and circuit simulations from main frames to engineering work stations. He is now with Philips Semiconductors, where he is interested in automatic optimization of circuits and spiral inductors.

Edsger W. Dijkstra was born in 1930 in Rotterdam, The Netherlands. He studied at Leyden University from 1948 until 1956, when he received his degree in Theoretical Physics. He worked as a programmer at the Mathematical Centre in Amsterdam from 1952 until 1962, when he was appointed as full Professor of Mathematics at the Technical University, Eindhoven. In 1973 he became Research Fellow of Burroughs Corporation, from 1984 until 1999 he has occupied the Schlumberger Centennial Chair in Computer Sciences at the University of Texas in Austin. He is now Professor Emeritus.

Ann Dünki is the Chief Information Officer for the Telekurs Group, the nucleus of the Swiss banking industry's digital interactions. Based at the ETH between 1971 and 1978 and working in the area of networked communications, she there came in contact with the world of Pascal and Modula and Wirth. She left the ETH for a career first in industry and afterwards in the e-based financial sector. Concerns today include digital authentication and authorization, directory based infrastructures, and intelligent objects. She plays an electronic keyboard (sort of), dabbles with the world of digital photography, and is still buoyed by the wonder within Niklaus Wirth's community.

Hans Eberle is a Senior Staff Engineer at Sun Microsystems Laboratories in Mountain View, California. He was an Assistant Professor of Computer Science at ETH Zurich from 1993 until 1998. From 1988 until 1993 he was a Principal Engineer at the Systems Research Center of the Digital Equipment Corporation in Palo Alto, California. He received his diploma in Electrical Engineering and Ph.D. in Technical Sciences from ETH Zurich in 1984 and 1987, respectively. He worked in Niklaus Wirth's group from 1984 until 1987.

In 1984, **Michael Franz** read Wirth's book "Algorithmen und Datenstrukturen" while he was doing military service in Germany, prompting him to apply to ETH. To his surprise, an entrance examination was required, and even more surprisingly, he passed. And so began Franz' tenure in the School of Wirth. In 1989, Franz graduated with an Engineer's Degree from ETH and received a full Fulbright scholarship for Ph.D. studies in the USA. Franz subsequently declined this scholarship, opting instead to remain at ETH and completing a Ph.D. under Niklaus Wirth in 1994. After two further years at ETH as a Senior Research Associate and Lecturer, Franz became an Assistant Professor of Computer Science at the University of California, Irvine. There, Franz currently leads a research group of 12 Ph.D. students and one post-doctoral researcher, working on the three main threads of dynamic optimization ("accelerate a program while it is already running"), mobile program representations ("alternatives to the Java Virtual Machine"), and component-oriented languages and software systems ("paradigms beyond object-oriented programming").

franz@ics.uci.edu

Stephan Gehring first met Niklaus Wirth in 1985 during Wirth's sabbatical at Xerox PARC in Palo Alto, California, even before Stephan started his studies in Computer Science at ETH Zurich. After receiving his diploma in 1991, he joined Wirth's group in 1992 where he worked on CAD tools for Field-Programmable Gate Arrays. He received his Ph.D. in 1997 and is currently a Member of Research Staff at Interval Research Corporation in Palo Alto, California.

stephan.gehring@ieee.org

Robert Griesemer studied Informatik (Computer Engineering) at ETH Zürich from 1983–1988. After some exposure to the Oberon System, he decided to apply for a position at Niklaus Wirth's Institute for Computer Systems. He worked with Oberon and Oberon-2 under the guidance of Hanspeter Mössenböck and Niklaus Wirth. Robert's studies led to Oberon language extensions for vector computers. After his doctorate in 1993, he spent a year in the Sather language group at ICSI in Berkeley, USA. He joined Longview Technologies (aka Animorphic Systems), a newly founded startup company in Palo Alto, California, in 1994. At Longview, he was instrumental in designing and implementing Smalltalk and Java virtual machines. Since 1997 Robert has been with Sun Microsystems where he continues to work on the Java HotSpot™ Virtual Machine technology originally developed at Longview. He is the technical leader of the client compiler group.

Jürg Gutknecht: Long after my first 3-year experience with computer programming (in industry) and after the completion of my Dr. Math. thesis I met Niklaus Wirth for the first time in 1981 in his office at ETH and soon after in his weekend house in Rehetobel near Heerbrugg, where I was teaching math at that time. A short demo of the Lilith by his assistants caught me instantly, and I took a sabbatical leave from my teaching job and joined Wirth's team. My first project was Andra (whose revision was later called Lara), a novel WYSIWYG text system for Lilith along the Xerox Bravo lines. Later I helped Wirth to develop a new and super-fast one-pass Modula-2 compiler. In 1985, when both Wirth and I spent a sabbatical at Xerox PARC (for me it was a sabbatical within a sabbatical), our long-term close collaboration started in a small office shortly after one of the famous PARC-lunches. It started with some sort of brainstorming on the principles of a new language and operating system, later to be called Oberon. Back in Zurich I was elected as (assistant) professor of Computer Science at ETH, and I finally quit my teaching job in Heerbrugg. From 1986 till 1989 Niklaus and I developed Oberon, where development in this case included design, implementation, weekend after weekend of discussions, filing down one rough edge after the other and testing new ideas, more often than not in front of a "black screen". After 1989 our paths of research forked but until this very day we are both building our new intellectual constructs on the simple, clear and sound platform of Oberon.

gutknecht@inf.ethz.ch

Jirka Hoppe is assistant vice director at UBS, Switzerland (largest Swiss bank), responsible for the definition of the software architectures in the bank. He received his diploma in Electrical Engineering at the Swiss Federal Institute of Technology in 1973. For the next nine years he worked in N. Wirth's team in the areas of programming languages (Modula, Modula-2), compilers, operating systems, computer hardware (development of the computer Lilith) and networks. His Ph.D thesis (1978) deals with types and concepts of operating systems. For the next year he joined the company Diser and tried to manufacture, sell and improve Lilith. After the company breakdown, he worked for another nine years at Océ Wissenschaftliches Forschungsinstitut AG, Zurich, where he was involved in document processing, document management, full text search engines, and document archival.

Kathleen Jensen worked for Niklaus Wirth from 1971–74, and is the co-author of the Pascal Users Manual and Report. After leaving ETH she joined Digital Equipment Corporation where she held a number of senior positions in Services and Engineering. She currently resides in England.

Svend Erik Knudsen was born in Fredriksberg, Denmark in 1947. In 1962, he moved with his family to the eastern part of Switzerland from where he went to school in Liechtenstein. He received his diploma in Physics and Ph.D. in Technical Sciences from ETH Zurich in 1975 and 1983 respectively. Since 1984, he has been employed at ETH's computing services. He worked in the group of Professor Niklaus Wirth from 1976 until 1984 in the areas of programming languages (Pascal and Modula-2) and operating systems (Medos).

Knudsen@id.ethz.ch

Srdjan Mitrovic studied Electrical Engineering at ETH Zurich from 1981–1987. During that time he enjoyed many courses taught by Niklaus Wirth and got intimately acquainted with Pascal and Modula-2. He graduated with a doctorate at the Technical Computer Engineering and Networks Laboratory at ETH in 1993 under supervision of Albert Kündig, where he developed a Sisal compiler for the ADAM data-flow architecture. From 1993–1996 Srdjan held various post-doctoral positions at the Lawrence Livermore National Laboratory in California, where he studied multi-threaded code generation techniques for the Tera multithreaded architecture. Srdjan joined Longview Technologies in Palo Alto, California, in 1996. He adapted Longview's virtual machine technology to Java and implemented Longview's first Java compiler. Since 1997 he has been with Sun Microsystems, where he manages the client compiler group.

Hanspeter Mössenböck is a professor of Computer Science at the Johannes Kepler University of Linz. He studied Computer Science in Linz specializing in compilers and compiler generators. After a PostDoc year at the University of Zurich he became an assistant professor at ETH Zurich in 1988, where he worked with professor Niklaus Wirth for six years.

moessenboeck@ssw.uni-linz.ac.at

Matt Morrise received his B.S. and M.S. in mathematics from Brigham Young University. He was at Signetics for 10 years where he worked on circuit simulation, schematics capture physical design and other IC related software projects, all on the Lilith and Eve. He is currently at Intel working on timing analysis tools in their microprocessor group. His interests include FLTK and Python.

Martin Odersky barely managed to finish his Diploma in Mathematics in 1985, because he fell in love with Modula-2 and got too deeply involved in constructing a Modula-2 compiler. The next logical step was to come to Zurich and start work as an assistant of Wirth. Interest shifted from Modula-2 to Oberon, and so he finished 1989 with a thesis on language definition techniques, applied to Oberon. Afterwards he worked at IBM research, Yale University, the University of Karlsruhe and the University of South Australia. Since 1999 he heads the programming methods laboratory at EPFL.

Farrell Ostler received B.S. and M.E. degrees from Brigham Young University in Provo, Utah. In the summer of 1978 he went to Zurich, meeting Niklaus Wirth for the first time, to assist in building and debugging the first Lilith prototype. He also worked in Zurich in the summer of 1979 and the fall of 1980, the latter time to help install a series of Liliths that he had helped to build under a contract awarded to BYU by the ETH. In 1982 he joined Professor Wirth's group as an Assistant. He received the Doctor of Technical Sciences degree from ETH in 1986. He joined Signetics (later to become part of Philips Semiconductors) in 1987 to design a floating-point accelerator for circuit simulation, a project that evolved into a second-generation Lilith computer called Eve. Since then he has been involved in integrated circuit design.

Gustav Pomberger studied electrical engineering and computer science; Ph.D. in technical sciences in 1980; designer of electrical machines 1968 to 1976; graduate assistant at the University of Linz 1976 to 1984; visiting researcher at ETH Zurich in 1982; professor of computer science at the University of Zurich 1984 to 1987; since 1987 professor of software engineering at Johannes Kepler University of Linz; 1992 to 1999 head of C. Doppler Laboratory for Software Engineering. Gustav Pomberger has been befriended with Prof. Wirth for more than 15 years, enjoying intensive scientific and private interchanges, shared travel adventures and aeronautical enterprises (flying gliders and motorized gliders).

pomberger@swe.uni-linz.ac.at

Peter Rechenberg, born 1933 in Berlin, Germany, studied Electrical Engineering and received a Ph.D. in Computer Science from the Technical University of Berlin. Since 1975 he is Professor of Computer Science at the University of Linz, Austria (1999 retired). His working fields are Programming languages, Compilers and Software Engineering. His interest in Modula-2 and Prof. Wirths work in general led to the connection with Wirth and his group. Rechenberg is the author and co-author of several books about Programming Languages and Computer Science in general.

rechbg@soft.uni-linz.ac.at

Peter Schulthess was born 1946 in Zürich and studied Electrical Engineering at the ETH. 1972 he obtained a Master of Science in EE from the Georgia Institute of Technology. 1978 he finished his dissertation [8] with Prof. K. Bauknecht and N. Wirth as thesis advisors. After spending a year with the IBM Advanced Networking Group in Yorktown Heights he returned to ETH to work on local area networking and virtual machine architecture. In 1983 he was appointed professor for applied computer science in Augsburg. Since 1989 he has been directing the distributed systems laboratory of the University of Ulm. His current research areas are distributed operating systems, virtual presence scenarios and telematic services.

schulthess@informatik.uni-ulm.de

Clemens Szyperski coincidentally followed Niklaus Wirth's path from Electrical Engineering to Computer Science. After graduating in EE from the Aachen University of Technology, Germany, he joined Wirth's team at ETH in 1987, where he first worked on distributed systems and then on extensible operating systems in the group of Hanspeter Mössenböck, which led to his PhD in 1992. His stay in Zurich covered the period of the rise and full blossom of Oberon. After a postdoc in Berkeley at the ICSI with more work on programming languages, he returned to Zurich in 1993 to co-found Oberon microsystems. Oberon microsystems from the beginning focused on component software. This and his academic work led to one of the major themes of his work in his subsequent position as Associate Professor at the Queensland University of Technology in Brisbane, Australia, from 1994, where he received tenure in 1997. The spirit of Oberon and components did not leave his mind and so he first published his award-winning book Component Software: Beyond Object-Oriented Programming with Addison-Wesley in 1998 and then joined Microsoft Research at its Redmond facility in Washington, USA, in 1999, where he is now working full-time on next-generation component-software principles and technology.

www.research.microsoft.com/users/cszypers/

Josef Templ studied computer science at the Johannes Kepler University of Linz (Austria) and moved to ETH Zurich as an Assistant of Prof. H. Mössenböck in the group of N. Wirth. At ETH he ported the Oberon compiler and system to the Sun SPARC/Solaris platform in order to make Oberon available on a non proprietary platform. In 1994 he received a Ph.D for his work on "Metaprogramming in Oberon". He then founded "Software Templ OEG", a company focussing on advanced software projects covering the whole spectrum from systems software to e-business. Among the company's products is "ofront", a translator from Oberon-2 to C, that makes Oberon available on virtually every computing platform. The company also implemented the very first Java just-in-time compiler for a RISC platform by leveraging the experience collected with the Oberon project.

Bernhard Wagner received a B.S. degree from Pierre et Marie Curie University, Paris VI, France and the M.S. degree from Ludwig Maximilians University, Munich, Germany, both in mathematics. As an engineer with Siemens AG, responsible for the Pascal compiler, he learned about Prof. Wirth's work and later got the opportunity to work close to him in Jirka Hoppe's group. As a result, a Ph.D. in computer science was granted to Bernhard Wagner by the ETH Zurich, Switzerland in 1986. After a year as a visiting assistant professor at Brigham Young University, Provo UT, he joined Ciba Specialty Chemicals, the former Ciba-Geigy AG in Basel where he works as a software specialist. His interests include distributed operating systems and computer languages. Dr. Wagner may be reached at bwagner@acm.org.